PHENOMENOLOGY AND THE PHILOSOPHY OF TECHNOLOGY

Phenomenology and the Philosophy of Technology

Edited by Bas de Boer and Jochem Zwier

https://www.openbookpublishers.com

©2024 Bas de Boer and Jochem Zwier. Copyright of individual chapters is maintained by the chapter's authors

This work is licensed under the Creative Commons Attribution-NonCommercial 4.0 International (CC BY-NC 4.0). This license allows you to share, copy, distribute and transmit the text; to adapt the text for non-commercial purposes of the text providing attribution is made to the authors (but not in any way that suggests that they endorse you or your use of the work). Attribution should include the following information:

Bas de Boer and Jochem Zwier (eds), *Phenomenology and the Philosophy of Technology*. Cambridge, UK: Open Book Publishers, 2024, https://doi.org/10.11647/OBP.0421

Every effort has been made to identify and contact copyright holders of images included in this publication, and any omission or error will be corrected if notification is made to the publisher.

Further details about CC BY-NC licenses are available at
http://creativecommons.org/licenses/by-nc/4.0/

All external links were active at the time of publication unless otherwise stated and have been archived via the Internet Archive Wayback Machine at https://archive.org/web

Digital material and resources associated with this volume are available at
https://doi.org/10.11647/OBP.0421#resources

ISBN Paperback: 978-1-80511-379-9
ISBN Hardback: 978-1-80511-380-5
ISBN Digital (PDF): 978-1-80511-381-2
ISBN Digital eBook (EPUB): 978-1-80511-382-9
ISBN HTML: 978-1-80511-383-6

DOI: 10.11647/OBP.0421

Cover image: photo by Engin Akyurt, leather fabric texture, November 12, 2022; https://unsplash.com/ photos/background-pattern--50ez9-BEMg
Cover design: Jeevanjot Kaur Nagpal

Contents

About the Contributors   vii

Introduction: Articulating the Phenomenological Legacy of the Philosophy of Technology   1
Jochem Zwier and Bas de Boer

PART I

THE PHENOMENOLOGICAL METHOD IN THE PHILOSOPHY OF TECHNOLOGY

1. Ecological Hermeneutic Phenomenology: A Method to Explore the Ontic and Ontological Structures of Technologies in the World   27
Vincent Blok

2. Towards a Hermeneutic Phenomenology of Technology   53
Alberto Romele

3. The Institution of Technology   73
Darian Meacham

PART II

THE PHENOMENON OF TECHNOLOGY

4. The Activist Potential of Postmodern Phenomenology of Technology   97
Robert Rosenberger

5. Technological Mediation without Empirical Borders   121
Martin Ritter

6. Seeing the Phenomenon: The Radical Disembodiment of *In Vitro* Human Reproduction   143
Dana S. Belu

7. Artificial Intelligence and the Need to Redefine Human Traits   165
Galit Wellner

PART III

PHENOMENOLOGY AND TECHNOLOGICAL PRACTICES

8. Nothing in Practice:
Entanglements of Sartre's Nothingness and Social Media Practice 189
Annie Kurz

9. Attending to the Online Other:
A Phenomenology of Attention on Social Media Platforms 215
Lavinia Marin

10. Three Embodied Dimensions of Communication:
Phenomenological Lessons *for and from* the Field of Augmented and Alternative Communication Technology 241
Janna van Grunsven, Bouke van Balen, and Caroline Bollen

Epilogue 267
Jochem Zwier and Bas de Boer

List of Figures 277

Index 279

About the Contributors

Bouke van Balen is a PhD candidate in Philosophy and Ethics of technology at UMC Utrecht (Neurology & Neurosurgery), TU Delft (Ethics & Philosophy of Technology), and TU Eindhoven (Human-Computer Interaction). In this interdisciplinary project, he is embedded in a lab of neuroscientists at the UMCU that develop implantable communication Brain-Computer Interfaces (BCIs) for independent home-use. His research is on the intersection of philosophy of technology, phenomenology, embodied cognition, neuroscience, and ethics. He is specifically interested in how BCIs can and should shape the perceptions and experiences of communication and subjectivity of people with severe communication problems due to paralysis. His project is part of the ESDiT (Ethics of Socially Disruptive Technologies) consortium.

Dana S. Belu is Professor of Philosophy at *California State University, Dominguez Hills*, USA, where she teaches in the Philosophy Department and in The Women's Studies Department. She is the author of *Heidegger, Reproductive Technology & The Motherless Age* (Palgrave Macmillan, 2017) and of numerous publications on feminist phenomenologies of reproduction. Her latest article 'Thinking about Mothers Thinking: Maternal Authenticity in Ruddick and Heidegger' is forthcoming in *The Question of Gender in Being and Time*, edited by Patricia Glazebrook and Suzanne Claxton (Rowman and Littlefield, 2024), https://www.csudh.edu/philosophy/faculty/dana-belu. Professor Belu serves as an Associate Editor for *csuglobal*, an online and interdisciplinary journal that interfaces the California State University system with California and with the globe, https://digitalcommons.humboldt.edu/csuglobaljournal/

Bas de Boer is an Assistant Professor in the philosophy section at the University of Twente. His research focuses on how technologies shape our understanding and experience of ourselves and the world we live in, with a specific focus on technologies in healthcare. His research interests are in philosophy of science, philosophy of medicine, and (post)phenomenology of technology. He authored *How Scientific Instruments Speak: Postphenomenology and Technological Mediations in Neuroscientific Practice* (Lexington Books, 2021).

Caroline Bollen is a **postdoctoral researcher** at Delft University of Technology (Ethics & Philosophy of Technology) and Eindhoven University of Technology (Human Technology Interaction). She has an interdisciplinary background in medical biology, neuroscience, and science in society. In her PhD project, she developed a novel account of empathy as a normative concept that is applicable in a social environment that is more and more mediated by communication technologies. In her research, she emphasizes social and epistemic (in)justices, and she explores how many accounts of empathy exclude autistic empathetic experiences and expressions. **This** project is part of the ESDiT (Ethics of Socially Disruptive Technologies) consortium.

Vincent Blok is Professor in Philosophy of Technology and Responsible Innovation at Wageningen University. He is also scientific director of the 4TU Centre for Ethics of Technology. He holds a PhD degree in philosophy from Leiden University with a specialization in philosophy of technology. His books include *Ernst Jünger's Philosophy of Technology. Heidegger and the Poetics of the Anthropocene* (Routledge, 2017), *Heidegger's Concept of Philosophical Method* (Routledge, 2019), *The Critique of Management. Toward a Philosophy and Ethics of Business Management* (Routledge, 2021), and *From World to Earth. Philosophical Ecology of a Threatened Planet* (Boom, 2022 (in Dutch). See www.vincentblok.nl for more information about his current research.

Janna van Grunsven is an Assistant Professor in TU Delft's ethics and philosophy of technology section. With the support of an Veni personal grant from the Dutch Research Council, she conducts research at the intersection of embodied cognition, philosophy and ethics of technology, and disability studies. In her project, *Mattering Minds: Understanding the*

Ethical Lives of Technologically Embedded Beings with 4E Cognition, she is particularly interested in the notion of moral visibility, i.e., the idea that people's expressive embodied behaviour is often (but certainly not always) directly seen by others as constraining and motivating a range of moral actions. Specifically, she examines how different technologies can promote or subvert people's moral visibility and, with that, their ability to flourish as embodied beings, situated in a technological environment. Her work has appeared in journals such as *Social Epistemology, Ethics and Information Technology, Techné: Research in Philosophy and Technology, Phenomenology and the Cognitive Sciences,* and the *Journal of Consciousness Studies.*

Annie Kurz is an interdisciplinary artist and designer and a lecturer in design and media theory. Currently she is a doctoral researcher at the University of Art and Design Offenbach am Main, Frankfurt (Hessen State University of Art and Design). During her stay in New York City, her art and research interests into digital technologies gravitated towards utilizing methodologies developed by Don Ihde and postphenomenology, which she considers best equipped to understand situated knowledge of designers. Her recent work, forthcoming book and doctoral thesis are preoccupied with the so-called phenomenon of 'digital detoxing' and apps related to the practice.

Lavinia Marin is an Assistant Professor at the Ethics and Philosophy of Technology Section, TU Delft, the Netherlands. Her current research investigates the conditions of possibility for epistemic and moral agency (both at the individual and group level) for users of social networking platforms using approaches from ethics and situated cognition. In addition, she is involved in a 4TU.CEE research project focused on conceptualizing experiential ethics education for engineers.

Darian Meacham is an Professor of Philosophy at Maastricht University and Principal Investigator for Ethics and Responsible Innovation at the Brightlands Institute for Smart Society. He is the Editor-in-chief of the Journal of the British Society for Phenomenology. He previously lectured at University of the West of England (UWE) in Bristol and received his PhD from the University of Leuven. His work focuses on the relation between phenomenology and naturalism, enactivism, philosophy of technology, as well the work of Patocka and (European) politics.

Martin Ritter is Deputy Director at the Institute of Philosophy of the Czech Academy of Sciences and Senior Researcher at its Department of Contemporary Continental Philosophy. He is also affiliated with the Center for Environmental and Technology Ethics - Prague. From 2007 to 2020, he taught philosophy at Charles University, Prague. From 2020 to 2022, he was a visiting scholar in the research group Philosophy of Media at the University of Vienna. Besides numerous journal articles especially on phenomenology, critical theory, media philosophy, and philosophy of technology, he has recently published two monographs: *To Liberate the Future by an Act of Cognition. Walter Benjamin's Theory of Truth* (Filosofia 2018, in Czech), and *Into the World. The Movement of Patočka's Phenomenology* (Springer 2019).

Alberto Romele is an Associate Professor of Communication and Media (semiotics, pragmatics, and hermeneutics) at the ICM, the Institute of Communication and Media, Sorbonne Nouvelle University. He has been a researcher at the IZEW, the International Center for Ethics in Sciences and Technology, University of Tübingen, an associate professor of philosophy and ethics of technology at the Catholic University of Lille, and a postdoc at the University of Porto. He holds a PhD from the University of Verona. His research focuses on digital hermeneutics, the imaginaries of Artificial Intelligence (AI), and, more recently, the use of popular images in communication on science and technology. His research has appeared in journals such as *Theory, Culture & Society, Surveillance & Society*, and *AI & Society*. He is the author of two monographs: *Digital Hermeneutics: Philosophical Investigations in New Media and Technologies* (Routledge, 2019); *Digital Habitus: A Critique of the Imaginaries of Artificial Intelligence* (Routledge, 2023).

Robert Rosenberger is an Associate Professor in the School of Public Policy and is currently serving as the President-Elect of the Society for Philosophy & Technology. His research in the philosophy of technology explores the habitual relationships people develop with everyday devices, with applications in design and policy. This includes lines of research into the driving impairment of smartphone usage, the educational advantages of computer-simulated frog dissection, the roles of imaging devices in scientific debates, and the critique of hostile design and architecture (especially anti-homeless design). His edited and co-edited books include *Postphenomenological Investigations: Essays on Human-Technology Relations* (Lexington Books, 2015), *Postphenomenology and Imaging: How to Read Technology* (Lexington Books, 2021), and the interview book *Philosophy of Science: 5 Questions* (Automatic Press / VIP, 2010). His polemical mini-monograph is entitled *Callous Objects: Designs against the Homeless* (University of Minnesota Press, 2017).

Galit Wellner lectures at Tel Aviv University. Dr. Wellner specializes in philosophy of digital technologies and their inter-relations with humans. She is an active member of the postphenomenology community. Her book *A Postphenomenological Inquiry of Cellphones: Genealogies, Meanings and Becoming* was published in 2015 in Lexington Books. She translated into Hebrew Don Ihde's book *Postphenomenology and Technoscience* (Resling, 2016). She also co-edited *Postphenomenology and Media: Essays on Human–Media–World Relations* (Lexington Books, 2017). Galit is interested in the ways in which digital technologies transform medical and scientific practices.

Jochem Zwier is a researcher in philosophy of technology and Managing Director of the 4TU Centre for Ethics of Technology at Wageningen University. His work is situated at the intersection of philosophy of technology and environmental thought. His research interests include phenomenology, hermeneutics, and philosophical anthropology.

Introduction: Articulating the Phenomenological Legacy of the Philosophy of Technology

Jochem Zwier and Bas de Boer

Open any textbook about the philosophy of technology and you are likely to encounter opening sentences like 'our world is saturated with technological artifacts', 'it is impossible to imagine any aspect of human life that is not affected by technological developments', or, more grandiose, 'we live in a technological age'. Such observations stage technology as a theme that is worthy of philosophical analysis, or even as *the* theme deserving philosophical reflection today. After all, if, as purported, 'technology fundamentally shapes the human condition', and if this condition always entreats philosophy, it appears not only legitimate but necessary to philosophically question technology.

Echoing the time-honoured pair of *existentia* and *essentia*, of the *that* and the *what*, the fact that technology is relevant then quite naturally leads to the question of what it is, which is to say what it is essentially. Yet mainly after developments in the twentieth century, the quest for finding a historically unchanging, universally valid, and therefore essentialist answer to the question of what technology is has been largely abandoned. This is not to say that essential characterizations of technology such as 'means to an end' or 'human made' have become impossible or mistaken, but that their limits have become apparent. A social media platform is human made and serves communicative ends, but this tells us little about how it shapes our experience of the world, how it affects information, misinformation, or disinformation, how it shapes the meaning of friendship, how it constitutes one's identity, etc. Accordingly, the *what*-question gradually made way for such *how*-questions.

Be that as it may, how-questions obviously allow for various types of answers. For example, when asked how a social media platform shapes the identity of users, one could offer a technical answer: it does so by using such and such algorithms, which operate on the basis of such-and-such hardware and software. Alternatively, one could offer (social) scientific answers: it does so by mobilizing such and such psychological mechanisms on the part of users, by tying in with such and such economic or political powers, etc. While these are all answers to a how-question, they already interpret this question to be framed in technical or (social) scientific terms. And while this may lead to fruitful results, it also raises another how-question, namely: how is it that the question appears *as* a technical question or *as* a question to be answered by referring to psychological or economic mechanisms? As the difference between a technical and psychological framework in the above example makes clear, the question itself does not immediately make evident how the theme in question appears, nor how it is to be approached.

1. Phenomenology

It was the ambition of phenomenology to develop the original or primordial how-question. In cultivating this ambition, phenomenology became an influential school in (continental) philosophy. Its roots can be traced back to the work of Franz Brentano in the second half of the nineteenth century, and the work of Edmund Husserl and Martin Heidegger is often singled out as giving phenomenology a prominent place in the philosophical landscape. It has influenced many different fields, ranging from ethics and anthropology to science studies and the philosophy of technology. As noted, it addressed the primordial question of how it is that things appear or 'show themselves' (*phainesthai*). Phenomenology critically responded to what it saw as a bias in the prevalent understandings of its day, according to which how-questions were presupposed to be questions for positive science (be it physics, psychology, social science, or other), without acknowledging this presupposition *as* presupposition. Positive science was quietly accepted as the golden road leading to a universal objectivity: rather than being treated as one particular way of understanding how reality appears and works, it was taken to be reality's final description, or at least as the principal method able to offer such a description. Phenomenology criticized the idea that the theoretical frameworks and formidable abstractions of the technical and scientific disciplines self-evidently open to the final description of things.

This critique revolved around the meaning of the empirical. While the sciences are clearly empirical in the sense that they formulate their theories and hypotheses with reference to sense-data, phenomenology precisely questioned the sense of such data. The sciences tend to dissect such data into parts which are then taken to behave according to mechanistic laws. Accordingly, we might think we see a cow, but when we 'really' look at it (e.g., with a scientific gaze, perhaps aided by scientific instruments), we see that it 'is' an interoperative collection of organs, cells, organelles, or molecules. Or, more radically, we see a thing, but what is 'really' happening is photons hitting our eyes triggering neural responses. While arguably somewhat of a caricature, such examples showcase the scientific tendency to dissect, abstract, and sort empirical sense-data to fit mechanical explanations, and then privileging these explanations as conclusive.

Phenomenology questioned neither the sophistication nor the fruitfulness of such analyses, but objected to the idea that they are to be regarded as the sole or ultimate way to make sense of the world. Instead, as it developed, phenomenology came to the idea that the positive sciences precisely lost sense of the world by mistaking their abstract representations for original experience. Hence the famous phenomenological motto to go back 'to the things themselves', to describe things not from the pre-formatted perspective of the sciences, but as Husserl said, to accept a thing 'simply as what it is presented as being' (Husserl, 1983, p. 44), which is to say the way it is presented to and constituted by thought. A central notion in Husserl's phenomenology is that thought is 'intentional', which is to say that it is necessarily directed toward objects in a specific way, meaning that the object appears in a specific way. When I see or 'intend' a tree as a species of oak, my experience of it is already structured in a particular way that differs from remembering the tree, avoiding the tree on a bike ride, etc. Intentionality thus expresses the 'how' of things appear in relation to thought or consciousness, which became an important point of departure for both Heidegger's and Maurice Merleau-Ponty's reinterpretations of phenomenology.

Particularly after its crossings with existentialism and the philosophy of life (*Lebensphilosophie*) in the work of Heidegger, Jean-Paul Sartre, and their followers, the Husserlian emphasis on how experienced things are constituted by and for consciousness was gradually replaced by a focus on experience as lived experience: on how things are encountered by existing in a life-world. According to the analyses that followed, how things are encountered in lived experience differs significantly from how they appear from scientific or other theoretical perspectives. In everyday existence and lived experience, one does not first encounter external and naked objects to then furnish them with qualities and meanings through theoretical and rational operations. Instead, things always already appear as fitting in a meaningfully structured whole in which we ourselves are included.

To the question 'what is a table?', phenomenology accordingly avoids answering by alluding to objective properties (length, weight, colour), but first asks: how does the table appear? In everyday existence, the table is not first encountered as a quality-bearing object standing over against subjective consciousness, but primarily appears as something for me to sit at. When I grab a pencil to make a quick note, I do not so much grasp an external object but immediately grasp something that meaningfully shows itself as being for-writing. When I enter the classroom, I do not observe fifty similar objects and one reversed object, but I immediately grasp the difference between the lecturer's table and the student's tables, and I immediately know where I am supposed to sit.

The meaningfully structured whole in which things already appear as having their place is what Heidegger called *world*. Rather than something external that consciousness must somehow bridge, the world is something in which human existence is already included, famously expressed in the notion of being-in-the-world. We accordingly do not first experience photons on our eyes, synthesize these into the object 'tree', and then deduce that it could be used to make timber for our subjective needs. Rather, described phenomenologically, 'the wood is a forest of timer, the mountain a quarry of rock; the river is water-power, the wind is wind "in the sails"' (Heidegger, 1996, p. 66). Things are not bestowed with meaning by means of theoretical reflection, but instead always already appear in a meaningful way to human existence as it practically engages with the world. Again, this is not to say that phenomenology discounts the fecundity of theoretical and scientific explanations, but it challenges their primacy and instead views them as a particular and derivative mode of being-in-the-world.

1.1 Heidegger

With respect to technology specifically, this phenomenological idea is developed in Heidegger's distinction between the ready-to-hand (*Zuhandenheit*) and the present-at-hand (*Vorhandenheit*). In his analysis of tool use in *Being and Time,* Heidegger shows that our primary interaction with tools is not one in which tools appear as objects in front of us but instead recede from view (Heidegger, 1996, §§15–16). A screwdriver, for instance, does not appear as an object with certain properties (as present-at-hand) but immediately appears as something 'in-order-to' do something else, such as driving a screw into the wall (as ready-to-hand). I am already familiar with the screwdriver as well as with the instrumental totality in which I am immersed and can simply start using the screwdriver immediately without explicitly thematizing it.

Rather than just an anthropological or sociological observation regarding tool use, this rather drastically repositions the subject. Modern philosophy had considered the subject as an isolated thinking substance that then somehow accesses the world to engage with things, leading to numerous difficulties related to how such isolation and subsequent accessing should be considered. Heidegger's phenomenological analyses serve to show how the subject, or rather *Dasein* (Heidegger precisely uses this term to avoid connotations that the modern concept of subject has) is always already in-volved with the world, or simply is in-the-world.

With respect to the aforementioned question of 'how' things appear, the result is that phenomenology becomes particularly sensitive to how we are already involved or included in a particular way of appearance. Philosophy need not first establish how our experience of things likes rocks or trees could be possible by coming up with metaphysical materialist or idealist principles, but instead asks and describes how we have already understood them. Such understanding or pre-understanding is not so much produced or construed by a subject as it is quietly accepted. The technical or practical engagement articulated in readiness-to-hand demonstrates this involvement particularly well.

Moreover, limiting our scope to questions concerning technology, this idea of already-being-involved and already-having-understood remains central in Heidegger's later questioning of technology. In asking what technology is, he argues that while technology is obviously a means to an end and something made and used by human beings, it primarily designates 'how' the world appears to us: how, in Heidegger's terms, it reveals the world. He argues that the mode of revealing particular to modern technology has the character of an enframing (*Gestell*) that challenges reality forth to appear as standing-reserve (*Bestand*). This amounts to saying that modern technology constitutes a relationship between humans and the world in which the latter principally appears as a resource that is constantly available for humans to be instrumentalized and used.

Although we cannot here delve into the intricacies of Heidegger's analysis (several of the contributions to this volume will do so) it is important to underline its relevance to our topic of phenomenology and technology. On the one hand, technology here takes on decidedly philosophical significance, not so much because of what it implies morally, but because of what it implies ontologically for the very being of the world and of human existence. On the other hand, Heidegger's diagnosis has come to function as a springboard for further discussions in philosophy of technology, at times further articulating the notion of technology as enframing, at other times criticizing and outright rejecting this articulation of technology. As will become clear from both the later part of this introduction as well as the contributions to this volume, such discussions are ongoing.

1.2 Merleau-Ponty

Another important encounter between phenomenology and technology can be found in the work of the French philosopher Merleau-Ponty. Like Heidegger, he took as a point of departure that to exist as a human being implies being-in-the-world that cannot be sidestepped. In doing so, he moved away from Husserl's focus on how experienced things are constituted for thought or consciousness, and understood the human being as always already involved in the world in which everything has a meaningful place and is interpreted against a horizon of familiarity. And precisely because human beings are always immersed in this world already, they naturally pass over the question of how their being-in-the-world is constituted. For Merleau-Ponty, the task of the phenomenologist is to find a way that enables description of that what humans are always already immersed in.

While Heidegger develops his phenomenology from an analysis of the existential structure of *Dasein*, Merleau-Ponty takes *embodiment* as a founding category.[1] Our body is, on Merleau-Ponty's account, not an object amongst other objects as the modern (Cartesian) worldview would have it, but is what Husserl called a 'zero-point of orientation' and the 'medium of all perception' (Husserl, 1989, p. 61). Being-in-the-world presupposes the existence of a body from which intentional relations originate: our body 'is the vehicle of being in the world [...] [through which we are] united with a definite milieu, merg[e] with certain projects, and [are] perpetually engaged therein' (Merleau-Ponty, 2012, p. 84). The central question then becomes how to describe the ways in which embodiment is constitutive of world.

The notion of embodiment does not refer to our body as an object with definite boundaries but instead, precisely because the body is a zero-point of orientation, our body is primarily to be understood in terms of what Merleau-Ponty calls the 'I can' (Merleau-Ponty, 2012, p. 139). The notions of motor intentionality and habit are crucial for understanding the constitution of the I can. Motricity is the primary mode of intentionality because inhabiting a world implies a familiarity with the objects around us and the capacity to interact with them. Concretely, when reaching for an object such as a glass, we are not imagining beforehand what is the exact distance between my body and

---

1 In this introduction, we limit ourselves to Merleau-Ponty's *Phenomenology of Perception*. In his later works, most notably in *The Visible and the Invisible*, Merleau-Ponty attempts to ground the ontology of world proper in his embodied phenomenology. Discussing this development is beyond the scope of this introduction. For a discussion of this aspect of his work, see for example de Boer and Verbeek (2022) or Landes (2013, pp. 161–180).

the object, but rather respond immediately to the object's solicitation without any mediating representations. Motricity, then, is to be understood as a positioning in the environment through a body schema: a pre-reflective unconscious manner of experiencing the environment and one's capabilities to act in it (e.g., Merleau-Ponty, 2012, p. 101; see also Gallagher, 1986).

Our body schema forms the horizon for how other objects appear to us, and shapes the possibilities for perception and action (i.e., the 'I can'). The body schema is not something static, not something that remains the same over a lifetime, but is instead dynamic in that is modified in light of past experiences and actions. It allows for tools to be incorporated, and it becomes modified when the objective properties of the body change. For instance, when being sufficiently familiar with using a cane, this cane becomes part of the body schema of the blind person, or the body schema might change when someone loses a leg. This possibility of incorporation has formed an important inspiration for the philosophy of technology.

Merleau-Ponty captures this dynamism with the notion of habit: 'my own body is the primordial *habit*, the one that conditions all others and by which they can be understood' (Merleau-Ponty, 2012, p. 93, my emphasis). When going down the stairs I do not need to remember the distance between the respective steps consciously, nor do I need to explicitly establish the distance that I am about to travel when leaving the door of house. The world that I inhabit as an embodied subject already presupposes the presence of a relationship between a manifold of virtual coordinates that I do not need to be made explicit (Merleau-Ponty, 2012, p. 131). These virtual coordinates are not properties of an external world waiting to be found by the embodied individual, but are the result of a process of *sedimentation* through which world is constituted in the first place. The possibility of walking down the stairs unproblematically 'only remains around me as my familiar domain if I still hold "in my hands" or "in my legs" its principal distances and directions, and only if a multitude of intentional threads run out toward it from my body' (Merleau-Ponty, 2012, pp. 131–32). Put differently, sedimentation is grounded in motor intentionality, but in turn shapes how motor intentionality concretely manifests and how the environment appears as a place of familiarity for me.

Merleau-Ponty's work paved the way for an understanding of intentionality as constituted by the embodied interactions between individuals and their surroundings, resulting in the world that one is at home in and in which objects attain familiarity. In the context of the philosophy of technology, as we will see, he is one of the key inspirations—besides Heidegger—for analyzing how technologies co-shape embodiment and help to constitute novel body schemas, as a result of which new forms of being-in-the-world can emerge.

2. Phenomenology and the Philosophy of Technology

We noted that the phenomenological starting point from lived experience and practical engagement with things in-the-world opened up new avenues for philosophy of technology. On the one hand, the phenomenological critique of the primacy of theory made it possible to consider technology beyond the platitude stating that 'technology is applied science'. For, if practical engagement comes before scientific reflection, and if practical engagement involves technology, then technology cannot be limited to an application of science. Moreover, inspiration from phenomenology meant that the questions about technology no longer solely revolved around what technology is (something already discussed by Aristotle), how it should be considered a human category (as discussed in the works of Ernst Kapp and Arnold Gehlen), or its role in the process of political-economy (as analyzed by Karl Marx). With reference to the above-mentioned how-questions, the phenomenological question became how technology shapes our experience of the world, how it plays a role in the way things appear, or how we ourselves appear as its users.

Fast forwarding to how phenomenology has inspired philosophical explorations of technology in recent decades, at least two groups with an explicit phenomenological slant can be discerned, namely postphenomenology's questioning of the role of technology *in* experience; and what we might call the terrestrials who question the technological world on earth. A brief survey of these schools of thought should not only clarify whether, why, and how they study technology phenomenologically, but should also indicate their limits, unfinished businesses, and unchartered territories, which is where the present volume is situated.

2.1 Postphenomenology

Don Ihde describes postphenomenology with the following equation: 'pragmatism + phenomenology = postphenomenology' (Ihde, 2012, p. 117, p. 128). Limiting our focus to the second aspect of the equation, three ways in which phenomenology inspires postphenomenology can be discerned: (1) the understanding of technologies as mediators of human-world relations, (2) the characterization of technologies as revealing the world in a particular way, and (3) the focus on how technologies shape lived experiences by constituting specific ways of embodied being-in-the-world.

With respect to the first point on mediation, postphenomenology takes Heidegger's work as a central-point of reference.[2] More specifically, it departs from Heidegger's observation in *The Question Concerning Technology* that the essence of modern technology is in itself nothing technological; it is not to be found in the workings of technological artefacts or a particular way of thinking. Rather, 'technologies must be understood *phenomenologically*, i.e., as belonging in different ways to our experience and use of technologies, as a human-technology relation, rather than abstractly conceiving of them as mere objects' (Ihde, 1993, p. 34). Heidegger's analysis of tool use in *Being and Time* is a key source of inspiration for this idea. His analysis, which can be viewed as a more praxis-oriented reinterpretation of Husserl's intentionality, shows that tools (or technologies) are not experientially present when put to use, but rather enable specific relationships with reality (e.g., the hammer establishes a relationship with a nail that appears as 'hammer-able'). As mentioned, he calls this primary mode in which tools appear the ready-to-hand (*Zuhandenheit*), which he contrast with a mode of appearance as present-at-hand (*Vorhandenheit*), in which they appear as objects with describable qualities that are ultimately foreign to us (Heidegger, 1996, §§15–16). This understanding of technologies in terms of the ready-to-hand is central to the postphenomenological notion of technological mediation, which indicates that our encounter with the world is always

---

2 In this chapter, we focus on theoretical contributions to postphenomenology that explicitly discuss their phenomenological legacy, thereby leaving out the many fascinating empirical analyses of human-technology relations that postphenomenologists have provided.

mediated by the technologies that we use (e.g., de Boer, 2021; Ihde, 1979; Verbeek, 2005).

With respect to the second point on the revealing of the world, as early as in *Technics and Praxis* (1979), Don Ihde indicates that because technologies mediate human-world relations, they have a crucial role in shaping how human beings experience reality. This is because technologies amplify certain aspects of reality, while turning our attention away from other aspects (Ihde, 1979, p. 121). Postphenomenologists thus emphasize that technologies are no neutral intermediaries but actively shape how reality becomes present to human beings (e.g., Rosenberger & Verbeek, 2015). Whereas Heidegger speaks of Technology in terms of enframing as the singular way in which reality appears as resource (*Bestand*), postphenomenologists tend to translate this insight to specific technologies that each involve a particular way of revealing reality (e.g., Ihde, 1991, p. 52). For instance, a thermometer reveals temperature in a numerical manner, thereby putting our bodily experience of warmth into the background. The idea that specific technologies reveal reality in a specific manner, then, forms the foundation for postphenomenology's call to investigate how exactly the non-neutrality of technologies manifests, and how they shape human-world relationships. This investigation, so postphenomenologists maintain, should refrain from singular overarching determinations such as Heidegger's enframing, to instead proceed by analyzing concrete technologies as they are used within particular practices (e.g., Rosenberger & Verbeek, 2015, pp. 9–10).

The focus on concrete human-technology relations brings us to the third way in which postphenomenology is inspired by phenomenology: namely a focus on how technologies give rise to particular forms of embodied being-in-the-world (e.g., Ihde, 2002). A central point of reference here is Merleau-Ponty's *The Phenomenology of Perception* mentioned before, in which Merleau-Ponty gives a variety of examples of how tools structure one's embodied being-in-the-world by becoming integrated into one's body schema (e.g., Merleau-Ponty, 2012, p. 144). It is relevant that technologies help to constitute embodiment for two reasons: on the one hand, by becoming part of one's embodiment, technologies actively shape how the world is perceived by an experiencing subject, whilst becoming transparent for the subject in question (e.g., Ihde, 1993,

p. 108). On the other hand, because technologies give rise to ingrained habits that in turn shape the projects in which people intend to engage (e.g., de Boer, 2020; Rosenberger, 2014).

These three points amply showcase that several central starting-points in postphenomenology are directly inspired by key concerns of the phenomenological movement: the focus on intentionality, the transparency of tools in use, and the ideas that understanding embodiment is critical for understanding being-in-the-world and that technologies shape the existence of humans qua embodied beings. Various chapters of the present volume pick up on this trail.

2.2 Terrestrial Turn

Phenomenology has further inspired a recent call for what is called a terrestrial turn in the philosophy of technology. To make sense of this call, it is fruitful to briefly contrast its aims with those of postphenomenology. While postphenomenology champions itself for its ability to perform detailed analyses of concrete technologies and/or human-technology relations, those who we may refer to as terrestrialists[3] maintain that this renders postphenomenology blind for the larger whole within which these relations occur (e.g., Lemmens et al., 2017, p. 115). This is deemed problematic because we live in the age of the Anthropocene, a new geological epoch characterized by the planetary impact of human (technological) activity (cf. Zwier & Blok, 2017).[4] Whereas postphenomenology might very well be capable of analyzing human-technology relations on the ontic level of particular artefacts and uses, they—so the terrestrialists maintain—remain unable to articulate the ontological shift occurring in the Anthropocene. This shift is not so much about particular artefacts, embodiments, and uses, but concerns the whole of being or the world as such, which on the one hand appears as a resource that must be manipulated to safeguard

---

3   Although this term suggests a similarity with what Latour (2017) has called the *terrestrials*, this school of thought typically bears no close of affinity to Latour's work.
4   Note that this criticism is different from the more common critique that postphenomenology does not pay sufficient attention to the socio-political conditions underlying specific human-technology relations (e.g., Coeckelbergh, 2017, p. 36; Feenberg, 2015).

habitability, while on the other hand hinting at the limits of total manipulation in the guise of an increasingly unruly planet. Articulating and investigating this becomes the self-set task of the terrestrialists. The idea to think technology terrestrially reflects central concepts in Heideggerian phenomenology: the difference between the ontic and the ontological, and the understanding of the essence of modern technology as enframing.

The central entry-point to a terrestrial analysis of Technology is Heidegger's distinction between the ontic and the ontological. Basically put, echoing the former remarks about being-in-the-world, this marks the difference between the beings and objects *in front of us* (ontic), and *how* we encounter things in a pre-structured and pre-understood meaningful whole in which we find ourselves (ontological) (cf. Zwier, Blok, & Lemmens, 2016). For the terrestrials, this distinction is of crucial relevance because it articulates Technology on an ontological level. This opens up the possibility to reflect on 'the relation between being and thinking that [...] structures the way in which objects are encountered' (Zwier & Blok, 2019, p. 624), and to be concerned with 'the whole of Being as the inclusive mode of appearance' (Zwier & Blok, 2017, p. 233). Insofar as philosophy of technology is to proceed phenomenologically, it should focus on this ontological level, as 'consideration of [the ontological] mode is precisely the concern of phenomenology' (Zwier et al., 2016, p. 314).

The distinction between the ontic and the ontological gives rise to a rehabilitation of—or better, a renewed critical interest in—Heidegger's notion of enframing. Recall that, for Heidegger, enframing denotes the essence of modern technology through which reality is revealed to human beings in terms of a challenging-forth. As Cera puts it, this revealing is characteristic of our current 'age of totalized technology, [which] is first and foremost the epoch in which "being" means "being raw material (*Rohstoff*)." Everything that is, is makeable' (Cera, 2017, p. 250). In a similar vein, Blok maintains that the Anthropocene is to be understood as an ontological phenomenon because it disrupts 'the way in which reality as a whole appears—the world as challenged forth—and the way human being is responsive to this new reality—human being as challenged forth' (Blok, 2022, p. 5). In this line of thinking, phenomenology remains important because it opens up an ontological mode of questioning that allows articulation of how reality as a whole appears in the age of the Anthropocene.

The next concern for the terrestrialists is how it is possible to articulate this whole phenomenologically. On the one hand, borrowing from Heidegger, they maintain that the whole of the Anthropocene can be experienced through fundamental moods (*Grundstimmungen*): 'I will interpret both man's worldhood and animal's environmentality according to a *pathic presupposition*: namely, those *fundamental moods* (*Grundstimmungen*) that refer each of them to their respective findingness (*Befindlichkeit*)' (Cera, 2017, p. 261). Via the fundamental moods, it becomes possible to have an experience of one's place in an ontological whole that structures our relation with reality. On the other hand, it is maintained that—in the Anthropocene—the ontological can, *pace* Heidegger, be experienced on the ontic level, because of how, remarkably, the Earth is both a particular being and the contingent condition of any understanding of being and therefore of ontology. Accordingly, '[T]he Anthropocene [...] brings into view the Earth as ontic-ontological condition of possibility for responsiveness to the call of being' (Zwier & Blok, 2017, p. 235), whilst this experience can take place in our relationships with ontic technologies: '[T]echnology fosters [...] responsivity to being' (Zwier & Blok, 2019, p. 644). Whatever one makes of such analyses and claims, it may be clear that phenomenology here appears as a method that not only fleshes out the mediations and embodiments of particular technologies and human beings, but further addresses the ontological.

3. Overview of the Book

From the above two sections, it should have become clear that phenomenology is an important inspiration for these recent trends in the philosophy of technology, both of which explicitly position themselves in relation to the phenomenological tradition. However, insofar as our discussion is representative of the field, it also seems that mainstream philosophy of technology draws from phenomenology in quite a limited way: since discussions of phenomenology are often limited to the works of Husserl, Heidegger, and Merleau-Ponty, more recent developments within the phenomenological movement remain unaddressed. Besides offering a survey of recent developments in the phenomenology of technology, the present edited volume also asks why it is that many philosophers take phenomenology to be an appropriate starting-point for a philosophy of technology; if and why the 'big names' of twentieth century remain to be a main reference-point; as well as whether and how different ways of phenomenologically approaching technology are surfacing. To develop such questions systematically, we have divided the chapters in this book into three sections: (1) philosophy of technology and the phenomenological method, (2) technology as phenomenon, and (3) phenomenology and technological practice.

The *first* section of the book is concerned with how *phenomenological methods* inform the philosophy of technology. The purpose of this section is to explore what it means to inquire into something *phenomenologically*, and the extent to which contemporary investigations into technology rely on key thinkers in the phenomenological tradition. Furthermore, the aim of this section is to explore to what extent phenomenology can be combined with other philosophical schools (e.g., hermeneutics, pragmatism, actor-network theory), and what the methodological implications of such combinations would be. These questions are especially pertinent since much contemporary philosophy of technology champions itself for conducting 'empirical analyses of technology'. If such analyses are to be treated differently from those conducted by psychologists or sociologists, it is necessary to clarify how the world studied by the phenomenologist appears differently than the objects of the positive sciences. The section thus aims to contribute to the question of method in the philosophy of technology.

The *second* section of the book is concerned with the question of how the phenomenological tradition informs how technology appears as phenomenon and object of inquiry. Is this phenomenon something that can be analyzed as a whole, being a particular kind of thinking or relationship with the world, or should we rather speak about *technologies*, about particular artefacts that co-shape the embodied experience of users? The current tendency is to focus exclusively on individual technological artefacts, while being hesitant to take allegedly essentialist understandings of 'Technology with a capital T'. Rather, so it is sometimes argued, philosophy of technology should be a philosophy *from technologies* (Rosenberger & Verbeek, 2015, p. 10), and should be concerned with exploring how novel technological developments challenge existing phenomenological analyses and concepts. Simultaneously, philosophers routinely speak of the human being as technically conditioned, thereby seeming to reintroduce a more general conception of technical thinking that echoes Husserl's and Heidegger's analyses of technics. This section serves to address the basic question of what philosophers of technology refer to when claiming to provide analyses of 'technology'.

The *third* section is concerned with how philosophy of technology qua phenomenological enterprise informs how people make and make use of technologies. It accordingly asks whether and how phenomenological insights can be translated into technical action. On the one hand, one of the explicit goals of philosophy of technology is to inform design practices and make designers sensitive to the lived experience of prospective users (e.g., Verbeek, 2011). On the other hand, it is often argued that citizens —and democracy more generally—can benefit from a better insight into how technologies shape their experience and understanding of themselves and the world around them (e.g., Feenberg, 2017). How can phenomenology—as a method—play a role in these respects? As such, this section is primarily concerned with how phenomenological reflections are and can be practically applied.

3.1 The Phenomenological Method in the Philosophy of Technology

The first section focusing on methodical and methodological considerations comprises contributions from Vincent Blok, Alberto Romele, and Darian Meacham, all of whom are concerned with what it means to question technology phenomenologically.

In the chapter 'Ecological Hermeneutic Phenomenology: A Method to Explore the Ontic and Ontological Structure of Technologies in the World', Blok sets out to develop a phenomenological method to study technology in a way that moves beyond the one-sided essentialist or 'ontology-only' approach developed by Heidegger, as well as the 'ontic', 'empiricist', or 'thing-only' approach found in postphenomenology. Blok's phenomenological method instead seeks to demonstrate that a pre-understanding or *acceptio* such as the understanding of time as linear finds its footing or 'founding' in things (e.g., mechanical clocks). As a result, ontological enactment *and* ontic content become central to what a phenomenon is, where neither can be 'bracketed' or viewed as derivative. The chapter suggests that this relation between the ontic and the ontological must be thought of as a transduction in order to address or 'move across' (*trans*) what is thematic *and* what remains non-thematic with respect to any phenomenon. Finally, the chapter explains why the proposed method bears the name of *ecological* hermeneutics, because if the ontological *acceptio* or 'enactment' (e.g., linear time) is always 'founded' in things (e.g., mechanical clocks), things today do not just appear *in* the world, but explicitly appear in terms of the ecological constraints *of* planet Earth.

Sharing Blok's emphasis on hermeneutics whilst presenting a differing articulation of it, the chapter 'Unveiling the Interplay: A Hermeneutic Phenomenology of Technology' by Alberto Romele aims to show why the philosophical study of technology cannot be limited to phenomenology, but necessarily requires a hermeneutic approach. By elucidating the relation between phenomenology and hermeneutics, Romele criticizes the idealist tendencies in Husserlian phenomenology, as well as the ontological hermeneutics developed by Heidegger and Gadamer. The chapter instead advocates an ontic and pragmatic hermeneutic approach. To make this approach relevant for the philosophy of technology, Romele argues that the 'material hermeneutics' as practiced in postphenomenology falls short and must be unmasked as a 'material idealism'. Notwithstanding its self-professed 'empirical' interest in 'the things themselves', such idealism jettisons everything about the appearance of things that cannot be captured in terms of 'technological mediation', thus ignoring the sphere of symbolic, social, and cultural mediations that always already shapes how 'the things themselves' are and can be interpreted. The chapter closes by illustrating how a hermeneutic phenomenology of technology opens to a multidisciplinary political hermeneutics of technology.

In the third chapter entitled 'The Institution of Technology', Darian Meacham explores if the concept of 'institution' can help to better articulate how phenomenology can contribute to the philosophy of technology. He analyzes the development of this concept throughout

Merleau-Ponty's work and shows how it arose in response to György Lukács's criticism that phenomenology would be inapt to deal with political affairs and/or to articulate the totality that humans are immersed in. Roughly speaking, Meacham defines institutions as durable forms of common life. By focusing on institutions, he addresses Lukács's criticism by acknowledging the possibility of intersubjective relations that are shared over time as well as the creation and maintenance of social and technical objects through expressive actions. Meacham sketches the beginnings of a phenomenological method of studying technologies as institutions, which enables us to articulate how they structure different domains of intersubjective life.

3.2 The Phenomenon of Technology

The four chapters in this section each answer how their understanding of technology is informed by the phenomenological tradition, but also provide a critique of the limited conceptualization of technology offered by this very tradition. Is phenomenology sufficient to fulfil the task(s) of a philosophy of technology as it is understood in the field? Are prevalent approaches such as postphenomenology on the right track when taking 'concrete technological artefacts' as their primary object of concern? And to what extent are the concepts developed in past phenomenological accounts still useful for understanding questions around new and emerging fields such as Artificial Intelligence (AI)?

In the chapter 'The Activist Potential of Postmodern Phenomenology of Technology', Robert Rosenberger suggests that one of the key tasks of a phenomenological philosophy of technology should be to contribute to the goals and aims of political activism. In this sense, his chapter concurs with more general developments in the phenomenology tradition towards a critical or activist phenomenology. He argues that postphenomenology offers a fruitful starting-point for an activist phenomenology because it provides three avenues that can be directly applied to political debates in general and political activism in particular: (1) the notion of technological mediation enables us to understand how the political context as well as the relevant political actors are co-shaped by technological developments, (2) the notion of multistability helps to reveal the alternative ways in which technologies can be used other than their dominant stability, and (3) our perception in general is mediated by the hidden political assumptions of the technologies that we use routinely.

Martin Ritter's chapter 'Technological Mediation without Empirical Borders' provides a critique of the postphenomenological understanding of 'technology' as something referring to empirically observable artefacts. He argues that postphenomenology suffers from three main shortcomings: (1) it fails to engage with the question of what constitutes a technology, (2) it mistakenly reduces technological mediations to observable interactions between humans and technologies, and (3) its commitment to the empirical turn in the philosophy of technology and its corresponding emphasis on case studies provides only limited access to postphenomenology's self-proclaimed object of study: human-technology relations. In offering these critiques, the chapter presents a substantial general critique of the empirical turn in the philosophy of technology, as well as pointing towards the need to find a language to articulate how the notion of 'technological mediation' is not bounded by particular empirical circumstances.

Dana Belu's chapter 'Seeing the Phenomenon: The Radical Disembodiment of In Vitro Human Reproduction' discusses the radical technologization of women's reproductive body in assisted reproductive technology (ART). This discussion centres around the claim that neither phenomenology nor social constructivism is by itself able to discuss this technologization. The reason for this is that phenomenology is insufficiently empirically sensitive to what is involved in ART, whereas (critical) social constructivism remains trapped in a 'productivist' dialectic that misses relations between nature and technology that fall outside the scope of production. By critically discussing and recombining Heidegger's and Andrew Feenberg's work, the chapter claims that ART frames women's bodies neither as subjects nor objects of technical action, but as resources. However, such technologization is itself forgotten, leading not only to self-objectification but—particularly in the case of IVG (*in vitro gametogenesis*)—to the dissolution of the subject/object boundary rather than the subject becoming a more or less stable object. The chapter explores the notion of vocation, as well as Heidegger's meditative questioning of technology to explore the limits of such technologization.

In 'Artificial Intelligence and the Need to Redefine Human Traits', Galit Wellner argues that digital and virtual technologies like AI not only change how we experience the world, but also transform human mental capacities. While industrial technologies predominantly concern embodiment relations (e.g., extending or replacing manual labour), technologies like AI bear on the mind, notably in terms of imagination and attention. Wellner argues that Ihde's phenomenological analyses insufficiently articulate this contrast because of their emphasis on embodied perception, which appears less relevant in technologies like cryptocurrency and generative AI. Turning to the theme of attention, the chapter first presents Husserl's classical phenomenological interpretation of attention as 'searchlight', as well as Merleau-Ponty's critique of this interpretation. Wellner subsequently indicates the limits of Merleau-Ponty's 'field of attention' which, like Ihde, unduly prioritizes embodiment and fails to account for the phenomenon of multi-tasking. Wellner accordingly calls for supplanting the phenomenological first-person perspective with a layered approach focusing on plateaus, where embodiment relations make way for embrainment relations.

3.3 Phenomenology and Technological Practices

The three chapters in the final section all show how a phenomenological perspective yields novel insights about the relationships between users and technologies in everyday life. Phenomenology sheds a specific light on the problems that technologies might pose, about how we can develop more desirable practices around such technologies, or about how design choices can be better aligned with the lifeworld of users. In doing so, they point to the practical benefit of adopting a phenomenological perspective when inquiring about how technologies shape our lifeworld.

Annie Kurz's chapter combines postphenomenology and Sartrean phenomenology to analyze how social media technologies shape our subjectivity. Her focus is on how our self-understanding changes as a result of the ways we manifest ourselves online, and specifically by the profiles we (need to) make in order to become visible on social media platforms. She uses Sartre's notion of 'nothingness' to indicate that self-understanding always implies a relationship to something that one is not. Elaborating on this notion, she indicates that one particular form of not-self, namely one's online presence, has become key in self-development due to the ubiquity of social media. To capture this dimension of social media use, she introduces the *absence relation*; a human-technology relation that is explanatory for how many individuals or professions rely on social media even when not directly using it. Recognizing this aspect of social media use enables us to question the extent to which many aspects of our (professional) lives should be reliant on manifesting oneself in an online environment.

Lavinia Marin draws from phenomenology to lay bare another aspect of the ubiquitous presence of social media. By taking the phenomenology of attention as a starting-point, she shows that attention is—rather than only a scarce resource, as analysts departing from the perspective of the attention economy would have it—foundational for our moral relations to other beings. She argues that there is a distinctive form of other-oriented attention that enables us to perceive other beings as living beings that are worthy of care. This mode of attention presupposes a form of affectivity and involves the recognition of the other as a moral being capable of forming judgments, as well as someone having certain vulnerabilities. Her analysis shows that by prioritizing homogenous interactions and standardization, social media platforms hinder us from engaging in this mode of attention, thereby undermining our capacity to recognize others as surprising, changing, and fallible beings.

In the last chapter, Janna van Grunsven, Caroline Bollen, and Bouke van Balen show how the phenomenology of communication can inform the field of augmented or alternative communication technology (AAC tech). AAC tech is a set of technologies developed for people who are unable to use some of their bodily expressive resources due to congenital or acquired disability. This inability often makes it very difficult for those people to communicate. Developers of AAC tech often take a cognitivist starting-point, thereby missing out on the subtle ways in which embodiment shapes communication. The phenomenological description of the lived experiences of these people offers a fruitful starting-point for recognizing the often-forgotten embodied dimension of communication, and enables the authors to formulate desiderata for how AAC tech should be developed: AAC tech should take into account (1) embodied address, (2) embodied enrichment, and (3) embodied diversity. Focusing on the lived experience of potential users of AAC tech has, according to van Grunsven, Bollen, and van Balen, not only direct practical applications for technology development but also the potential to inform phenomenology methodologically: focusing on a limit case such as the one discussed in this chapter elucidates that communication takes place in a wide variety of ways and that it is not the task of the phenomenologist to lay bare a general or essential structure of communication that can be taken as a standard.

In closing, we recall the ambition of phenomenology to develop the original or primordial how-question: how is it that things appear or show themselves the way they do? In what was perhaps a comment on defecting followers, or perhaps a self-criticism, Husserl once remarked that, with respect to the idea of phenomenology uncovering the primordial 'how' in transcendental consciousness and thus offering a solid ground for the positive sciences, 'the dream is over' (*Die Traum ist ausgeträumt*) (Husserl, 1970, p. 389). In the philosophy of technology, few researchers indeed would still embrace this eidetic understanding of phenomenology as capable of revealing essences. However, this does not mean that the phenomenological project is exhausted; rather, it shows how phenomenology continues to reinvent itself in light of the central problems of different times. The three trajectories pursued in this volume demonstrate how phenomenology can be of ongoing interest in posing and reframing problems arising in the interactions between humans and technologies.

References

Blok, V. (2022). The ontology of technology beyond anthropocentrism and determinism: The role of technologies in the constitution of the (post) Anthropocene world. *Foundations of Science, 28*, 987–1005, https://doi.org/10.1007/s10699-022-09829-1

de Boer, B. (2020). Experiencing objectified health: Turning the body into an object of attention. *Medicine, Healthcare and Philosophy, 23*, 401–411, https://doi.org/10.1007/s11019-020-0994-0

de Boer, B. (2021). *How scientific instruments speak: Postphenomenology and technological mediations in neuroscientific practice*. Lexington Books.

de Boer, B., & Verbeek, P.-P. (2022). Living in the flesh: Technologically mediated chiasmic relationships (in times of a pandemic). *Human Studies, 45*, 189–208, https://doi.org/10.1007/s10746-022-09625-7

Cera, A. (2017). The technocene or technology as (neo)environment. *Techné: Research in Philosophy and Technology, 21*(2–3), 243–281, https://doi.org/10.5840/techne201710472

Coeckelbergh, M. (2017). *Using words and things: Language and the philosophy of technology*. Routledge.

Feenberg, A. (2015). Making the gestalt switch. In R. Rosenberger & P.-P. Verbeek (Eds), *Postphenomenological investigations: Essays on human-technology relations* (pp. 229–236). Lexington Books.

Feenberg, A. (2017). *Technosystem: The social life of reason*. Harvard University Press.

Gallagher, S. (1986). Body image and body schema: A conceptual clarification. *The Journal of Mind and Behavior, 7*(4), 541–554.

Heidegger, M. (1996). *Being and time* (J. Stambaugh, Trans.). State University of New York Press.

Husserl, E. (1970). *The crisis of the European sciences and transcendental phenomenology* (D. Carr, Trans.). Northwestern University Press.

Husserl, E. (1983). *Ideas pertaining to a pure phenomenology and to a phenomenological philosophy: First book* (F. Kerseten, Trans). Martinus Nijhoff.

Husserl, E. (1989). *Ideas pertaining to a pure phenomenology and to a phenomenological philosophy: Second book* (R. Rojcewicz & A. Schuwer, Trans.). Kluwer.

Ihde, D. (1979). *Technics and praxis*. D. Reidel Publishing Company.

Ihde, D. (1991). *Instrumental realism: The interface between philosophy of science and philosophy of technology*. Indiana University Press.

Ihde, D. (1993). *Postphenomenology: Essays in the postmodern context*. Northwestern University Press.

Ihde, D. (2002). *Bodies in technology*. University of Minnesota Press.

Ihde, D. (2012). *Experimental phenomenology: Multistabilities* (2nd edition). State University of New York Press, https://doi.org/10.1515/9781438442877

Landes, D. A. (2013). *Merleau-Ponty and the paradoxes of expression*. Bloomsbury, https://doi.org/10.5040/9781472548061

Latour, B. (2017). *Facing Gaia: Eight lectures on the new climatic regime* (C. Porter, Trans.). Polity Press.

Lemmens, P., Blok, V., & Zwier, J. (2017). Toward a terrestrial turn in philosophy of technology: Guest editors' introduction. *Techné: Research in Philosophy and Technology, 21*(2–3), 114–126, https://doi.org/10.5840/techne2017212/363

Merleau-Ponty, M. (2012). *Phenomenology of perception* (D. A. Landes, Trans.). Routledge.

Rosenberger, R. (2014). Multistability and the agency of mundane artifacts: From speed bumps to subway benches. *Human Studies, 37,* 369–392, https://doi.org/10.1007/s10746-014-9317-1

Rosenberger, R., & Verbeek, P.-P. (2015). A field guide to postphenomenology. In R. Rosenberger & P.-P. Verbeek (Eds), *Postphenomenological investigations: Essays on human-technology relations* (pp. 9–41). Lexington Books.

Verbeek, P.-P. (2005). *What things do: Philosophical reflections on technology, agency, and design.* Pennsylvania University Press.

Verbeek, P.-P. (2011). *Moralizing technology: Understanding and designing the morality of things.* University of Chicago Press.

Zwier, J., & Blok, V. (2017). Saving earth: Encountering Heidegger's philosophy of technology in the Anthropocene. *Techné: Research in Philosophy and Technology, 21*(2–3), 222–242, https://doi.org/10.5840/techne201772167

Zwier, J., & Blok, V. (2019). Seeing through the fumes: Technology and asymmetry in the Anthropocene. *Human Studies, 42,* 621–646, https://doi.org/10.1007/s10746-019-09508-4

Zwier, J., Blok, V., & Lemmens, P. (2016). Phenomenology and the empirical turn: A phenomenological analysis of postphenomenology. *Philosophy & Technology, 29,* 313–333, https://doi.org/10.1007/s13347-016-0221-7

PART I

THE PHENOMENOLOGICAL METHOD IN THE PHILOSOPHY OF TECHNOLOGY

1. Ecological Hermeneutic Phenomenology: A Method to Explore the Ontic and Ontological Structures of Technologies in the World

Vincent Blok

1. Introduction

Socially disruptive technologies like Artificial Intelligence (AI) and synthetic biology show that a phenomenological approach that focuses on the micro level of artefacts and the way they mediate experience, like postphenomenology, is no longer sufficient. It can already be questioned whether the introduction of the prefix *post-* comes at the expense of the phenomenon of phenomenology, as a pragmatist understanding of the human-technology relation (Ihde, 1990) neglects the existential, environmental, political, and economic involvement of human existence in the constitution of meaning beyond any functionalist or instrumentalist orientation (cf. Schutz, 1967; Blok, 2014). The focus on 'technologies in their particularities' (Ihde, 2009, pp. 21–22) testifies to a liberal faith in technological progress that stresses the individual characteristics of particular technologies—which can be redesigned and enhanced by the designer to serve society—rather than the structural characteristics associated with the existential, environmental, political and economic reality that cannot be remedied by individual designers.

For example, in order to feed the world in 2050, it is argued that the application of digital technologies in precision livestock and smart farming is urgently needed (European Commission, 2020). By studying how digital technologies mediate experience from a postphenomenologist perspective, we can for instance argue positively that unlike in the past, when farmers had to manage their animals as a collective herd, modern farmers are now able to engage in an individualized approach to animal care, guided by the data provided by sensors, decision support systems, and other digital tools. We can also argue more negatively that unlike in the past, when farmers were in control of their stables, they now function more as data managers who mainly manage their herds indirectly. This perspective can also raise all kinds of ethical questions, like the pain involved in the application of sensors or the ownership of the data that the animals provide. Such questions call for value sensitive redesign, for instance decentralized data processing, storage, and destruction in order to increase farmer control. What this descriptive analysis will not reveal are broader phenomena like dataism or pan-computationalism in the digital age, i.e., the idea that all physical systems—the soil and the weather, the plant and the animal, the farmer and the citizen—consists of computational data. We speak of a World of data with capital W, meaning that data is not so much a characteristic of the physical entities we encounter in the world, like the soil in which the plants are rooted and grow under the influence of weather conditions, but where data concerns a metaphysical structure that characterizes the whole of being as computational data, and affects the meaning of human and non-human living and acting in the World (Blok, 2023a). It is this type of broader phenomena that characterize the World in which we live today, that raise societal concerns about the industrialization, surveillance, instrumentalization, and commodification of agricultural production and consumption, and can no longer be neglected in contemporary phenomenology of technology. Digital technologies like an AI application or digital twin are in fact not 'particular' technologies, but interconnected and interdependent technologies in an ecosystem or World of data beyond the individual artefact.

This raises, however, a methodological question. Originally, the level of analysis of phenomenology of technology was found at the level of underlying ontological structures that govern the technological world, resulting in conceptualizations of the technologization of the world as a reservoir of resources that is present for exploitation (Heidegger,

1977), or as instrumental rationalization of social life (Ellul, 1964). Later, this essentialism and determinism was rejected in favour of an empirical or practical turn to concrete artefacts and practices, for instance the postphenomenological analysis that deviates from the 'high altitude' of Heidegger's focus on technology 'in general' and concentrates on the concrete human-technology relation (Ihde, 2010). Recently, I have criticized both versions of phenomenology for their one-sided orientation on either the ontological level, which neglects the role of concrete disruptive innovations like the steam engine or AI in the constitution of the World in which we live and act, or on the ontic level, which overlooks how new artefacts like AI-driven applications are embedded in a particular ontological structure of the World (Blok, 2022). Ihde does acknowledge a macro-perspective that situates the micro-perspective on the human-technology relation of new artefacts in a broader cultural context (Ihde, 1990). However, he is not able to analyze how the two perspectives are intertwined (Scharff, 2020), yet constitute different domains that cannot be reduced to each other. As long as we extrapolate from the micro-perspective to the macro-perspective, we quantitatively *generalize* based on the content of the human-technology relation, while neglecting the *qualitative* difference between the ontic level of new artefacts and the ontological structure of the World, as we will see. While traditional phenomenology can be criticized for its essentialist bias, resulting in its alienation of concrete technologies and practices, postphenomenology can be criticized for its descriptive bias, resulting in its alienation of the ontological dimension of the World in which each and every technology remains embedded. In this regard, we can argue that phenomenology of technology till now cannot claim to do justice to the full phenomenon of phenomenology yet.

This raises the question of what a phenomenology of technology looks like, that considers both the ontic and ontological structure of new and disruptive technologies in an integrated manner. In section 2, we first consult the traditional concept of phenomenology to find an entry point for our methodological considerations. It will become clear that Heidegger provides a progressive concept of hermeneutic phenomenology, although we are critical of his essentialism and linguistic focus in which there seems to be no room for the phenomenological consideration of ontic phenomena. The discussion of Heidegger results in a methodological concept of an empirically informed ecological hermeneutic phenomenology that enables us to research how new and emerging technologies impact the World in which we live and act in section 3. In section 4, we critically reflect on the *epoché* of phenomenology and show that a methodological concept of ecological hermeneutic phenomenology engages in an ecological transduction from technology as thematic artefact to technology as co-thematic ontological structure in which each and every artefact is grounded. In section 5, we draw conclusions.

2. What Is the Phenomenon of Phenomenology?

As the pragmatist understanding of the human-technology relation commits to an instrumentalist orientation of phenomenology (see section 1), we return to its original conceptualization as it is developed in the work of Edmund Husserl and Martin Heidegger. In his *Ideas* from 1913, Husserl finds the starting point of phenomenology in what we simply and directly experience, without committing to any claim about the factuality of what we experience:

> We proceed in the first instance by showing up simply and directly what we see; and since the Being to be thus shown up is neither more nor less than that which we refer to on essential grounds as 'pure experiences', 'pure consciousness' with its pure 'correlates of consciousness', and on the other side its 'pure Ego', we observe that it is from *the Ego, the* consciousness, *the* experience as given to us from the natural attitude, that we take our start. (Husserl, 1972, p. 101)

Contrary to the positive sciences, phenomenology does not research the 'reality' of what we experience but focuses on the way these experiences of the world are given in our intentional consciousness of this world. Husserl's phenomenology is transcendentally oriented, as he asks for the conditions of possibility of the correlation between the way the world is given to us (*noema*) and our consciousness of this world (*noesis*) and finds this condition in 'pure consciousness in its own absolute being' (Husserl, 1972, p. 140).

Heidegger is critical of Husserl's phenomenology, because pure consciousness presupposes that we have a position in front of the phenomena that can subsequently become accessible via perception, while we are in fact always already living and acting in a meaningful world in which we are at home and know how to live and act (Heidegger, 1996). In other words, Husserl's phenomenology reduces the relationality of the way the world is given to us and our understanding of the world to one of the relata, namely the transcendental subjectivity of pure consciousness that constitutes the meaning of the world and human being-in-the-world. Contrary to Husserl, Heidegger believes that the relationality of the givenness of the world and our understanding of the world cannot be reduced to one of the relata. He rejects Husserl's *transcendental* phenomenology and innovates phenomenology by engaging in the *hermeneutics* of this relationality of our living and acting in the world (Blok, 2021).[1] Hermeneutic phenomenology explicates the self-evident understanding of the meaning of the World as it is articulated in concepts like 'subject' and 'object', 'matter' and 'form', 'nature' and 'technology' etc.

In order to do justice to the relationality of the phenomena, Heidegger proposes the following definition: 'What is phenomenology? What is phenomenon? Here this can be itself indicated only formally. Each experience—as experi*encing*, and what is experi*enced*—can "be taken in the phenomenon", that is to say, one can ask: 1) after the original *"what"*, that is experienced therein (content), 2) after the original *"how"*, in which it is experienced (*relation*), 3) after the original *"how"*, in which the relational meaning is enacted (*enactment*). But these three directions of sense (content-relational-enactment-sense) do not simply coexist. "Phenomenon" is the totality of sense in these three directions' (Heidegger, 2010, p. 63). We consider a simple example to illustrate what Heidegger has in mind. If I say that my desk is two metres wide, I in the first instance say something about the content of the phenomenon that I experience in the world, namely about my experience of the wideness of my desk. But in my experience of my desk, also a particular *relation* between me and the desk is assumed that determines how the desk appears; the desk appears *as* measurable. Only

---

1 Although contemporary efforts in continental philosophy of technology to articulate the conditions of possibility of the world are valuable (Smith, 2015; Lemmens, 2021), it is questionable whether they can move beyond the orientation on the transcendental subject and can acknowledge the relationality of phenomena that constitute the world—whether it is found in a fundamental position of pure consciousness or technological artefacts—as long as it employs a 'transcendental' approach.

if the desk appears *as* measurable, it makes sense to measure my desk and say that it is two meters wide. Also, in my measuring of my desk, a particular understanding of human existence in the world is assumed that determines how the desk appears, namely me *as* the one who is the measurer of the wideness of the desk. In my experience of the desk in front of me, this specific relation between me and the world is always already enacted and articulates the meaning of my living and acting in the world, *before* I can determine the content of any particular being-in-the-world, like the wideness of the desk. It is not only the meaning of the content of my experience of beings in the world that is phenomenon in Heidegger's hermeneutic phenomenology, but precisely the meaning of the relation and enactment that co-determines this content. In the whole of content, relation, and enactment, the meaningful World in which I live and act as measurer of my desk as measurable entity is constituted.

Can we conclude that Heidegger's hermeneutic phenomenology already provides a method to research the ontic and ontological structure of new and disruptive technologies in an integrated manner, as he asks for the content, relational, and enactment sense? This is not the case. A first reason is that, although Heidegger speaks about the content-relational-enactment-sense in his conceptualization of phenomenology, it is also clear that his criticism of Husserl's transcendental phenomenology is embedded in his criticism of the metaphysical tradition that finds its point of departure in a domain of beings and asks for the being of these beings. Contrary to the metaphysical tradition, Heidegger's phenomenology is not taking beings as point of departure, but Being: 'According to the usual interpretation, the "question of being" means asking about beings as such (metaphysics). But if we think along the lines of *Being and Time,* the "question of being" means asking about being as such' (Heidegger, 1989, pp. 20–21). In this regard, even if Heidegger speaks about the content sense in his early concept of phenomenology, he is not so much interested in the ontic phenomena—the content of my experience of the desk I am writing at—but primarily in the ontology of the desk that is primarily constituted in the relational and enactment sense.

This is confirmed in *Being and Time,* where Heidegger characterizes phenomenology in the following way: 'The expression "phenomenology" signifies primarily a *methodological conception*. This expression does not characterize the what of the objects of philosophical research as subject-matter, but rather the *how* of that research' (Heidegger, 1996, p. 50). This 'how' does not mean only the 'how of philosophical research' or the method of phenomenology, but at the same time also the 'how of the objects of philosophical research' or the relation that has to be thought from out of this relation itself. Phenomenology not only involves a shift from the relata (beings) to the relationality of our living and acting in the World (Being), but also a shift to a particular enactment of this relation in order to let that which shows itself be seen in the very way in which it shows itself. Phenomenology characterizes the 'how' (relation) of being-in-the-world and at the same time the 'how' (enactment) or the way in which philosophy reflects on this relation.

In the first instance, hermeneutic phenomenology *explicates* the self-evident understanding of our living and acting in the World by following the indication towards the relation and enactment sense in philosophical concepts like 'object' and 'subject', 'theory' and 'practice', 'matter' and 'form'; it provides access to the meaningful World in which we are always already at home by articulating the dominant meanings of the World and concepts we live with in our daily life and practices. In the second instance, hermeneutic phenomenology consists in the *destruction* of these dominant meanings of the philosophical concepts in light of their original meaning (*theorein, hule, eidos*, and so on) in order to articulate a critical or progressive meaning of these concepts. By questioning the original meaning of the philosophical concepts that determine our living and acting in the World in order to explore new meanings, it becomes possible to critically assess the appropriateness of these concepts. This means that hermeneutic phenomenology not only acknowledges that our interpretation of the meaningful World in which we are always already at home is pre-structured and guided by the philosophical tradition, but also always remains open to revision, open to a new exploration of meaning. In this respect, a hermeneutic circle between our being at home in a pre-structured meaning of the World, our destruction of this meaning and our exploration of new meanings is characteristic for Heidegger's hermeneutic phenomenology (Heidegger, 1996, p. 62).

With this, it becomes clear that Heidegger's hermeneutic phenomenology is intrinsically linguistic (Blok, 2021, pp. 44–52). In his *Introduction to Phenomenological Research*, Heidegger argues that the point of departure is found in a turn of speech that has a 'fundamental methodological significance for the philosophical problematic' (Heidegger, 1994, p. 33). Language is not understood here as an instrument in the hands of man but concerns the meaning of the words that articulate and structure the meaningful world in which we always already live and act (Blok, 2021, pp. 44–52).

The linguistic orientation of Heidegger's hermeneutic phenomenology confronts us with a second reason why Heidegger's hermeneutic phenomenology does not yet provide a method to research the ontic and ontological structure of new and emerging technologies in an integrated manner. On the one hand, it is clear why a hermeneutic phenomenology that takes not beings but Being as the point of departure relies on language, as language is not a being nor an instrument in the hand of human beings, but a relational phenomenon that articulates the meaningful World in which we live and act. On the other hand, if we want phenomenology to take the ontic and ontological structure of new and disruptive technologies into account, we have to move beyond the linguistic focus of hermeneutics and engage in an *ecological* hermeneutics of material—ontic—phenomena.[2]

By phenomenology as ecological hermeneutics, we don't mean the interpretation of material beings, as opposed to Being itself, through interpretative tools and technologies like lenses, sensors, computers, etc. (Ihde, 2022). For Ihde, material hermeneutics involves the extension of hermeneutics from texts to physical entities that mediate our experience. On the one hand, it is indeed important to acknowledge that hermeneutics is not intrinsically connected with linguistics in the strict sense of the word, as language is primarily about meaning, and material entities like trees and steam engines, humans and AI systems are meaningful and as such, can be subject to hermeneutics. These material entities have a voice that has to be heard in phenomenology. But this doesn't imply, first, that material hermeneutics should be limited to the meaning of material beings in the world and the way they mediate experience, but should actually consider both the meaning of the material entity (content-

---

2   We choose the notion of 'ecological' hermeneutics here, rather than material- or thing-hermeneutics, because our concept of hermeneutics does not only consider things in the World but also the materiality of the ecological conditions on which they depend, which extends to the ecosystems of planet Earth that provide the materials these things are made from and the fuels to energize them, as we will see in the next sections.

sense) *and* the meaning of the World in which they appear (relational and enactment-sense) in an integrated manner. The materiality that our ecological hermeneutic phenomenology is interested in is therefore not limited to material *beings*, nor to the materiality of these beings as presented to our understanding (World). It also encompasses the materiality of these beings as they withdraw from human experience (Earth) (see section 5).

3. Phenomenology as Method

How can we use ecological hermeneutic phenomenology as a method to research the ontic and ontological structure of new and disruptive technologies in an integrated manner, finding a middle ground between the one-sided orientation on either the ontological level (Heidegger's phenomenology) or on the ontic level (postphenomenology)? Although we were critical about the 'essentialism' of Heidegger's phenomenology in the previous section, we consult now a late seminar which provides an opening to develop an integrated concept of ecological hermeneutic phenomenology.

In the *Zollikon Seminars* from 1959–1969, Heidegger introduces the phenomenon of phenomenology by consulting Kant's idea that *being* is not a real predicate, but merely the positing of a being (Kant, 1990). If we say that an artefact like a table is in the room, the *being* of this table is not a predicate that can be derived from the table itself, like its colour or form. If we analyze, unravel, or decompose the table, we never find its *being*. To the extent that we can nonetheless experience that the table exists, we have to conclude that its being is always taken for granted and assumed in our dealings with tables in our daily practice. To what extend do we *assume* the existence of the table? Heidegger distinguishes between three meanings of this assumption: (1) to expect, for instance, I assume that the delivery service will deliver my new table today; (2) to suppose, for instance, I suppose this table is made from wood or that it is a Jugendstil table; (3) to accept, for instance, my acceptance and openness for the *being* of the table. Heidegger distinguishes between the *suppositio* and the *acceptio* of the existence of the table. The *suppositio* refers to a hypothesis about the table that can be proven to be true or false, such as whether it is made from wood or whether it is a Jugendstil (German

Art Nouveau) table, while the *acceptio* refers to the basic assumption of the table's existence itself, which doesn't need to be proven but rather *shows itself from itself* (i.e., directly). For Heidegger, it is this *acceptio* that provides access to the phenomenon of phenomenology. On the one hand, we accept the existing table as it shows itself from itself. This existing table we perceive is an *ontic* phenomenon, i.e., it concerns a being. On the other hand, we accept the existence of the table as it shows itself from itself. The existence of the table is not perceivable like its colour or form, but shows itself from itself as an *ontological* phenomenon, i.e., it concerns the *being* of the table (Heidegger, 1987).

Contrary to Kant, Heidegger argues that the human does not *posit* ontological phenomena, as if the existence of the table is dependent on the perception of the transcendental subject. Ontological phenomena are also not objective, as if the existence of the table is only a matter for the table itself. Humans make and use tables to write letters on and have conversations at. These ontological phenomena are not subjective nor objective but *relational*, as the existence of the table shows itself from itself in my living and acting in the World. I enact this relation, as I exist myself and make or use these tables. At the same time, the ontological phenomenon of existence is not a neutral general characteristic of all beings, as the example of the table can make clear. Heidegger argues that the existence of the table can for instance consist in its being ready-at-hand as a useful thing (*Zuhanden*) or as present-at-hand (*Vorhanden*) in the room. Although we tend to perceive *human* existence in a similar way as the existence of non-human beings, namely as present-at-hand, Heidegger argues that we are not in the room in the same way. If I experience the existence of a table, I am not present-at-hand in the room like the table, but I am situated here at my place in the room and at the same time there at the table. Only thanks to this distinction between my place here and the table there, can I experience the table and its existence. My existence in the room is characterized by my *situatedness* here and there in the room, while the table is not situated but present-at-hand in the room according to Heidegger (1996).

For the purpose of this chapter, we will refrain from discussing Heidegger's comparison of the characteristics of the existence of the table in comparison with those of human existence. More important is the acknowledgement of a difference between ontic phenomena (the existing *table* in front of me) and ontological phenomena (the *existence* of the table in front of me), that ontological phenomena are not neutral or general characteristics of all beings but articulate a variety of ways of being-in-the-world, and the acknowledgement that ontological phenomena are not *posited* by the transcendental subject but are *accepted* by human existence. Any *suppositio* about the table—for instance that it is in Jugendstil style—can be proven or rejected, but that does not hold for the existence of the table. We have to *accept* the existence of the table and also that I have a relation with the table through making and using it. Its existence cannot and also does not have to be proven, but it is a prerequisite for any suppositions regarding the table; the table must exist in a particular way before I can say something true or false about it.

According to Heidegger, science and technology only have access to ontic phenomena—the table, the molecular structure of the wood it is made from, the DNA of the wood, etc.—and can develop hypotheses about these beings and their mechanisms, which can subsequently be engineered in science and technology. Ontological phenomena demand a different, singular method that cannot be undertaken by science and technology, namely a method that is open for the *acceptio* in each and every supposition. Heidegger's objective is not to reject the suppositions of science and technology in favour of the *acceptio* of phenomenology, but by engaging in the phenomenology of the *acceptio* in each and every scientific supposition, we develop a knowing relation without being absorbed by its suppositions:[3] 'to say the same thing about the same thing' (Heidegger, 1987, p. 30). Because we attribute existence to the table as it belongs to the table, while ontological phenomena (the acceptance of the existence of the table) cannot be perceived like ontic phenomena (the perception of the existing table in front of me), the methodological question emerges of how we have access to these ontological phenomena, and how they become the

---

3   In this chapter, we concentrate on the methodological dimension of the concept of phenomenology, and not on the existential dimension that is central in Heidegger's concept of phenomenology. For him, the actual engagement with phenomenology requires a transformation of human existence, namely from the human as the subject of the supposition or hypothesis underlying ontic phenomena to the human as openness (*Dasein*) for the *acceptio* in each and every supposition. By engaging in a phenomenology of the *acceptio* in each and every scientific supposition, we develop a free relation to science and technology. This existential dimension of phenomenology is beyond the scope of this article.

Sache of phenomenology.

Heidegger starts with an ontic phenomenon like an apple that falls from a tree on the ground, which is described according to the Newtonian laws of gravity as a point of mass changing its location from one location in space to another. We can then ask what is presupposed in this description of the apple. What is presupposed is the natural scientific concept of nature, according to which the apple does not fall *from* the tree *to* the ground but changes its location in law-governed fashion within a homogeneous space and time. By asking what is presupposed in this description of the apple, we encounter the *suppositio* that the apple is a point of mass that changes its location in law-governed fashion. Based on this supposition, we experience the apple as point of mass. We can then also ask what is *accepted* in this supposition about the apple, namely the existence of homogeneous space and time in which an apple can be found; only if the existence of a homogeneous space and time is accepted, the apple does not fall *from* the tree *to* the ground as its natural place, but changes its location in space and time in law-governed fashion.

The move from the *suppositio* to the *acceptio* is not the product of abstraction and generalization. If I see a green apple in front of me and say, 'there is a green apple', then 'there is a green apple' corresponds with the thematic perception of the green apple in front of me. There is, however, no thematic perception that corresponds with the 'existence' of the apple. We will not find the existence as characteristic of the apple if we look at the apple. With regard to the greenness of the apple, we can generalize inductively or deductively from one instance of a green apple to the general concept of 'apple' as such, or from a general idea of 'greenness' to the singular apple that falls under this category. But the generalization from the green apple to greenness and from greenness to colour is not possible in case we want to articulate the 'existence' of the apple. How should we proceed if we want to articulate the *acceptio* of existence in a phenomenological way?

We first consult the phenomenology of Husserl, as he distinguishes between two ways of having access to being, namely generalization and formalization (Husserl, 1972). Generalization is a method to understand things in terms of more and more general concepts. Green, for instance, is a colour, and colour is a sensory quality. It seems to be the case that we can go on with generalization, from a green apple in front of me to colour, to sensory quality, and to object as such. Green is then a sensory quality, and all sensory qualities of an object, whereby object as such is the most general concept. And yet, there is a rupture in the increasing generalization. The question is whether the generalization from green apple to colour is the same as that from green apple to object as such. According to Husserl, this is a rupture, because the generalization from one particular green apple to green and to colour is determined by the subject matter itself and remains also testable based on this subject matter, whereas the generalization of the same particular green apple to object as such is not determined by that subject matter. The concept 'object' does not 'lie' in the material content of the green apple, like the general green lies *within* the various particular green apples.

For this reason, Husserl speaks about *formalization* instead of generalization, a generalization which is not based on the *material content* of green apples, but a generalization which is empty in content. If we say that 'the stone is an object', we are not reliant on the stone but are precisely free of its material content and formalize towards the concept of 'object'. Moreover, we do not have to generalize step by step in order to find the highest generalization 'object' as such. Husserl therefore calls 'object' a formal-ontological category which is not the product of generalization but of formalization. Does this distinction help to understand how phenomenology has access to the *acceptio* involved in each supposition, namely not via generalization, but rather via formalization?

We can argue that the *acceptio* of existence, just like the concept 'object', does not lie in the material content of green apples, like the general green lies within green apples. If we want to thematize the *acceptio* of homogeneous space, rather than spatial beings like apples, the method of generalization does not help. Although the apple is spatial, the abstraction of the singular apple in front of me and generalization will not result in the concept of space as being is not a real predicate, i.e., spatiality is not a characteristic of the apple like its colour or its form and the abstraction from particularities of the apple will never lead to the concept of space. Rather, every spatial being is *in* space, and the concept of space is therefore not the product of abstraction of any particular space. This is also missed by the effort to abstract from the spatiality of the green apple and formalization towards space as such. As spatial beings are *in* space, any abstraction of this spatiality and any formalization that is empty in content misses the access point to the *acceptio*. We should not neglect the content sense of the phenomena, i.e., the spatiality of spatial beings like the apple, and therefore, we are hesitant to conclude that formalization provides access to the *acceptio* of space and call for an *ecological* hermeneutic phenomenology. How should we proceed if we want to articulate space in a phenomenological way, if we cannot rely on generalization and formalization?

Because the apple is spatial, we don't have to formally renounce from the material content of the apple but should hold on to the materiality of the apple that exists in space, that is extended and therefore something spatial. When we pick up the apple and take a bite of it, then this spatiality of the apple is not perceived thematically. At the same time, space is perceived nonthematically in each and every thematic perception of *spatial* beings like apples. In order to get access to the *acceptio* of space in the perception of the apple, phenomenology should not generalize or formalize from the spatiality of the apple but on the contrary, adhere to the thematically perceived—the apple as spatial being—and thematize the *acceptio* in each and every thematic perception, the spatiality of the apple which is itself unthematic but necessarily given. Heidegger provides the example of a cup in space: 'What happens to the cup when we look away from it and turn toward space as the theme? The process of thematization is reversed. Nevertheless, if I make space the theme, I cannot leave the cup out of consideration. Space as a theme is where the cup exists. Therefore, if I were to leave the cup out of consideration completely, I would not be able to apprehend the character of space as that where the cup exists. I must merely let the cup become nonthematic' (Heidegger, 1987, p. 39). Access to the *acceptio* of space is provided by phenomenologically reversing the thematic order: we let the thematic content—the cup in space—become nonthematic, and the nonthematic—the spatiality of the cup—thematic.

Although Heidegger provides an indication of how to proceed if we want to articulate space in a phenomenological way, we also have to be critical towards his approach. Although Heidegger's phenomenology clearly starts with ontic phenomena, as the example of the cup in space makes clear, his concept of phenomenology focuses on the relational and enactment sense of the phenomenon (see section 2). His phenomenological analysis reveals for instance that the apple that changes its location in a law-governed fashion accepts homogeneous space and raises critical questions about the *acceptio* because I am not in space like the apple that changes its location. In this effort, his method of phenomenology neglects the content sense in his analysis. On the one hand, this is understandable, as the focus on the content sense runs the risk of neglecting the relational and enactment sense, and Heidegger blames the theoretical attitude of Husserl's method of phenomenology for solely concentrating on the content sense (Heidegger, 2010, p. 63). On the other hand, Heidegger's focus on the relational and enactment sense of the *acceptio* runs the opposite risk of neglecting the content sense of the phenomena, as we will see show in the remainder of this section.

Here we have to come back to the essentialism of Heidegger's phenomenology (section 2). According to Heidegger, each and every ontic phenomenon like the existing table *presupposes* ontological phenomena like the existence of the table, but not the other way around. Ontic phenomena like existing tables and apples *accept* existence, as existence is already nonthematically accepted in each and every thematic perception of a table or apple, but ontic phenomena do not *affect* ontological phenomena like existence as such. This is consistent with Heidegger's criticism of the metaphysical tradition, that it finds its point of departure in a domain of *beings* and asks for the being of these beings by abstracting from these beings, and with this, by thinking their *being* out of these beings via generalization or formalization. Also in Heidegger's phenomenology, a domain of beings is the point of departure—existing tables—but for him, the ontological phenomenon of existence has nothing to do with existing tables and is also not affected by ontic phenomena like tables; for this reason, he argues right at the start of *The question concerning technology*: 'The essence of technology is by no means anything technological' (Heidegger, 1977, p. 7). And yet, we can question whether this is true, whether ontic phenomena indeed have no ontological impact.

The example of the invention of the mechanical clock that increasingly replaced elemental clocks can make this clear. A mechanical clock measures intervals of time and takes time as homogeneous linear-chronological time for granted. The invention of the mechanical clock is *grounded* in the *acceptio* of time as linear chronological time. Only if I accept time as linear chronological time, it makes sense to invent an artefact that counts intervals of time like a mechanical clock. The *acceptio* of time as homogeneous time is, however, not of all times. While time is circular in elemental clocks and oriented on the cyclical movements of the sun or plant life cycles, for instance, time appears as linear in mechanical clocks. What explains the shift in the *acceptio* of time as circular to time as linear chronological? The invention of the mechanical clock is not only grounded in the *acceptio* of linear chronological time, but paradoxically enough also *founds* this shift in our *acceptio* of time, to the extent that the innovation of the mechanical clock destructs the *acceptio* of time as cyclical and constructs the *acceptio* of time as linear and chronological. In other words, the *acceptio* of time is not always the same but changes, and this change of the *acceptio*—time as linear and chronological—does not only affect ontic phenomena, the invention and evolution of the mechanical clock that counts intervals of time as grounded in the *acceptio* for time as linear chronological—but also the other way around, as the invention of ontic phenomena—the mechanical clock—affects the ontological phenomena involved—it *founds* the *acceptio* of time as linear and chronological. The shift in our *acceptio* of time does not happen with the first invention of the mechanical clock, but is *founded* by the invention, dissemination, and use of the mechanical clock and of accompanying phenomena like calendars, forecasting, etc. (Blok, 2022). In this regard, we can question Heidegger's assumption that ontic phenomena do not affect ontological phenomena, and with this, we can question Heidegger's essentialist concept of phenomenology and argue that phenomenology should not only take ontic phenomena as the point of departure for the phenomenological analysis of ontological phenomena, while neglecting the possible impact of ontic phenomena—the invention of the mechanical clock—on the ontological phenomena—the impact of this invention on the *acceptio* of time as linear and chronological.

In our proposal for a concept of an ecological hermeneutic phenomenology, we therefore engage in an empirical turn to consider the content sense of ontic phenomena—the invention, evolution, and dissemination of the mechanical clock—and their ontological impact on the relational sense and the enactment sense that founds and grounds the World in an integrated manner.[4] In the founding *of* and grounding *in* the *acceptio* of time as linear and chronological time, through the invention of the mechanical clock, our understanding of the World and our living and acting in the World changes. If I watch the clock at the railway station and conclude that the train I expected to catch is already gone, I, in the first instance, say something about the *content* of the phenomenon that I experience in the world, namely about the physical clock in front of me that indicates that the train left the station too early. But in my experience of the clock, also a particular *relation* between me and the World is assumed that determines how clocks and trains appear. If the clock indicates that the train left the station *too early*, the appearance of the train is chronologically calculated in terms of the passage of time. It is expected to arrive in five minutes, for instance (future), is entering the station right away (present), or can already have left the station (past). Only if the relational sense between me and the train is linear and chronological does it makes sense to be at the railway station at eight o'clock to catch the train, *wait* for the train that is five minutes late, *expect* the train to come within five minutes, etc. Only if the train appears *as* linear and chronological being does it makes sense to watch the clock at the railway station and say that the train left the station too early. Also, in our experience of the clock and conclusion that the train left the railway station too early, the enactment of this relation by human existence determines our living and acting in the World, namely *as* linear, chronological being who tries to be at the railway station at three-thirty, five minutes before the train is expected to arrive, for instance. In my walking to the railway station, this specific relation between me and the World is always already enacted and articulates the meaning of my living and acting in the World, *before* I can determine whether I have to hurry up to catch the train, or can take it easy and have a coffee at a terrasse. In the linear, chronological World, human existence is understood as a non-cyclical, irreversible process along an axis running from a past to a future (Jünger, 1979). The ontological impact of the innovation of the mechanical clock (content sense) impacts being (relational sense) and thinking (enactment sense)

---

4 For the further elaboration of the paradoxical relation between founding and grounding, see Blok (2022).

at once and constitute the World in which we live and act.[5]

Because ontic phenomena like the invention, dissemination, and adoption of the mechanical clock turns out to have an ontological impact on the relational and enactment sense that constitute the World in which we live and act, we can criticize Heidegger's one-sided orientation on ontological phenomena. We don't reject Heidegger's method of phenomenology as such but move beyond the essentialist bias of his concept of phenomenology, in which ontic phenomena only function as a point of departure for considering ontological phenomena. Instead, we propose a concept of an *empirically* informed *ecological* hermeneutic phenomenology as a method for researching both ontic and ontological phenomena in an integrated manner. Ontic phenomena—a thing like the mechanical clock in front of me—not only *accept* ontological phenomena—linear, chronological time—but also the other way around; ontological phenomena like linear, chronological time presuppose ontic phenomena like the invention, evolution, and dissemination of mechanical clocks. Ecological hermeneutic phenomenology should therefore research what is taken for granted in ontic *and* ontological phenomena in an integrated manner, and consider the content, relation, and enactment sense that constitute the World in which we live and act.

We call our concept of empirically informed ecological hermeneutic phenomenology *transductive*. Phenomenology does not abstract from the thematically perceived—the perception of a thing like the mechanical clock in front of me—but on the contrary, adheres to the thematically perceived and thematizes what is taken for granted in each and every thematic perception—the *acceptio* of time as linear and chronological—which is itself unthematic but necessarily given in the evolution and dissemination of the mechanical clock. The thematization of the ontological phenomena by letting the ontic phenomena become nonthematic does not proceed inductively or deductively, but proceeds as if we look at them sideways, laterally, by passing by, or *transductively* (from *leading through* or *across*),[6] namely *leading through or across* the

---

5   We call this founding *of* and grounding *in* the constitution of the World, namely of the World in which time appears as linear chronological and human existence lives and acts in this World.

6   Our concept of transduction deviates from the one Simondon introduces in

ontological phenomena by letting the thematic (ontic) phenomena—the mechanical clock—become nonthematic and thematizing that which is concomitantly unthematically but necessarily given—the *acceptio* of time as linear mechanical—as ontological phenomena. The concept of time as linear and chronological, which we take for granted, becomes evident through its manifestation by the transductive articulation of the *acceptio* of time in each and every experience of the ontic phenomena. This transduction of the *acceptio* of ontological phenomena from the experience of ontic phenomena provides access to the phenomenon of phenomenology.

4. The Rehabilitation of the Content Sense in Phenomenology

The content sense of ontic phenomena like mechanical clocks is not limited to the clock *as we experience* them. Traditional phenomenologists like Husserl argue that the way the world of positive facts is given to us (noema) is correlated to the subjective way of apprehending this world (noesis). Seen from this perspective, the content sense is limited to the phenomena as we simply and directly experience them. For this reason, Husserl argues that we should not commit to any claim about the factuality of what we experience, and brackets (*epoché*) the existence of the world external to consciousness in order to focus on the way these facts present themselves to our conscious self-experience. 'The genuine transcendental epoché makes possible the "transcendental reduction"— the discovery and investigation of the transcendental correlation between world and world-consciousness' (Husserl, 2012, p. 164). The same holds for postphenomenologists, who focus their research on cases of technologies that stay close to human experience and articulate the human-technology relation (Bosschaert & Blok, 2023).

But the content sense of sundials, hourglasses, mechanical clocks, atomic clocks, etc. is not limited to the way we experience them, as they

---

his work (Combes, 2013), as transduction for him concerns the process of productively differentiating and individuating new beings at an ontic level (a new species in biological evolution, a new technology in technological evolution), while we conceptualize transduction as leading through the *acceptio* in each and every such production at an ontological level.

are made from (scarce) materials, bear the traces of the material and energy they were made from, the ecological conditions to which they are adaptive, etc. This materiality of the ecological conditions is not only correlated, but also *un*-correlated being that can be observed if we think of technological artefacts like AI-driven devices and look *under the hood*, and experience the *black box* that informs its operations, the material stubbornness or obstinacy of technologies that allow certain designs and do not allow others, and their capacity to remain a misfit in the ecosystem in which they are embedded. Especially in times of global warming, we experience the dependency of technologies on the biosphere of planet Earth that provides scarce materials but also the elements like water, wind, and fire that can make them wear out and can take their existence away.

The content sense of ontic phenomena like the mechanical clock does not only concern the things *as we experience them*, as in traditional phenomenology, but also the *materiality* of these ontic phenomena like the mechanical clock *beyond* what we can directly experience. This has consequences for our method of phenomenology. In fact, the content sense of the materiality of ontic phenomena like mechanical clocks *res-cends* (from *res-*, matter, thing), rather than trans-*cends*, our living and acting in the World in which we encounter and experience these clocks. While Husserl's concept of phenomenology commits to an *epoché* regarding the real existence of the phenomena and engages in a *transcendental reduction* to get access to the phenomenon of phenomenology, our acknowledgement of the ecological conditions of ontic phenomena beyond our experience enforces our rejection of the *epoché* of phenomenology. In fact, the phenomenological *epoché* testifies to a *state of exception* (Agamben, 2005), a suspension of our commitment to the materiality of the ecological conditions of planet Earth, while this materiality precisely calls for a *state of inclusion*. Therefore, contrary to traditional phenomenology, ecological hermeneutic phenomenology engages in a *res-cendental transduction* to get access to the phenomenon of phenomenology. Ontic phenomena like the mechanical clock *hold, interiorize,* or *contain* this materiality of the ecological conditions and we should therefore reject the *epoché* in favour of the res-cendental transduction of the content, the relational, and the enactment sense that constitutes the World.

This *res* concerns not only the materiality of ontic phenomena like clocks, but also encompasses the broader ecological context. It includes the Earth as the source of scarce materials needed to build the mechanical clock, the environment in which factories are established to build these clocks, and the role of the Earth as a dumping ground for waste materials produced by these factories, etc. In other words, it concerns the ecological conditions on which these ontic phenomena depend for their existence. The material substantiality of planet Earth is the condition of possibility of every technology and its functioning, which means that technologies like mechanical clocks do not only have an ontological impact on the relational sense and the enactment sense of the World but are also *constrained* by the materiality of planet Earth. For instance, the emergence of quartz clocks since the 1980s is dependent on small and cheap electronic oscillators that are regulated by quartz crystals and resulted in more accurate timekeeping compared with mechanical clocks. As such a dependency, we can consider the content sense of ontic phenomena like the materiality of quartz clocks as a constraint of the relational and enactment sense that structures our living and acting in the World; without the availability of material recourses to make mechanical clocks, no innovation, evolution, and dissemination of this invention could have taken place and with this, no transformation of the relational and enactment sense of time as circular time (elemental clocks) to time as linear, chronological time (mechanical clocks) would have emerged. The invention, evolution, and dissemination of ontic phenomena like the mechanical clock constitutes the relational and enactment sense of the linear, chronological World on the one hand, but is constrained by its materiality (content sense) on the other. An ecological hermeneutic phenomenology acknowledges both the relational and enactment senses that structure the World *and* the content sense of the ecological conditions of planet Earth as a pattern of constraints for each and every technology that constitutes the World.

This acknowledgement of the materiality of the ecological conditions of planet Earth as a constraint also makes it possible for phenomenology to extend its social engagement and ecological involvement beyond a purely functionalist or instrumentalist orientation. While many philosophers of technology still take for granted the material conditions of Earth's biosphere, such as the provision of scarce materials, fuels, and waste disposal for our technologies, climate change requires philosophers of technology to engage in a 'terrestrial turn' in order to consider the planetary context in which these technologies emerge and function (Lemmens et al., 2017). Our proposal for an ecological hermeneutic phenomenology of technology enables us to actually engage in the social and ecological conditions of new and emerging technologies.

5. Conclusion

In this chapter, we critiqued the one-sided focus on either the ontological level of technology, which overlooks the role of concrete disruptive innovations in shaping the World in which we live and act, or the ontic level, which neglects how new and emerging technologies are embedded in a particular ontological structure of the World. Because the invention, evolution, and dissemination of new and emerging technologies has an ontological impact on the World in which we live and act, phenomenology as a method of philosophy of technology should move beyond the essentialist bias of traditional phenomenology and the descriptive bias of postphenomenology.

We developed a methodological concept of an empirically informed ecological hermeneutic phenomenology that enables us to research how new and emerging technologies (content sense) impact being (relational sense) and thinking (enactment sense) at once and constitute the World in which we live and act. With the rehabilitation of the content sense of new and emerging technologies, we move beyond the essentialist bias of Heidegger's phenomenology. The rehabilitation of the content sense also moves beyond the descriptive bias of postphenomenology, as it is not limited to new and emerging technologies *as we experience* them. While traditionally, phenomenology commits to an *epoché* regarding the real existence of the phenomena, our acknowledgement of the materiality of ontic phenomena beyond our experience forced us to reject the *epoché* of phenomenology. Ecological hermeneutic phenomenology is a methodology to engage in a rescendental transduction from the content sense of new and emerging technologies to the relational and enactment senses that co-constitute the World in which we live and act. The materiality of planet Earth is a *constraint* for the content sense of new and emerging technologies and the way they impact the relational and enactment senses that *structure* our living and acting in the World.

In the context of this chapter, we only applied our methodological concept of ecological hermeneutic phenomenology to the case of the mechanical clock and did not yet consider the way digital technologies constitute the World of data in the digital age (see section 1). Our hypothesis is that the method of ecological hermeneutic phenomenology enables us to transduct from the content sense of individual digital technologies like AI applications and digital twins to the relational and enactment senses of the World of data, and to critically reflect on the dataism or pan-computationism that characterizes the situation of the World today (Blok, 2023a). The exploration of this hypothesis is beyond the scope of this chapter and remains open for future research.[7]

References

Agamben, G. (2005). *State of exception*. University of Chicago Press.

Blok, V. (2014). Being-in-the-world as being-in-nature: An ecological perspective on Being and Time. *Studia Phaenomenologica, 14*, 215–235, https://doi.org/10.5840/studphaen20141411

Blok, V. (2021). *Heidegger's concept of philosophical method. Innovating philosophy in the age of global warming*. Routledge.

Blok, V. (2022). The ontology of technology beyond anthropocentrism and determinism: The role of technologies in the constitution of the (post) anthropocene world. *Foundations of Science, 28*, 987–1005. https://doi.org/10.1007/s10699-022-09829-1

Blok, V. (2023a). *Philosophy of technology in the digital age. The datafication of the world, the homo virtualis, and the capacity of technological innovations to set the World free*. Wageningen University.

Blok, V. (2023b). The earth means the world to me: Earth- and world-interest in times of climate change. In M. Di Paola & G. Pellegrino (Eds), *Handbook of Philosophy of Climate Change* (pp. 1–17). Springer, https://doi.org/10.1007/978-3-030-16960-2_105-1

Bosschaert, M., & Blok, V. (2023). The 'empirical' in the empirical turn: a critical analysis. *Foundations of Science, 28*, 783–804, https://doi.org/10.1007/s10699-022-09840-6

---

7 I would like to thank the reviewer of this chapter for their valuable feedback that enabled me to further improve the chapter's argument.

Bostrom, N. (2003). Are we living in a computer simulation? *The Philosophical Quarterly, 53*(211), 243–255.

Combes, M. (2013). *Gilbert Simondon and the philosophy of the transindividual.* MIT Press.

Ellul, J. (1964). *The technological society.* Vintage Books.

European Commission (2020). *A farm to fork strategy for a fair, healthy and environmentally friendly food system.* European Commission: COM 2020/381.

European Commission (2023). *Destination Earth*, https://digital-strategy.ec.europa.eu/en/policies/destination-earth

Heidegger, M. (1977). *The question concerning technology and other essays* (W. Lovitt, Trans.). Harper.

Heidegger, M. (1983). *Einführung in die Metaphysik, Gesamtausgabe Band 40.* Vittorio Klostermann.

Heidegger, M. (1987). *Zollikoner seminare.* Vittorio Klostermann.

Heidegger, M. (1994). *Phenomenological interpretation of Aristotle* (R. Rojcewicz, Trans.). Indiana University Press.

Heidegger, M. (1996). *Being and time* (J. Stambaugh, Trans.). State University of New York Press.

Heidegger, M. (2010). *The phenomenology of religious life* (M. Fritsch & J. A. Gosetti-Ferencei, Trans.). Indiana University Press.

Hui, Y. (2012). What is a digital object? *Metaphilosophy, 43*(4), 380–395.

Husserl, E. (1972). *Ideas 1. General introduction to pure philosophy* (W. R. Boyce Gibson, Trans.). Collier Books.

Husserl, E. (2012). *Die Krisis der europäischen Wissenschaften und die transcendentale Phänomenologie.* Felix Meiner Verlag.

Ihde, D. (1990). *Technology and the lifeworld: From garden to earth.* Indiana University Press.

Ihde, D. (2009). *Postphenomenology and technoscience: The Peking lectures.* State University of New York Press.

Ihde, D. (2010). *Heidegger's technologies; postphenomenological perspectives.* Fordham University Press.

Ihde, D. (2022). *Material hermeneutics: Reversing the linguistic turn.* Routledge.

Jünger, E. (1979). Das Sanduhrbuch. In *Sämtliche Werke, Band 12*, (pp. 101–250). Klett-Cotta.

Kant, I. (1990). *Kritik der reinen Vernunft.* Felix Meiner Verlag.

Korenhof, P., Blok, V., & Kloppenburg, S. (2021). Steering representations—Towards a critical understanding of digital twins. *Philosophy & Technology, 34*, 1751–1773. https://doi.org/10.1007/s13347-021-00484-1

Lemmens, P., Blok, V., & Zwier, J. (2017). Toward a terrestrial turn in philosophy of technology: Guest editor's introduction. *Techné: Research in Philosophy and Technology, 21*(2–3), 114–126, https://doi.org/10.5840/techne2017212/363

Lemmens, P. (2021). Thinking technology big again. Reconsidering the question of the transcendental and 'Technology with a capital T' in the light of the Anthropocene. *Foundations of Science, 27*(1), 171–187, https://doi.org/10.1007/s10699-020-09732-7

Scharf, R. C. (2020). Postphenomenology, a technology with a shelf-life? Ihde's move from Husserl toward Dewey. In G. Miller & A. Shew (Eds), *Reimagining philosophy and technology, reinventing Ihde* (pp. 63–86). Springer.

Smith, D. (2015). The internet as idea. For a transcendental philosophy of technology. *Techné: Research in Philosophy and Technology, 19*(3), 381–410, https://doi.org/10.5840/techne2015121140

Schutz, A. (1967). *The phenomenon of the social world*. Northwestern University Press.

2. Towards a Hermeneutic Phenomenology of Technology

Alberto Romele

1. Introduction

The aim of this chapter is to discuss the significance of combining phenomenology and hermeneutics when studying technology from a philosophical perspective. The chapter is divided into two parts. The first section examines the relationship between phenomenology and hermeneutics. Hermeneutics challenges the idealism of Husserlian phenomenology, recognizing that our interaction with the world and its phenomena is always predetermined by symbolic, linguistic, and social factors. Instead of advocating for an ontological hermeneutic as Martin Heidegger and Hans-Georg Gadamer did, we propose an ontic and pragmatic, and partially realist, hermeneutic approach. On the other hand, drawing primarily on Paul Ricœur's work, we also demonstrate that there is a phenomenological assumption in all hermeneutics (namely, the assumption of meaning), and a hermeneutic assumption in all phenomenology (namely, the assumption of *Auslegung*—meaning exegesis, explication, and interpretation in German).

In the second section, we apply these ideas to the field of philosophy of technology, specifically postphenomenology. Our argument is that a hermeneutics of technology (which corresponds to an expanded version of program 2 introduced by Don Ihde) challenges the material idealism of postphenomenology as it currently exists (which corresponds to the development of program 1 alone). We also demonstrate that it is necessary and possible to establish a deeper connection between these two approaches, which we refer to as a 'hermeneutic phenomenology of technology'. From an ontological perspective, this approach highlights the complex relationships between the conditions of possibility that individual technological artefacts are always embedded within. From a methodological perspective, it brings together studies that focus on the materiality of technological artefacts and their mediations, as well as those that examine conditions of possibility in different domains, such as symbolic, linguistic, cultural, social, and economic. Although most of the chapter is theoretical, in the conclusion we briefly mention our empirical research, in which we attempt to put these ideas into practice.

2. Hermeneutics and Phenomenology

The relationship between hermeneutics and phenomenology has always been complex. An illustrative example can be found in Heidegger's dedication of his seminal work, *Being and Time*, to Edmund Husserl 'in friendship and admiration' in 1927. However, concurrently, Heidegger confided to Karl Jaspers that, 'if the treatise has been written "against" anyone, then it has been written against Husserl' (Husserl, 1997, p. 22. In Crowell, 2013, p. 58). Simultaneously, Husserl struggled to see how Heidegger's work could contribute to his project of transcendental phenomenology. In a 1931 letter to Roman Ingarden, Husserl referred to Max Scheler and Heidegger as his two 'antipodes'—in this regard, see Crowell (2005). Over the subsequent years, the rupture between the two thinkers became definitive, driven not only by intellectual differences but also by Heidegger's alignment with the ideals of National Socialism.

It is essential to note that Heidegger's hermeneutical project remains fundamentally transcendental. Heidegger consistently seeks to go beyond preconceptions, such as values and worldviews, which are predefined. Beneath these preconceptions, he relentlessly searches for the 'sense of Being' that underlies the formation of our preconceptions. The answers to this inquiry may vary across historical and cultural contexts, but the central question always revolves around the sense of Being. Furthermore, for Heidegger, this issue is never limited to a specific *Dasein* that formulates a particular response to the ontological question concerning the Being of beings. Instead, his inquiry delves into why and how there exists a Being among beings, namely *Dasein*, that poses the question about Being. For Heidegger, the projectuality of *Dasein* arises precisely from its capacity to pose such an ontological question. Nonetheless, Heidegger does not display an overt curiosity regarding the multiple ways in which life projects of single *Daseins* are either realized or thwarted. Consequently, it can be argued that the *Kehre* (the 'turn') in Heidegger's thought does not represent a mere turning point but rather embodies its most authentic realization.

However, the discussion we wish to engage in within this context does not concern ontological hermeneutics à la Heidegger. We believe that ontological hermeneutics represents the failure of the very essence of hermeneutics. Paradoxically, ontological hermeneutics is anti-interpretive. According to ontological hermeneutics, effective interpretive activity is that which prepares us to receive a sense that originates from an external source, specifically the sense of Being—in the subjective sense of the genitive. This perspective is evident both in the later Heideggerian philosophy, post-*Kehre*, and in the teachings of Gadamer. Although Gadamer emphasizes the significance of dialogue, he posits that meaning does not arise from the interaction of the two participants but rather breaks through as an Event between them. Likewise, a work of art does not possess inherent value; its value lies only in its ability to convey the sense of Being. The role of the spectator/reader/listener of an artwork, in turn, is not to construct meaning but to receive it in the appropriate manner. When we speak of anti-interpretive tendencies, we mean that human beings are virtually deprived of their capacity for initiative, since the only possible initiative is that which leads to a meaning that is already always determined by Being itself. In addition to being anti-interpretive, ontological hermeneutics is also anti-communicative: indeed, the only successful communication is that which subjects the two interlocutors to the aegis of the meaning of Being. We have previously developed this critique of ontological hermeneutics in detail, as can be found in Romele (2014).

Our focus here centres on how a non-ontological hermeneutic approach can contribute to the deconstruction/destruction of Husserlian transcendental phenomenology. By 'non-ontological hermeneutics', we mean an ontic, and more specifically pragmatic, hermeneutics. An ontic hermeneutics concerns itself with the diversity of preconceptions that mediate our relationship with the world. It is worth noting that the term 'preconception' can be somewhat misleading. As we will explore later, our connection to the world is mediated not only by symbolic and conceptual elements but also by material and technological factors. A pragmatic hermeneutics is preoccupied with, or at least acknowledges, the processes of creation and reception of meaning, the character of which is symbolic—that is, historical, social, cultural, and so forth.

One of the main problems with symbolic mediations is their tendency to be themselves always symbolically mediated. We are confronted with what Charles Sanders Peirce and Umberto Eco referred to as 'unlimited semiosis'. On the one hand, there is an interpreter who tries to grasp the link between a signifier and a meaning; on the other hand, there is an interpretant which is a second signifier which points out in what sense a certain signifier can be said to convey a given meaning. But since this second signifier is itself a sign, in order to be understood it needs another sign—that is, another signifier (see Volli, 2002, p. 27).

Indeed, semiosis is never truly unlimited; it extends only as far as one finds satisfaction, typically when temporary consensus is reached between interlocutors. Pragmatic hermeneutics acknowledges that the truth value of an interpretation of the world is never absolute but always contingent upon the context. Furthermore, we should not presume that the validity of an interpretation of a specific aspect of the world within a particular context is solely determined by its utility to the greatest number. It is evident that certain interpretations of the world may serve the interests of a select few, while others may benefit no one at all. To assume that there is no vested interest behind our interpretations of the world is, of course, naïve. However, to believe that there is always a hidden agenda behind our interpretations might be an overestimation of our capabilities.

Lastly, it is important to clarify that when we refer to 'signs', we are not exclusively talking about symbolic or conventional signs, such as the letters of the alphabet. For most human beings, who are unavoidably engaged in interpretation, the world is composed of signs. The assertion that 'we cannot not interpret' does not imply that we are constantly engaged in interpretation. Interpretation is an activity we engage in when something ceases to be self-evident to us. As the concept of 'hysteresis' teaches us, we often persist in applying our interpretations of the world even when they no longer effectively explain our experiences.

Yet, behind every interaction with the world lies an interpretation, at times active and dynamic, and at other times passive and habitual—for a comprehensive overview, see Michel (2019). In short, what we mean is that instead of distinguishing between interpretive and non-interpretive states, one should distinguish between different degrees of interpretation, the two poles being the quasi-absence of interpretation (an 'unintelligent' habit) on the one hand, and the most driven creative activity (what the Romantics called 'genius') on the other. The point is that interpretation is a state that, despite its intensity, characterizes a specific way of being and of dwelling in the world.

This approach, which acknowledges the constant mediation between the self and the world and recognizes the contextual nature of this mediation, has profound implications for phenomenology, especially Husserlian idealism.[8] Paul Ricœur (1991) offers a comprehensive discussion on how hermeneutics can be positioned in opposition to Husserlian idealism. For instance, within Husserl's philosophy, there is a pursuit of scientific rigor (distinct from that found in the natural sciences) that drives him to seek an 'ultimate grounding', to explore 'real beginnings', and to grapple with the concept of 'paths toward the beginning' devoid of any presuppositions. However, as we have just observed, hermeneutics considers presuppositions as an integral aspect of our existence in relation to the world.

In Ricœur's words (1991, p. 29), 'the ideal of scientificity, constructed by Husserl as the ultimate justification, encounters its fundamental limit in the ontological condition of understanding'—which he immediately further elucidates as 'finitude'. From a hermeneutic perspective, the quest for the ultimate foundation is the result of a prejudice/illusion—

---

8   Husserl's idealism is considered the paradox par excellence of classical phenomenology. On the one hand, phenomenology requires us to be as close as possible to the things themselves and to suspend our judgements to let things appear as they appear. On the other hand, however, this proximity to the things themselves and this suspension of all judgements and prejudices is seen as only the first step in an epistemological process that should enable us to grasp things in their purest ideality—that is, in their authentic being. As is well known, Husserl revised his idealist positions in the last part of his life. The interesting move proposed by Ricœur in his interpretation of Husserl is to show that the presuppositions of the critique and revision of idealism via hermeneutics were already present in two works belonging to the idealist period, such as the *Logical Investigations* and the *Cartesian Meditations*. In this respect, see below.

specifically, the prejudice/illusion that objectivity serves as the foundation for 'true' and 'just' knowledge—though this bias remains concealed within itself. Pierre Bourdieu (1990) introduces the concept of the 'scholastic point of view', famously characterizing it as the particular standpoint of those who believe they possess no particular standpoint on the world. Consequently, they regard their perspective on the world as the universal worldview. Bourdieu's critique is directed at academics in general, with philosophers being a particular focus. It could be said that idealist phenomenologists exemplify the philosopher archetype, embodying the academic ensnared by their own scholastic illusion. While phenomenology calls for a return to intuition, hermeneutics counters this by asserting that all understanding is inherently mediated by interpretation. In this sense, even the purest intuitions are, in essence, 'dead' interpretations.

Another crucial aspect emphasized by Ricœur is that of subjectivity. In Husserlian idealism, the realm of ultimate foundation resides within subjectivity, where all transcendence remains uncertain, and only immanence is beyond doubt (Ricœur, 1991, p. 33). In this context, it becomes evident that Heidegger's ontological hermeneutics already introduces a profound departure from this perspective. *Dasein* is distinguished from other beings precisely because it is ontologically constituted by the question that pushes it towards the sense of Being and hence Otherness. Regarding ontic hermeneutics, Ricœur provides a model based on the concept of text. Since the text has achieved autonomy in relation to its author, the interpreter's objective is not to reconstruct the author's intentions. If anything, it is to grasp the 'world of the text'.

To bring these ideas closer to the philosophy of technology, two points can be made. First, from a hermeneutic standpoint, every technology represents an alteration in our relationship with the world. In certain cases, technology is even materially constitutive of our own bodies and its intentionalities. In other words, technology (even when embodied) is always an otherness that pushes subjects beyond solipsism. Through technology, the self is always already open to a multiplicity of otherness. Second, it is essential not to romanticize (as Ricœur and other hermeneutic thinkers tend to do) the autonomy of the text—and consequently, the autonomy of every other hermeneutic technology—from the author's intentions. While it is true that technology can produce unforeseen effects, a critical hermeneutics must also explore the intentions of the author or creator, as this inquiry can reveal preconceptions and interests that may be unknown to the creator or deliberately embedded. An illustrative example is the debate surrounding the alleged racism of Robert Moses (Winner, 1980).

What we are saying, in short, is that there is a certain tendency in the philosophy of technology to make technologies autonomous from the intentions of their creators. In addition to Anglophone traditions, we are thinking here of French philosophy of technology, in particular Gilbert Simondon. The proliferation of autonomous technologies such as generative AI reinforces the idea that the consequences of a technology are always beyond the control of its designers. However, we think it would be necessary to pay more attention to those 'success stories', which we think are numerous, in which designers succeed in imprinting their intentions on technical artefacts while at the same time hiding the traces of those intentions. Just like a good novelist.

Now, while hermeneutics may seem to challenge phenomenological idealism, it is possible to envision a less confrontational relationship between phenomenology and hermeneutics. According to Ricœur, there exists a phenomenological presupposition of hermeneutics, just as there is a hermeneutical presupposition of phenomenology. The phenomenological presupposition of hermeneutics is that 'every question concerning any form of "being" ultimately pertains to the meaning of that being' (Ricœur, 1991, p. 38). It is well known that the phenomenological approach prioritizes the appearance (the *phainestai*) of things to the self. In *Being and Time*, Heidegger asserts that 'phenomenology' means '*apophainesthai ta phainomena*', or 'to let thatwhichshowsitselfbeseenfromitself in the very way in which it shows itself from itself' (Heidegger, 2007, p. 58). Heidegger acknowledges the primordiality of the appearing of beings for the *Dasein*. Yet, in a phenomenological (and, in some ways, still transcendental) attitude, he aims to demonstrate that appearance does not distort the essence of beings but fully reveals it. Heidegger contends that phenomenology seeks to elucidate how beings appear to us 'from themselves'—even if this 'from themselves' is ultimately related to the historicity of Being. For us, this represents an inherent contradiction. We propose a simpler solution, eliminating the need for an ultimate donation or revelation. Instead, we maintain that the foundation of a non-idealist phenomenology lies in the idea that the things of the world reach us through their appearance, which ultimately is nothing more than their always-being-meaningful-for-us.

To assert that the things of the world (beings) present themselves through appearance does not imply a complacency with immediate reality. In phenomenology, one of the pivotal concepts is *epoché*, the suspension of the conventional, everyday relationship with the world. One could describe *epoché* as the act of becoming conscious of a meaningful relationship to the world precisely through the temporary suspension of this lived experience of meaning. Consider Heidegger's famous example of the hammer: the breaking of the hammer, which makes its ready-to-hand appear, is an invitation of the thing itself to *epoché* with respect to its being ready-to-hand. Put simply, it is in the moment when we reflect on our relationship with worldly things that we discover that our connection is not primarily with the objects themselves but rather with things in the way they are meaningful and useful to us. This concept, as frequently highlighted by Ricœur, is not significantly different from what hermeneutics refer to as 'distanciation'. Hermeneutical distanciation involves becoming aware of the biases that mediate our connection to the world. It does not mean, however, to renounce to them. In Heidegger's terms, it therefore in no way means privileging the being present-at-hand of things.

An open point of discussion in our view relates to the linguistic nature of experience and, consequently, the appearance of the world to us. According to Ricœur, linguisticity does not occupy a primary role in hermeneutics, at least not in the hermeneutics of Heidegger and Gadamer. It is indeed true that Gadamer commences his major work, *Truth and Method*, not by delving into language but by discussing artistic experience. Additionally, Heidegger's practical dimension appears to have a broader scope than language. However, we believe that the prelinguistic models within hermeneutics are still constructed upon the linguistic paradigm of transmitting and reconfiguring meaning in a logical and linear manner. If this assertion holds true, then it would be reasonable to regard phenomenology as a corrective to the logocentrism—and particularly the textocentrism—that characterizes the entire hermeneutic tradition.

The hermeneutic presupposition underlying all phenomenology is 'the necessity for phenomenology to conceive of its method as an *Auslegung*, an exegesis, an explication, an interpretation' (Ricœur, 1991, p. 43). According to the French philosopher, *Auslegung* is already evident in both the *Logical Investigations* and the *Cartesian Meditations*. In the latter, the concept of *Auslegung* appears to resolve an essential paradox: the requirement that otherness must be phenomenologically constituted both 'within me' and 'as other than me' simultaneously. In this context, Ricœur (1991, p. 51) writes, '*Auslegung* does nothing more than unfold the surplus of meaning that, in my experience, indicates the place for the other'. Indeed, what does it mean to interpret? It means, above all, to acknowledge that there is something significant outside of us, whose meaning is not entirely contingent upon us. The act of interpreting the world begins with the conviction that there is something external to us that requires interpretation and understanding. One could describe *Auslegung* as the intersection of meaning intentions originating from the interpreter and those emanating from what is being interpreted. Otherness is no longer confined within me, as it might be in a solipsistic interpretation of phenomenology. The subject remains open to otherness, and otherness itself becomes a horizon of understanding. This, we might assert, ensures the openness of interpretive activity. In this context, one might employ the interpretive semiotic distinction between the immediate object and the dynamic object. Here, 'object' is not juxtaposed against 'subject'. The immediate object is what appears 'as the sign represents it' (in phenomenological terms, the thing in its appearance). On the other hand, the dynamic object, as Peirce famously elucidates, is 'truly efficient but not immediately present'. It is the raw data that eludes us. It is perpetually subject to interpretation but also beckons us to interpret it to some extent. Without this 'call', interpretation would not occur, and if there were no interpretation of something beyond itself, then there might not even be a subject, a 'self as another'. Incidentally, there is a huge difference between the ontic idea of dynamic object and the ontological idea of sense of Being. First, it is clear that the dynamic object is by nature multiple and minor, whereas the sense of Being is monolithic. Of course, for Heidegger there are the multiple variations of its historical giving, but these variations are, so to speak, for our own sake. Second, dynamic objects have affordances, but they certainly do not have or make sense. Dynamic objects are silent; in short, they are simply what they are and carry no message for us. We cannot go into the details of the discussion here, but two important references for us are Alain Robbe-Grillet's (1992) theory of the new novel and Maurizio Ferraris' (2014) new realism.

3. Phenomenology and Hermeneutics of Technology

In the preceding section, we delved into the essential relationship between phenomenology and hermeneutics. Phenomenology serves as the foundation of hermeneutics, at least for any hermeneutics that aspires to be more than just a technical guide for accurate text interpretation. Similarly, phenomenology requires hermeneutics to transcend solipsism. Hermeneutics, at its core, implies an orientation towards what exists outside of ourselves, guided by the belief that the external world is not merely a reflection of our consciousness but possesses its own messages and teachings. Even when hermeneutics is understood as a 'hermeneutics of the subject', it interprets the subject in light of the layers of otherness that exist in us independently of us and that can (and want to) communicate with us.

It is worth noting that this idea according to which something always exists outside of us—not as a singular Being but as a multitude of distinct beings—is what renders hermeneutics incompatible with certain exaggerations of deconstructionism, nihilism, or pragmatism in the vein of Richard Rorty. In this context, Eco (2000) recounts a dialogue between himself and Rorty that occurred during the Tanner Lectures in 1990. In response to Rorty's proposition of a radical interpretivism,[9] Eco argues that a screwdriver can indeed serve various purposes. Beyond just screwing, it can be used, for instance, to open a package. However, it would be unwise to employ it for cleaning one's ears, as it is too long and sharp for precise control by the hand. This perspective underscores the ontic and pragmatic nature of hermeneutics and underscores its

---

9   It is beyond the scope of this paper to answer the question of whether Eco's critique of Rorty is honest or whether it makes Rorty into a straw man. For example, are we sure that Rorty or, in the specific field of hermeneutics, Vattimo, would apply their radical interpretivism (or 'flexibilism') not only to texts and their contents, but also to other technical artefacts and their materialities?

realism and materialism—for insights into the limits of interpretation, see Eco (1994).

It is customary to view hermeneutics as a product of the linguistic turn that dominated philosophy and the humanities and social sciences for much of the twentieth century. However, this view is inaccurate, both in terms of historical and theoretical considerations. Historically, hermeneutics has consistently focused on the materiality of objects, particularly texts. It is not coincidental that the term 'material hermeneutics' first appeared not in Ihde or Peter-Paul Verbeek (2003) but in the work of philologist Peter Szondi (1995). Theoretically, hermeneutics—particularly existentialist and ontological hermeneutics as exemplified by Heidegger and Gadamer—represents a relatively brief episode, almost a misunderstanding, within a discipline that has always been concerned with objects and methodologies. Even when engaging with 'worldviews', hermeneutics does not assume immediate accessibility to them. Instead, understanding 'worldviews' necessitates a study of the 'Objective Spirit'—that is, the material concretizations of a culture or society. Think here of the later work of the later Wilhelm Dilthey and then of a broader tradition of hermeneutics that encompasses thinkers such as Ernst Cassirer and Erwin Panofsky. For instance, Panofsky developed 'iconology' as a method for investigating worldviews by analyzing the traces of these worldviews in artworks. Incidentally, it is worth mentioning that the same existentialist and ontological hermeneutics of Heidegger and Gadamer is developed according to a method of archaeology of texts and concepts that is very close to that of methodological hermeneutics—although with a certain fondness for interpretations that purport to be literal but are in fact often allegorical.

In this section, we aim to extend the discussion from the previous section into the realm of the philosophy of technology, specifically within the context of postphenomenology. Our first idea is that, to some extent, the hermeneutics of technology challenges certain phenomenological assumptions that underpin contemporary philosophy of technology. Our second idea is that, beyond this apparent conflict, we can and should explore a more intricate interplay between phenomenology and hermeneutics within the philosophy of technology.

In what sense does the hermeneutics of technology challenge the phenomenology of technology? To address this question, we must first clarify what we mean by the 'phenomenology of technology'. In this context, the phenomenology of technology refers to the tendency of postphenomenology to define itself in accordance with the 'program 1' of postphenomenology outlined by Ihde (1990). Specifically, we are referring to the tendency of the postphenomenological school to place the relationships among the self (I), technology, and the world at the core of its investigations. From a theoretical perspective, this involves the exploration of novel types of relationships—cyborg relations, immersive relations, and so forth. From a practical standpoint, it entails utilizing the framework of I-technology-world relations to examine the uses and mediations of specific technologies. This approach retains a phenomenological dimension, since it is concerned with the manner in which the world appears to us. It also assumes that this process of 'appearing' plays a central role in our relationship with the world and, consequently, in the manner in which we construct ourselves as subjects. However, it is also distinctly postphenomenological, as it no longer exhibits, at least on the surface, traces of transcendental idealism. Indeed, as one becomes increasingly aware of the near-inevitability of the presence of a third element between the subject and the world, one concurrently acknowledges the impossibility of rendering things to appear as they are in themselves (the concept of *'apophainesthai ta phainomena'* discussed earlier). Of course, traces of such an approach can already be seen in post-Husserlian phenomenology, notably in the works of Maurice Merleau-Ponty. Yet, the merit of Ihde's postphenomenology, which openly acknowledges its indebtedness to Merleau-Ponty, rather than Husserl, is its explicit emphasis on this aspect.

So, in what manner can we still invoke idealism within the context of postphenomenology? At first glance, there appears to be nothing idealistic about a philosophy that places material mediations, particularly technological mediations, at its focal point. This approach entails a complete acceptance that objects will never present themselves to us precisely as they intend to be seen. Instead, they will invariably differ from their intended appearances when presented to us. The objective of postphenomenology is not to eliminate technological mediations but rather to accentuate their role—not necessarily to embrace them unquestioningly, but also to subject them to scrutiny if they induce distortions with significant implications, especially from a societal perspective. However, on closer examination, postphenomenology exhibits a form of 'materialist idealism'. By this term, we denote postphenomenology's inclination to suspend (in the sense of the phenomenological *epoché*) the judgment towards all non-technological mediations. Often, these non-technological mediations—of a symbolic, social, or cultural nature—mediate the same technological mediations that interest postphenomenology. We are not suggesting that the relationship between these mediations must necessarily be hierarchical, but it is undoubtedly valuable to investigate cases where technological mediations are hierarchically subordinate to other forms of mediations. Such inquiries serve to deconstruct the materialist idealism inherent in certain strands of postphenomenology.

For instance, during our fieldwork at a lower limb prosthesis centre, we made two significant observations. First, we found that the concept of 'cyborg relations', at least in this context, does not hold true. The idea of a 'cyborg relationship' is more a product of imagery rooted in social and cultural influences than a technological reality. In reality, there is never a complete fusion between the human body and technology; instead, there exists a series of technological mediations. The prosthesis never seamlessly integrates with the body; it never becomes transparent in its usage. Various technologies mediate other technologies to bridge the insurmountable gap between humans and technology. For instance, a typical lower limb prosthesis consists of a rigid frame; within this frame lies a socket made of plastic or laminated material; the socket attaches to the body through a soft polyurethane or silicone liner worn between it and the residual limb; additional prosthetic socks, made from wool, nylon, or synthetic fabric, may be worn with the liner to ensure a better fit since the size of the residual limb can vary; these socks may come in different thicknesses. Furthermore, in the spaces that inevitably persist between the residual limb and the socket, sweat accumulates, especially in hot weather. Wearing a prosthesis, something many of us take for granted, entails having a part of one's own sensitive body encased in plastic, polyurethane, silicone, wool, nylon, or similar materials for extended periods. Amputees must clean or change their liners at least three times a day to prevent dermatitis and other medical issues. In these moments, the technology does not merge with the body but rather stands out, akin to Heidegger's famous example of the hammer—these observations are detailed in Romele (2023, p. 28).

Second, we discovered that the separation between the body and the prosthesis can indeed be bridged, but solely through symbolic, social, and cultural mediations. In other words, in this context, symbolic mediations serve as the conditions of possibility for a particular type of material relations. In our research, we specifically observed the presence of posthumanist and transhumanist protoimaginaries among both patients and staff at the prosthetic centre, even among individuals who might initially appear more 'realistic' and 'pragmatic'.

In summary, it can be argued that the hermeneutics of technology dismantles the empiricist bias that prevails in much of contemporary philosophy of technology. By 'empiricist bias', we mean the tendency to want to focus only on 'concrete artifacts'—while unwittingly smuggling in posthumanist and transhumanist proto-imaginaries. The reasons for this bias are well-documented and are closely linked to the discipline's 'empirical turn'. It can be argued that at a certain point, the philosophy of technology, having relinquished ontological and theological aspirations akin to those of Heidegger and Jacques Ellul, found itself caught between two conflicting forces: the technical aspects of engineering work and the socio-cultural considerations explored by disciplines such as media studies.

Of course, we are not the first to criticize the empiricism prevalent in postphenomenology and contemporary philosophy of technology. However, in this context, we also want to emphasize the importance of considering the relationship between the phenomenology and hermeneutics of technology. By the term 'hermeneutics of technology', we refer to something akin to Ihde's 'program 2' within postphenomenology. In this program, Ihde focuses on the cultural hermeneutics of technology, exploring how the use of a technology varies in response to cultural (and, although Ihde does not explicitly specify, social) differences. An illustrative example is Ihde's account of sardine cans left by Australian explorers in the New Guinea highlands in the 1930s. These cans were transformed into elaborate headdresses worn by New Guineans on special occasions. In this regard, there is already substantial research on 'technology transfer' from one culture or society to another. Similarly, in what concerns the social aspects, extensive research exists—although not primarily within the realms of postphenomenology or philosophy of technology—that investigates how the use of the same technology varies with changes in social class. For instance, studies have demonstrated that the Internet, at least in the early days of social networking, was used out of necessity by lower-income individuals, while it served as a platform for serious leisure among wealthier ones (Robinson, 2009).

It is worth noting that program 2 has been largely overlooked by the postphenomenological school, which has predominantly favoured program 1. This partiality has, to some extent, severed the original intent of Ihde's project. We contend that, therefore, postphenomenology is not just an incomplete project but rather a failed one. In a sense, Ihde recognizes the necessity of integrating these two programs when he introduces the concepts of micro-perceptions and macro-perceptions. Micro-perceptions are grounded in perceptual phenomenology, while macro-perceptions involve cultural and hermeneutical dimensions:

> What is usually taken as sensory perception (what is immediate and focused bodily in actual seeing, hearing, etc.), I shall call microperception. But there is also what might be called a cultural, or hermeneutic, perception, which I shall call macroperception. Both belong equally to the lifeworld. And both dimensions of perception are closely linked and intertwined. There is no microperception (sensory-bodily) without its location within a field of macroperception and no macroperception without its microperceptual foci. (Ihde, 1990, p. 29)

For us, program 2 should be understood in a broader context than Ihde himself presents. By solely confining it to a cultural and social hermeneutic of technology, one might erroneously conclude that technologies are perpetually ensconced within preexisting social and cultural frameworks. However, it is essential to remember that technologies themselves actively participate in the construction and reconfiguration of 'semiospheres'. Technologies are not mere neutral entities, transparent in their use, nor are they solely the embodiment of established social and cultural practices. They play an active role in the reconfiguration of these practices and the creation of new ones. In essence, one must comprehend the relationship between the material and symbolic aspects of technologies through the lens of the hermeneutic circle, denoting their interdependence. We insist that this is not simply an unfinished project, but a failed one, as a lintel supported by a single pillar would be. Just think of the determinism of certain orthodox readings of Karl Marx, according to which everything that is not material (be it religion, art, or law) is an illusion. This materialism prevented, among other things, an understanding of the power of imaginaries (symbols, culture, etc.) in the construction (as well as the deconstruction) of social reality—for a critique of the economic materialism of the young Marx, see Ricœur (1986). Focusing on programme 1 of postphenomenology leads to not only an incomplete answer, but precisely a wrong answer as to what a technological artefact is, its conditions of possibility, and its consequences. And it is no coincidence that even the most classical postphenomenology has in recent years incorporated more and more symbolic, value, and cultural elements without, however, reforming its theoretical framework.

If our prior assertions regarding the description of technological reality hold true, then they should also be valid and supportable from a methodological standpoint. In other words, to empirically study technological mediations, one must employ both phenomenology *and* hermeneutics, specifically adopting a hermeneutic phenomenology of technology. This implies that a technology should be scrutinized *both* in terms of its mediations and the conditions of possibility that enable these mediations. While hermeneutics has conventionally been concerned with symbolic, cultural, or linguistic conditions of possibility, a broader perspective demands hermeneutic phenomenology of technology to examine additional conditions of possibility—think of Cassirer, who explored various symbolic forms, including technology and economics, recognizing the latter's preeminence over the former. It could be said that technologies are all 'boundary objects' at the intersection of different domains that, precisely around the object, confront or conflict with each other. Of course, we can act 'as if' technology depends exclusively on itself or on only one of these conditions of possibility, but this will still be an epistemological and methodological fiction or convention. For example, I can pretend that Artificial Intelligence (AI) is only a technology, but I will not be able to understand how the current status of this technology also, and perhaps especially, depends on being embedded in a specific economic system that favours forms of consumption and waste. Nevertheless, it is evident that such an endeavour appears more akin to a collaborative research program encompassing multiple researchers, each with their own objects and methodologies, rather than an individual's pursuit. In the conclusion, we aim to show how we are trying to implement such a methodology in our research and thereby contribute to the development of a discipline.

Before proceeding, it is essential to provide an important clarification. There is indeed an empirical interpretation of the relationship between phenomenology and hermeneutics within the framework of postphenomenology, which we believe significantly differs from what we refer to as the 'hermeneutic phenomenology of technology'. Verbeek (2001, p. 128), in his explication of Ihde's work, elucidates that:

> [e]mbodiment relations and hermeneutic relations can be viewed as the extremes of a continuum: As we move on this continuum of embodiment to hermeneutic relations more toward the hermeneutic pole, the transformation that reality undergoes in the mediation is one of progressively higher contrast: the perception effected by the mediation deviates ever more sharply from unmediated perception. [...] The 'space' available for reality to express itself becomes more restricted as the mediation of our perception becomes more hermeneutic in nature.

In this context, phenomenology and hermeneutics are seen as two distinct but interconnected dimensions within the same discipline, and as methods for studying technological mediations. Yet, in our view, to put phenomenology and hermeneutics on the same plane of empirical analysis of technological mediations is to fail to recognize an important part of the specific contribution that hermeneutics can make to the philosophical study of technologies. The concept of 'hermeneutic mediation of technologies' should be understood not only in the subjective genitive sense but also in the objective sense, implying that technologies themselves are always *objects* of hermeneutic mediation.

4. Conclusion

Instead of retracing the various stages of this chapter, in the conclusion, we would like to briefly refer to our empirical work. Indeed, it is within these works that we strive not only to theorize but also, and above all, to practice a hermeneutic phenomenology of technology.

In our ongoing research, we focus on visual and textual representations of AI. The underlying idea is that to fully grasp the materiality of AI, including its practical efficacy, we must also consider the discourses surrounding AI. Science communication literature has long established that science communication goes beyond the straightforward transmission of knowledge and can substantially impact how science is perceived and engaged with by society (Bucchi, 1996). Science articles in popular media, for instance, are not just simplified science lessons; they are intricate entities that mobilize everyday conceptions, moral judgments, character depictions, and interpersonal relationships.

Recently, we conducted research analyzing the usage of the expression 'AI ethics' through discourse analysis of eight newspapers from four European countries. Our hypothesis was that 'AI ethics' had become a 'floating signifier'.[10] This concept, introduced by Ernesto Laclau (2005), refers to terms or concepts that are sufficiently polysemous to be interpreted, understood, and strategically employed in various ways by different social groups for hegemonic purposes. Our empirical analysis confirmed this hypothesis and revealed three distinct discursive uses of 'AI ethics': institutional use emphasizing normativity, academic use—particularly in the humanities and social sciences—focusing on critique, and business use approaching it as techno-solutionism. Our intention was not to pinpoint a definitive definition of AI ethics or assess the ethical nature of specific AI systems but to examine the different and often conflicting ways this term is used and understood. Paradoxically, before being an ethical concept, 'AI ethics' is deeply political. Different techno-political agendas compete over the definition of what should be considered 'AI ethics'.

This approach does not undermine the importance of addressing AI ethics but underscores that how we address concrete questions about AI ethics is always context-dependent, particularly within political and social contexts. It highlights the need to engage in what we term the 'politics of AI ethics'. This, in our view, exemplifies a 'phenomenological hermeneutics of technology'. Methodologically, we have attempted to integrate a material approach, such as discourse analysis (Jørgensen & Phillips, 2002), with theoretical analysis. Philosophy, in this context,

---

10 This unpublished research in English will be published in the French journal *Interfaces numériques*.

learns from other disciplines, notably media studies. Inspired by Ricœur's idea that there is no dichotomy between method and truth—as suggested, instead, by Heidegger and Gadamer—we believe that more extensive explanation is necessary for a deeper understanding. From a results perspective, our transcendental analysis (concerned with the conditions of possibility for a particular technological implementation) demonstrates that these very conditions significantly impact the reality of the AI systems that will be implemented.

One may question whether a politics of AI ethics can still be considered hermeneutic, as hermeneutics (and phenomenology) has historically been hesitant to engage in ethical and political reflections—and sometimes leans towards conservatism. However, it is crucial to note that there are efforts to develop political hermeneutics, as exemplified by Vattimo and Zabala (2014). Moreover, we have no qualms about asserting that hermeneutics should be open to insights from other disciplines and theoretical perspectives. The idea that hermeneutics and phenomenology, even when combined, can provide an exhaustive account of a technology and its multiple consequences is untenable. As we discussed earlier, at the core of hermeneutics lies a call to engage with otherness, to that which exists outside itself, and this extends to the discipline itself.

References

Bourdieu, P. (1990). The scholastic point of view. *Cultural Anthropology, 5*(4), 380–391.

Bucchi, M. (1996). When scientists turn to the public: Alternative routes in science communication. *Public Understanding of Science, 5*(4), 375–394, https://doi.org/10.1088/0963-6625/5/4/005

Crowell, S.G. (2005). Heidegger and Husserl: The matter and method of philosophy. In H.L. Dreyfus & M.A. Wrathall (Eds), *A companion to Heidegger* (pp. 49–64). Blackwell, https://doi.org/10.1002/9780470996492.ch4

Eco, U. (1994). *The limits of interpretation.* Indiana University Press.

Eco, U. (2000). *Kant and the platypus: Essays on language and cognition.* Harcourt.

Ferraris, M. (2014). *Manifesto of New Realism.* State University of New York Press.

Heidegger, M. (2007). *Being and time*. Blackwell.

Husserl, E. (1997). *Psychological and transcendental phenomenology and the confrontation with Heidegger (1927–1931)* (Th. Sheehan & R. Palmer, Trans.). Kluwer.

Ihde, D. (1990). *Technology and the lifeworld: From garden to earth*. Indiana University Press.

Jørgensen, M., & Phillips, L. (2002). *Discourse analysis as theory and method*. SAGE, https://doi.org/10.4135/9781849208871

Laclau, E. (2005). *On populist reason*. Verso.

Michel, J. (2019). *Homo interpretans: Towards a transformation of hermeneutics*. Rowman & Littlefield.

Ricœur, P. (1986). *Lectures on ideology and utopia*. Columbia University Press.

Ricœur, P. (1991). *From text to action: Essays in hermeneutics 2*. Northwestern University Press.

Robbe-Grillet, A. (1992). *For a new novel: Essays on fiction*. Northwestern University Press.

Robinson, L. (2009). A taste for the necessary. *Information, Communication & Society, 12*(4), 488–507, https://doi.org/10.1080/13691180902857678

Romele, A. (2014). The ineffectiveness of hermeneutics. Another Augustine's legacy in Gadamer. *International Journal of Philosophy and Theology, 75*(5), 422–439, https://doi.org/10.1080/21692327.2015.1027789

Romele, A. (2023). *Digital habitus: A critique of the imaginaries of Artificial Intelligence*. Routledge, https://doi.org/10.4324/9781003400479

Szondi, P. (1995). *Introduction to literary hermeneutics* (1st edition). Cambridge University Press, https://doi.org/10.1017/CBO9780511597503

Vattimo, G., & Zabala, S. (2014). *Hermeneutic communism: From Heidegger to Marx*. Columbia University Press.

Verbeek, P.-P. (2003). Material hermeneutics. *Techné: Research in Philosophy and Technology, 6*(3), 181–184.

Volli, U. (2002). *Manuale di semiotica*. GLF Editori Laterza.

Winner, L. (1980). Do artifacts have politics? *Daedalus, 109*(1), 121–136.

3. The Institution of Technology

Darian Meacham

1. Introduction

In this chapter I have a fairly straightforward aim. I ask whether the phenomenological concept of 'Institution' (*Stiftung*), which is sometimes translated (into both French and English) to 'foundation' or 'establishment', can help to better articulate how phenomenology or phenomenological methods can contribute to the philosophical examination of technology. I think that the answer is yes. Nonetheless, it is not clear from the outset that the concept of institution, as developed in the phenomenological tradition, can be rendered in a straightforward manner as a *method* or *tool* in the philosopher of technology's quiver. Moreover, the application of phenomenological methods in the philosophy of technology under the umbrella of postphenomenology has also come under recent criticism for being insufficiently attentive to questions of broader historical and political context (Cressman, 2020)—a classic critique of phenomenology—and for being insufficiently phenomenological (Ritter, 2021)—a common critique of applied versions of phenomenological philosophy. The aim here is not to intervene in these debates about the merits and shortcomings of postphenomenological methods in the philosophy of technology or whether postphenomenology is sufficiently phenomenological, but rather to understand how the concept of institution transformed phenomenological analysis and how this might be of some use in approaching the question of technology from a phenomenological perspective.

Though the concept of 'institution' (*Stiftung*) appears in the work of Edmund Husserl, Maurice Merleau-Ponty, Jean-Paul Sartre, Jacques Derrida, Claude Lefort, Cornelius Castoriadis, and more recently Roberto Esposito, the focus in this chapter will be on its role in Merleau-Ponty's thinking, with some reference to its Husserlian development. The reason for this is on the one hand scope and on the other that the manner in which Merleau-Ponty elaborates the concept makes its affinity to the philosophy of technology readily apparent. In the first section of the chapter, I will give a brief account of the development of the concept in Merleau-Ponty's thinking from earlier writing on perception and embodiment through to a form of synthesis of his readings of Max Weber, György Lukács, and Husserl that was at least in part meant to address and elaborate his own and other criticisms of transcendental phenomenology. In this second part, I will try to provide a more conceptual overview of the concept and how it developed from an element of Husserl's genetic phenomenology to a 'fundamental modality of time' (to use Lefort's expression) in Merleau-Ponty's onto-political turn in the mid-1950s. The difficulty with the concept of 'institution' is its fecundity: event, social object, form, and structure are all ways in which the concept can and has been utilized. To give the term its place in a method of phenomenological analysis, these different senses of the term will have to be separated analytically, to the extent possible. In the third part, I will examine how this concept may be able to contribute to a phenomenological approach to questions concerning technology.

2. Very Brief History of a Concept

The concept of institution is most closely associated, in Merleau-Ponty's thought, with the *Collège de France* lectures from 1955 and the subsequent 1961 course on Husserl's 'Origin of Geometry' text (Husserl, 2002). Lefort's use and further development of the concept in the development and elaboration of his own political phenomenology stemmed from a rigorous engagement with the entirety of Merleau-Ponty's oeuvre.[1]

---

[1] Derrida's own treatment of the 'Origin of Geometry' text marks another trajectory for the life of the concept, which is outside the scope of the present chapter.

However, Merleau-Ponty's engagement with the concept predates these 'later' writings and can already be discerned more than a decade earlier in the phenomenology of perceptual experience and embodied being in *Phenomenology of Perception* (1942). This early uptake was probably a consequence of Merleau-Ponty's close reading of Husserl's *Ideas II* manuscripts in the early 1940s. The application of the concept to historical—how one time has access to another time (Merleau-Ponty, 2003, p. 8)—and political analyses dates to a period when he turned again toward questions of politics in the texts gathered in *Adventures of the Dialectic* (1955) (Merleau-Ponty, 1973), following a break with Sartre and French communist politics.[2] The first sentences of the preface of *Adventures of the Dialectic* read: 'we need a philosophy of both history and spirit to deal with the problems we touch upon here. Yet we would be unduly rigorous if we were to wait for perfectly elaborated principles before speaking philosophically of politics'. The concept of institution seems then to be the imperfectly elaborated principle that will form the basis of Merleau-Ponty's philosophy of history. The period of the institution lectures and the publication of *Adventures of the Dialectic* (1955) was also a period of engagement with Weber and Lukács. Before proceeding to the concept of institution directly, it is necessary to touch upon the insights that are driving this often overlooked engagement, because I think that they are formative for the development of the concept of institution.

Merleau-Ponty's engagement with Weber merits broader consideration but here I will point to only two points of contact within the essay 'The crisis of understanding' (Merleau-Ponty, 1973): (1) the reconstruction of the 'horizon' of an action, and (2) the notion of 'elective affinity'. The first pertains to what Merleau-Ponty considers the form of activity proper to both the historian and the 'man of action'. The 'man of action' should be a kind of historian and likewise the activity of engaging in historical investigation is always a form of (political) action. To understand an action, it is necessary to reconstruct its horizon, which

---

2   Despite the falling out, Sartre seems to have closely followed Merleau-Ponty's turn toward history and politics in the 1950s, famously writing, in an eulogy following Merleau-Ponty's death, that Merleau-Ponty had taught him the meaning of history. The concept of institution takes an important role in the *Critique of Dialectal Reason* (1961).

is to say not just the 'perspective of the agent' or the subjective acts, but also the objective content or context which shapes the subjective acts. Merleau-Ponty calls doing history 'action in the realm of the imaginary' (Merleau-Ponty, 1973, p. 11). What does this mean? The historian engages in an imaginative reconstruction of the horizon of subjective acts and objective forces that shape concrete action.

Two key points here. First, neither the historian nor the 'man of action' (the political actor) can engage in this horizon reconstruction from the position of pure spectator; by acting in and on the realm of the historical imaginary that shapes action, the historian or political actor reshapes the historical horizon of action in the present moment. The imaginary that Merleau-Ponty refers to does not sit on the side of the subjective act, but is the web of meaning from which both the subjective act or volition (he uses both words here, though the scope of subjective act goes beyond that of volitions) and the objective content attain meaning. In other words, the imaginary pertains to the historical and material context of meaning formation.

Second point: Merleau-Ponty cautions his reader, or Weber's reader, that this does not amount to reconstituting in whole or in part the thought processes of 'great men' or historical actors. The ambition is much greater: 'the total meaning of what has been done'. But by 'total meaning', what he seems to mean is that the historian comes to be aware of a certain style or 'logical structure of the facts' in their temporal development. This logic that is revealed in historians' work becomes a 'key' to comprehending a further unfolding of events, intentions, and objective conditions. Merleau-Ponty refers to Weber's classic example of how Calvinism and nascent capitalism come together. What Weber's reading of Benjamin Franklin unveils is not the thoughts of one person, but rather how a style that is detected in Franklin becomes a heuristic key to understanding the objective trajectory that was developing historically in Western Europe at the time. It is important to emphasize here how the term 'objective' is being used here. It refers not just to material conditions, but also the public imaginary or symbolic dimensions that shape or condition the meaning of subjective acts and their material context.

To describe Weber's innovation, Merleau-Ponty uses two terms that also show the lineages of his (Merleau-Ponty's) thinking. He tells the reader that Weber has shown a method for restoring the 'anonymous intention' (a term coming from Husserl's analysis of passive synthesis) of a 'dialectic of a whole' (a term referring most directly here to Lukács's work). The intention is anonymous in the proper sense— it does not originate or belong to any one person or persons, but appears in the trajectory of the historical development of the objective. Without using the term 'institution', Merleau-Ponty provides a nearly verbatim description of what he was putting into his lecture notes for the lectures on institution and passivity that were contemporaneous to the publication of the *Adventures of the Dialectic*: 'symbolic matrices which have no pre-existence and which can for a longer or shorter time influence history itself and then disappear, not by external forces but through an internal disintegration or because one of their secondary elements becomes predominant and changes their nature' (Merleau-Ponty, 1973, pp. 16–17).

What is detected in a style—what Merleau-Ponty elsewhere helpfully calls a 'watermark'—which appears in the historical development of the objective are 'elective affinities between the elements of a historical totality'.[3] The sociologist Michael Löwy provides a clear explanation of this somewhat magical term in Weber's writing, which enthrals Merleau-Ponty: 'elective affinity is a process through which two cultural forms—religious, intellectual, political or economical—that have certain analogies, intimate kinships or meaning affinities, enter in a relationship of reciprocal attraction and influence, mutual selection, active convergence and mutual reinforcement' (Löwy, 2004). The elements that emerge and which can enter into these relations of affinity, Calvinism and nascent ideas of capitalism being the prime example, do not spring from an 'all powerful idea'—they are the sparks of a 'historical imagination' (Merleau-Ponty, 1973, p. 17) that develops in an indeterminate if not entirely haphazard fashion in an ongoing dialectic with the web of human speech, choices, movements, and expression more broadly. It is this not entirely haphazard fashion of development of the dialectic that appears as though it were a watermark on the objective content of history itself.

Merleau-Ponty's reading of Weber and its own affinity with the idea of institution that was coming from the phenomenological side can be

---

3   The term 'style' has its own Husserlian legacy which Merleau-Ponty is building on, see Meacham (2013).

read as a response to the critique that Lukács made of phenomenology already nearly a decade earlier; a critique that I think also animates some of the recent 'dialectical' criticism of (post) phenomenology as an approach in the philosophy of technology (Cressman, 2020). In the long essay on Lukács, '"Western" Marxism', that directly follows the essay by Weber in *Adventures of the Dialectic*, Merleau-Ponty provides a view of Lukács' historical materialism that bears a close resemblance to his (Merleau-Ponty's) reading of Weber: 'the relations among men are not the sum of personal acts or personal decisions, but pass through things, the anonymous roles, the common situations and the institutions where men have projected so much of themselves that their fate is now played out outside them[selves] [*desormais hors d'eux*]' (Merleau-Ponty, 1973, p. 32).

The point that I want to make here is that these readings of Weber and Lukács function as preparation for what can be read as a phenomenological response to Lukács's critique of phenomenology through the concept of institution. It is worthwhile then to look a bit more closely at that critique as it is phrased in the 1949 essay 'Existentialism' (Lukács, 1971). Lukács takes as his example an 'honest' phenomenologist, Wilhelm Szilasi—someone whose name is now forgotten, but who evidently Lukács held in higher esteem than, say Max Scheler, whom he refers to in the same essay as a charlatan. Szilasi attempts the well-worn move of the phenomenology lecturer, to provide a phenomenological analysis of the situation perceptually before him in terms of how the co-presence of others conditions or co-constitutes its appearance: 'this space with its variously worked boards is a lecture hall only because we understand this mass of wooden objects as such, and we do understand it so because from the outset we mean it as something presupposed in our common task—namely, lecturing and listening. [...] It is the way of being together that determines what the thing is'. Lukács makes several critical points. The first has to do with the level of abstraction. Szilasi refers to 'variously worked boards' and not to desks, benches, etc., so as not to deprive the intentional act of its constituting power or what Lukács calls the 'magical potency of the intentional experience'. This is not an oversight, but an essential dimension of the phenomenological analysis. Lukács goes on. What is also missing from the analysis, but precisely not from the experience itself, are the social and political conditions which shape the environment of the lecture. In this case, that it is taking place in Zurich and not Freiburg where Szilasi can no longer teach due to the Nazi regime. Moreover, the building, the heating system, and the furniture all bear what we above—using Merleau-Ponty's terminology—referred to as the style or watermark of 'a certain stage of development of industry and of society'. Lukács criticism is not that phenomenological method cannot account for socio-historical meaning, but that it places it on the side of individual subjectivity. It 'confronts consciousness with a chaos of things (and men) which only individual subjectivity can articulate and objectify'. To understand the critique, it is helpful to go back to Merleau-Ponty's own reading of Weber and Lukács. As Merleau-Ponty points out, Lukács's retort to Weber in *History and Class Consciousness* was that he remained confined to the traditional categories of subject and object (Lukács, 1923). When we are also able to relativize these categories, we can arrive at a 'sort of totality'. It is a *sort* of totality because it does not encompass all actual and possible being, but a 'coherent arrangement of known facts' (Merleau-Ponty, 1973, p. 31). In other words, it is a partial and historical totality that allows for what Merleau-Ponty will later refer to as 'coherent deformation' with the advent of lines of development and matrices in the historical imagination.

In short, the critique is that phenomenological analysis fails, by design, to appropriately account for the fundamental insight of Lukács's dialectical philosophy: that perceived empirical objects 'are to be understood as aspects of a totality, i.e., as aspects of a total social situation caught up in the process of historical change' (Lukács, 1971, p. 162). The theory of institution functions then as a phenomenological response to Lukács critique, but also as a development of Merleau-Ponty's own critique of transcendental phenomenology, which in *The Visible and the Invisible* he characterizes as the attempt on the part of reflective consciousness to methodologically walk back the path of constitution from the constituted object of experience to the 'zero point of subjectivity'; as though 'one could walk in either direction from Notre Dame to the Eiffel Tower or from the Eiffel Tower to Notre Dame' (Flynn, 2013; Merleau-Ponty, 1968). The analogy is interesting for our purposes here as Merleau-Ponty uses not only a historical example but a technological one. The point that he wishes to make with this example is that there is what we can call an institutional pathway or history that gives the historical path from Notre Dame to the Eiffel Tower its sense. The sense of both artefacts is emergent from this institutional history and cannot be thought without it. The idea of movement and the play of the French word *sens* as meaning both sense and direction is important here: sense is emergent in the movement of institutions. One can travel in both directions from the Eiffel Tower to Notre Dame, but it is not the same path. On the walk back, we see things differently, having been marked by the walk there. We can think this in a very literal sense of the perceptual experience of the walk to and from Notre Dame, but also in the historical sense, which runs through the perceptual. Notre Dame appears in an institutional and perceptual context that includes a history of architectural development through to the Eiffel Tower. To link back to Lukács's critique of phenomenology, we see in and through 'a certain stage of development of industry and of society'; there is no direct path from the constituted object of experience to 'the zero point of subjectivity', perceptual consciousness occurs in and through a historical totality. This is why Merleau-Ponty, in the 1955 lectures on institution, says that we should shift from thinking consciousness in terms of constituting/constituted to instituting/instituted.

Though presenting this as a critique of transcendental phenomenology, Merleau-Ponty is nonetheless insistent that the sprigs of institutional thinking can be found in the 'unthought' of Husserl's own work—itself an institution. And this idea of the 'unthought' (akin to the notion of horizon that Merleau-Ponty pulls from Weber's work) that reanimates an institution becomes key to the theory of institution itself. In the next section, we will focus somewhat more on the Husserlian legacy of the concept.

3. The Phenomenology of Institution

In this section, I will try to further unpack the phenomenological theory of institution that Merleau-Ponty attempts to develop on the basis of this reading of Weber and Lukács on the one hand and also his project of developing Husserlian phenomenology beyond the limitations pointed out by Lukács. Taking a step back, it is helpful to reiterate what it is that I mean, in the most basic sense, when I use the term 'institution'.

Perhaps one of the clearer explanations of what an institution is comes not from the phenomenological tradition (not entirely surprisingly) but from the conservative political theorist Yuval Levin: 'when I speak of institutions, I mean the durable forms of our common life. They are the frameworks and structures of what we do together' (Levin, 2020). In this section I will try to unpack this rather straightforward description in the phenomenological language of Merleau-Ponty, while trying to retain the central insight articulated by Levin.

3.1 Institutions in Personal Life

For both Husserl and Merleau-Ponty, an institution within subjective life refers to an event that becomes a durable form of sense (to use Levin's construction). Husserl in the language of constitution uses the term 'act', specifying that an institution is an act that opens a horizon of other potential sense-developments, whether conceived as events or acts. The horizon of potentiality exists in a form of latency in the initial event of the sense-bestowing act. This latency or horizon of potentiality can be more or less constrained depending on the history or institutional web that any one event or act occurs within. When potentiality within the web of institutions that constitutes a subjective life (Merleau-Ponty takes issue with the language of constitution here for reasons well-articulated by Lukács above) is actualized into sense-formation or an event it 'refers back' to the initial institution that facilitated it. Husserl and subsequently Merleau-Ponty use the term *Nachstiftung* or reinstitution to describe this. This back-referral awakens and also transforms the initial institution, affecting both its sense within the web of a subjective life, but also its intensity. If we can refer to these processes of sense formation as institutional pathways, no pathway operates in isolation. The entire nexus of a subjective life is in a constant process of being activated, reactivated, and transformed, however subtly.

The discussion of institution in personal life occurs for Husserl—and also when it is picked up by Merleau-Ponty—in the broader context of passive synthesis; meaning a form of synthesis that is not present to consciousness. Passivity, in this sense, is not opposed to activity. To put it in somewhat plainer terms, our subjective lives are instituted in ways that we are not aware of. Becoming at best partially aware of these processes in relation to an objective context is the activity of the historian or political actors as discussed in the first section. This process of reinstitution, the continuous activation and transformation of the temporal web of our subjective lives, takes place in what Husserl calls the 'background that is prior to all comportment and is instead presupposed by all comportment' (Husserl, 1989, p. 279). The institution can be described in terms of an active meaning structure that displays a sort of meta-stability or plasticity; it is subject to change and transformation without losing its identity. This explanation clarifies somewhat how Merleau-Ponty wishes to use the concept when he sketches the problem and defines the term in the *resumé* of his 1955 course at the *Collège de France* and how Lefort summarizes the idea in his introduction to those lectures:

> Institution in the strong sense is this symbolic matrix that creates an opening of a field, of a future according to its dimensions, from which comes the possibility of a common adventure and a history like consciousness. (Lefort in Merleau-Ponty 2003, p. 45)
>
> The concept of institution may help us to find a solution to certain difficulties in the philosophy of consciousness [...] there is nothing in the object that is capable of throwing consciousness back toward other perspectives [...] Thus what we understand by the concept of institution are those events in experience that endow it with durable dimensions, in relation to which a whole series of other experiences will acquire meaning, will for an intelligible series or a history—or again those events which sediment in me a meaning, not just as survivals or residues, but as the invitation to a sequel, the necessity of a future. (Merleau-Ponty, 2003, pp. 123–124)

Both of these descriptions help to demonstrate how the concept both retains its character as an element of phenomenological methodology while also addressing the critique of that methodology as one finds, for example, in Lukács work, as discussed above. This is, in other words, consciousness historicized. A 'history like consciousness' emerges from what is described above as the historical imagination of a material totality at a certain point in its development. But consciousness (an example of an institution) is also an institution that endows a particular sense to a series of future experiences, but also to the past. The force of the institution extends into an indeterminate future and a past that is also reshaped as its 'facts' are reinstituted by their contact with the trajectory of the new institution. Institution is what gives consciousness its history in both senses, a consciousness of history and the history of consciousness. I am using consciousness itself as an example here, but we could just as easily take another, the technology of writing or the invention of perspective in painting. Considered as institutions, these open particular pathways of historical development, not just for individual subjects (Lukács's critique of phenomenology) but for the material totality as meaningful in itself.

This should also help us to better understand the Eiffel Tower to Notre Dame comment from *The Visible and the Invisible*. The critique that Lukács makes is that the phenomenological method counts on the constituting act of the subject for the sense content of the experience. But in walking the path backwards, neither the subject nor the totality from which sense is instituted is the same. It is true that from the perspective of a philosophy of consciousness like the one Lukács and Merleau-Ponty are critiquing, there would be nothing in the object to throw consciousness off in new directions, because the object is constituted in its sense by the act of consciousness. But appearing in a constantly evolving historical and material socio-technical context (the 'totality') as it does, the object that one encounters on the walk back is now run through with different institutional significances than it was on the walk there. And what of the 'necessity of a future'? What the phenomenologist qua institutional analyst investigates are the appearances of what I earlier called 'watermarks' in experience—these appear as indicative of a style that expresses the elective affinities within a particular moment of the totality or of the historical socio-technical context and gives sense to a forward historical trajectory of the totality. Its institutionally conditioned but indeterminate horizon of potentiality appears in experience through the style or as a watermark in experience.

3.2 Institutions in Intersubjective Life

The account above addresses institution in personal life, but personal life is never solipsistic. The institutional life of consciousness that Merleau-Ponty sets out to describe is part of a 'common adventure' during which durable common forms of life are instituted. In fact, the history of this concept on the phenomenological side begins with Husserl's analysis of intersubjectivity in the famous sections of *Cartesian*

Meditations (Husserl, 1973) devoted to that topic. First, the institution of the sense of my own body as a *lived body* facilitates what Husserl calls the analogous apperception by which the bodies of others also appear as lived-bodies and not only object-bodies (*Körper*). (I will leave aside further discussion of the difficulties and productive problems in this account of inter-subjectivity.)

It is in this shift from personal to intersubjective or collective life that the concept of institution begins to take the full significance that Lefort attributes to it above. Events in the sense described in the paragraph above are not lived in solipsistic isolation, in the relation between subjective consciousness and object, but are experienced and sedimented as institutions in expressive relations with others. Perceptual and expressive life flows and congeals (institutes) at points in constant expression relations with others. Experience is shared, and an experience around which we communicate with others and moreover about which we communicate becomes an institution in intersubjective or public life. Its activity qua institution in sense formation is run through the experiences of others and expressions of that experience in communicative acts. The possibility of technologically preserving or meditating these experiences (for example in writing or oral tradition, recorded speech or images) alters the nature of the institutional structure of human experience, providing new possibilities for sedimentation of experiences outside of the scope of any individual life. This is why the advent of writing is so closely bound up with the concept of institution in Husserl's and Merleau-Ponty's work (as well as in Derrida's [1978]). The possibility of writing and recording facilitates the process of sedimentation wherein the initial expressive acts and intuition are sedimented but also forgotten or anonymized into formalizations or what Levin calls in another context the durable forms of collective life. It is this sedimentation that makes the forms of meaning durable and also easily transferable in formalizations across time and space. Here, writing functions as a technology that was itself instituted and whose meaning—the meaning of the possibility of communication across space and time using written language—shaped the institutional totality; and also as an institution that mediates experience and sense formation, i.e., the historical development of the totality in the manner described above.

3.3 Institutions as Social Objects

The public sedimentation in expression (of which written language is an example, but not the only one) of events and experiences transforms them from private to public institutions. To the extent that the institutional nexus that is created with the sedimentation of an experience in the temporal flow of consciousness can be considered an object, we can consider these public or communal experiences and events to also be objects. The theory of institution this way opens onto a phenomenological theory of social objects. Social objects are those that are formed and maintained in expressive and communicative acts. In this way, a public institution or social object resembles what Merleau-Ponty called, in the discussion of Weber, 'symbolic matrices'. These social objects/public institutions/symbolic matrices do things in social life; in other words, they exhibit powers to mediate meaning formation of other institutions at public or private levels. An institution's instituting power—how it mediates and conditions the sense-forming capacities of other institutions—is constrained by the web of other institutions that it is within. As Merleau-Ponty wrote about symbolic matrices, they disappear 'not by external forces but through an internal disintegration'. These institutions (let us stick with that term) require maintenance in communicative action. Without such maintenance, the instituting power that they exert on the web or totality of sense around them diminishes and can eventually fade away or be fundamentally transformed, as, for example, the Acropolis of Athens goes from being a centre of religious and political life to a tourist attraction, though its appearance is still conditioned by its former existence as a sacred place. In other words, the Acropolis, as an objective, material architectural accomplishment remains an institution, but the power that it exerts on the dynamics of sense formation around it has transformed.

Some institutions are intentionally constructed in communicative acts to exercise constraints on or transform others, within a certain sphere—laws and regulations would be a good example of this, and we can analyze institutional web or ecologies at many different levels. A relevant difference between three terms that I have run together here, perhaps somewhat hastily—social objects/public institutions/symbolic matrices—is that while a social object entails something that we can point to (e.g., an organization, nation, group, or idea) it is less clear that symbolic matrices necessarily entail the same solidity. When we talk about the instituting power of symbolic matrices, an object is not necessary. It can also refer to something we might call an imaginary line of force that organises elective affinities, creating a historical trajectory.

One can see that the way that I am talking about public institutions here comes quite close to the way the mediating powers of technologies are discussed in some forms of analysis. The above example of writing or recording technologies are apt ones. These are not just material processes but also exercise a power over sense formation within a web of meanings. The institution of writing technology seems to have a very general significance; this means something like, there is little if any communication—including non-written communication—that occurs within literate societies that is not somehow mediated by the sense-forming power of the institution of writing itself. Simultaneously, the institution of writing is continuously transformed at local levels in relation to the more local institutional ecologies where it is continuously reinstituted. At the local level, Lukács's example, which he uses to criticize phenomenological methodology, provides a good example of how the social object, in this case the lecture hall, can be analyzed qua institution. It does not appear in abstraction from a historical and material context, but only in that context, and its manner of appearance in that context then exercises an instituting power over the sense making activities that occurs within its vicinity. We can take the term vicinity here in a literal sense. In the lecture hall, one speaks, moves, and probably also writes and remembers in ways that are conditioned by the sense of the hall, which also bears the watermark of 'a certain stage of development of industry and of society'. The power or force is 'objective' but also imaginary or anonymous in the manner discussed in the first section above, but it is manifest in individuated expression which is always watermarked, to use that term again, by an idiosyncratic institutional life history. In this way the object as it appears is not constituted by subjective acts, but instituted in a process of sense-development that includes subjective act and intersubjective verification and modification without being reduced to this. The instituting force of the lecture hall qua social object weighs heavier perhaps on the person who had spent their formative years in that hall, or even ones like it, than on a person who is just visiting, for example—this is another way in which there is a subject that is 'instituted and instituting, but inseparably, not a constituting subject' (Merleau-Ponty, 2003, p. 35).

3.4 The Anonymous Horizon and Coherent Deformation

The idea of an 'anonymous horizon' plays an important role in the account of institutions and their instituting powers. Merleau-Ponty also uses the term unthought to denote the same idea, but this risks an over-subjective interpretation. We can try to unpack this idea of the anonymous horizon by returning to the quote at the beginning of this section where Merleau-Ponty tells us that institution provides the 'durable dimensions' to experience. This dimensionality should be understood in terms of a virtual horizon of objective potentials that unfurls from the event of the institution. I use the term objective again here to denote that this virtual horizon is the ideal dimension of the material totality that Merleau-Ponty referred to in his reading of Lukács. The institution qua event should be understood as the actualization or concretization of a horizon of objective virtualities or potentialities that have emerged from the dynamics of the institutional totality. But the actualization or concretization of a potential does not exhaust it.[4] An institution always has an anonymous horizon: affinities that are opened up without being actualized and which can lay dormant, so to speak, until they are actualized or not, but which still shape the development of sense in their vicinity and the further development of the anonymous horizon itself.

To illustrate the point, Merleau-Ponty provides another technical example: painting. A (good) painter does not learn by simply imitating the work or techniques of her predecessors. What marks out the great work of painting is that it seems to respond to a question about painting

---

[4] Though there is a clear link between Merleau-Ponty's philosophy of institution and Simondon's theory of concretization (Simondon, 2016), I am using the terms in a slightly different way but closely related way here. If, by concretization, Simondon means a process where the technological object becomes increasingly self-sufficient and incorporates more functions into itself (Bontems, 2018), I am using it here to mean a process whereby the individuation of an institution leads to it becoming more robust or resilient in relation to pressures from its institutional environment.

itself without that question having been actually posed. This happens because the artist, or great artist, explores the unrealized potentials of a tradition (what we could think of as a sub-ecology). Great painters respond in their work to questions that are latent within a moment in history, questions that we or they did not know were there, that we had an inkling of, but could not quite articulate until they are instituted in the event of a work that responds to them without intending to. Merleau-Ponty tries to explain this in the analysis of painting in the essay 'Indirect Language and the Voices of Silence':

> The difficult and essential point here is to understand that in positing a field distinct from the empirical order of events, we are not positing a Spirit of Painting which is already in possession of itself on the other side to the world that it is gradually manifested in. There is not, above and beyond the causality of events, a second causality which makes the world of painting a 'supersensible world' [...] but if circumstances lend themselves in the least to creation, a preserved and transmitted canvas develops a suggestive power in its inheritors which is without proportion to what it is—not only as a bit of painted canvas, but even as a work endowed by its creator with a definite signification. (Merleau-Ponty, 1964, p. 68)

These works then institute what Merleau-Ponty refers to as a 'coherent deformation' that reveals a 'subterranean logic'—there is no causal pathway in an institutional history by the concretization of virtualities, which lived a potential or underground life until being concretized by a new institution (Merleau-Ponty, 2003, p. 124). In the last paragraph of 'Indirect Language and the Voices of Silence', Merleau-Ponty brings the project of institutional analysis that he had been to that point exploring through the study of expression and painting back to the project announced in the first lines of *Adventures of the Dialectic*. (Recall, 'we need a philosophy of both history and spirit to deal with the problems we touch upon here. Yet we would be unduly rigorous if we were to wait for perfectly elaborated principles before speaking philosophically of politics'.). Political thought consists in the same kind of institutional analysis or pathway tracing entailed in the study of painting. He calls it the elucidation of an 'historical perception in which all our understandings, all our experiences, and all our values come into play' (Merleau-Ponty, 1964, p. 83). Political thought then becomes not a search for principles and values, but the activity of unearthing the subterranean logic of events in the development of the totality. It is not so much the art of the possible as Carl von Clausewitz wrote, but an art of deciphering the signs of the potential or imaginary dimension that shapes the objective historical totality in both its actual and potential or virtual dimensions.

3.5 Matrix Institutions

In Merleau-Ponty's 1955 course notes on institution in public life, a specific set of institutions are identified that he refers to as events-matrices or matrix-institutions (Merleau-Ponty, 2003, p. 44). Perhaps the best way to describe these are as institutions that exert enormous instituting power, opening what he calls a 'unified historical field' meaning that it is an institution that makes the potential (not actual) a series of further events. The two examples that he offers in the 1955 course are again technological in the broad sense of the word: the Neolithic revolution and the industrial revolution. These institutions, which cannot be described as singular events but rather something more akin to constellations of institutions with an elective affinity leading to a dynamic 'cultural nexus [noyaux]' that exerts enormous instituting power on the dynamics of their local institutional (and material) ecology, play a significant role in determining the capacities of other subsequent institutions.

3.6 Institution as Dimensionality of Time

This analysis of the concept of institutions helps us to understand the idea of an institution conveyed in the quotes that began this section as giving experience durable (read: stable and robust) dimensions and inaugurating a history. It also helps to clarify the relation between institutions as events and institutions as objects. The foundation of an institution is an event that alters the dynamics of an existing objective totality. But the event also has a product, the enduring meaning-structure which continues to exert power over sense-making in the now altered totality. It is as an enduring meaning structure, a social object, that the institution continues to structure and stabilize experience. It is this general structure of institutions interacting and co-shaping one another in an objective totality that gives coherence to experience as a temporal flow (Meacham, 2013). Institution in this sense becomes the fundamental idea for understanding the phenomenality of time, its appearance. This is the ontological significance of the concept. Experienced time is the individuation of what Merleau-Ponty calls in his later writing raw-being. I think that this can be understood in terms of a pre-individuated state of potentiality, that is concretized in the processes of institution that have been described above. Processes of individuation can thus be understood in terms of objectification—the becoming of objects in a meaningful web of relations.

4. Technology and Institutions

In the preceding sections, I provided an overview of Merleau-Ponty's concept of institution as developed though his engagement with Weber and Lukács and the prior development of the concept in Husserl's phenomenology. In Merleau-Ponty's rendering of the concept, it comes to replace constitution in the account of subjective meaning forming activity. It also provides an account for the possibility of intersubjective relations that are shared over time as well as an account of social objects that are formed and maintained in communicative and expressive actions. Finally, the concept takes on historical and ontological significance as the principle that drives the experience of temporality at the subjective, intersubjective, and historical scales. In the final section of this chapter, I want to turn to what had been promised in the introduction but has to this point been only touched upon in passing, the relation to technology.

As noted, Merleau-Ponty's descriptions and analyses of the concept of institution contain many technological examples: writing, architecture, painting, and also what we might call technological events (or event matrices) such as the Neolithic revolution or the industrial revolution. The definition of technology that I am using here is purposefully broader than the classic definition of the application of scientific knowledge for practical purposes. It amounts to something like the products of *techné*, the form of 'knowledge and ability which is directed to producing and constructing', or the broader sense of the German *Technik*, meaning 'the entire domain of all those procedures and actions related to skilled production of any kind' (Schadewaldt, 1979). There is a reason why the clearest examples of institutions in the senses that have been elaborated above come from this domain. Technics is the activity of producing enduring objects whose individuation or development arises out of a need or a trajectory of concretization that may not be anywhere explicit, but that appears in the temporal concretization of the object.

The study of technical objects can then proceed in the manner that Merleau-Ponty indicates institutional analysis in other domains can occur, by a tracing back of institutional pathways and trajectories within an objective totality. In this way, the relativization of subject and object occurs and priority is placed neither on the subjective side of action and expression nor on the objective side of abstracted material conditions—abstracted in the sense that they do not consider the dimension of historical imagination that is studied is the institutional development of the objective totality. This cannot be studied as a whole, but only through the examinations of intertwined and overlapping historico-material regions of the totality. What the institutional analyst seeks out are the elective affinities that give sense and direction (*sens*) to a series of events within such regions, which are identified retrospectively, though whole fields are devoted to trying to identify them prospectively. These affinities can be sought in a study of the style of development, use, transformation, and disuse of technical objects qua institutions. This examination is necessarily both descriptive and empirical; it is the product of embedded observation, as it is not possible to remove the gaze from the internal institutional dynamics of the objective totality, though techniques are possible to provide the required distance. These are the techniques that Merleau-Ponty seeks to elucidate through his studies of painting, science, politics, and also philosophy, where he attempts as early as in the *Phenomenology of Perception* to recast the phenomenological reduction in this way, as a tool for distancing from the lived-immediacy of event. Though, it remains the case that he makes no mention, to my knowledge, of *technics* as a distinct domain. These techniques of institutional analysis themselves, in philosophy, the arts, science, and politics, have their own institutional trajectories. What appears in the institutional analysis of these zones of practice is the 'logical structure' or 'subterranean logic' of what Merleau-Ponty refers to as 'the facts' or elsewhere the 'objective' in the manner that I have been describing.

Although the domain of technics does not receive specific attention in the cases of institutional analysis that occupied Merleau-Ponty's later writing—art, science, language, and politics—it nonetheless has a privileged role. Technics is a cross-cutting field across all the other institutional domains, such that one cannot study the history of art, science, politics, or philosophy for that matter as distinct from the history of technics. In this sense, the institutional analysis of technical development has a particular ontological significance. It is also in this sense, as a way of studying history that tries to take fuller account of the dimension of potentiality or virtuality that inhabits the material world and is a driver of temporality in its experiential sense, that Merleau-Ponty's phenomenology of institution, which though incomplete, offers rich resources for a philosophy of technology.

References

Bontems, V. (2018). On the current uses of Simondon's philosophy of technology. In S. Loeve, X. Guchet, & B. Bensaude Vincent (Eds), *French philosophy of technology* (pp. 37–49). Springer.

Cressman, D. (2020). Contingency and potential: Reconsidering a dialectical philosophy of technology. *Techné: Research in Philosophy and Technology,* 24(1–2), 138–158. https://doi.org/10.5840/techne202027114

Derrida, J. (1978). *Edmund Husserl's origin of geometry: An introduction.* University of Nebraska Press.

Flynn, B. (2013). Lefort as phenomenologist of the political. In M. Plot (Ed.), *Claude Lefort: Thinker of the political* (pp. 23–33). Palgrave Macmillan.

Husserl, E. (1973). *Cartesian meditations: an introduction to phenomenology.* Kluwer.

Husserl, E. (1989). *Ideas pertaining to a pure phenomenology and to a phenomenological philosophy. Second book studies in the phenomenology of constitution.* Kluwer.

Husserl, E., & Merleau-Ponty, M. (2002). *Husserl at the limits of phenomenology: Including texts by Edmund Husserl/Maurice Merleau-Ponty.* Northwestern University Press.

Löwy, M. (2004). Le concept d'affinité élective chez Max Weber. *Archives de sciences sociales des religions,* 127, 93–103. https://doi.org/10.4000/assr.1055

Lukács, G. (1973). *Marxism and human liberation: Essays on history, culture and revolution.* Dell Publishing Company.

Lukács, G. (1971 [1923]). *History and class consciousness: Studies in Marxist dialectics*. MIT Press.

Meacham, D. (2013). What goes without saying: Husserl's concept of style. *Research in Phenomenology, 43*(1), 3–26. https://doi.org/10.1163/15691640-12341241

Merleau-Ponty, M. (1968). *The visible and the invisible* (A. Lingis, Trans.). Northwestern University Press.

Merleau-Ponty, M. (1973 [1955]). *Adventures of the dialectic* (J. Bien, Trans.). Northwestern University Press.

Merleau-Ponty, M. (2003). *L'Institution, La Passivité. Notes de course au college de France (1954–55)*. Editions Belin.

Ritter, M. (2021). Postphenomenological method and technological things themselves. *Human Studies, 44*, 581–593. https://doi.org/10.1007/s10746-021-09603-5

Schadewaldt, W. (1979). The concepts of 'nature' and 'technique' according to the Greeks. In C. Mitcham & R. Mackey (Eds), *Research in philosophy and technology* (pp. 159–171).

Simondon, G. (2016). *On the mode of existence of technical objects* (C. Malaspina & J. Rogove, Trans.). University of Minnesota Press.

PART II

THE PHENOMENON OF TECHNOLOGY

4. The Activist Potential of Postmodern Phenomenology of Technology

Robert Rosenberger

Introduction

People working in the phenomenological tradition of philosophy have sometimes disagreed about the potential for these ideas to contribute to activist projects. I have met some who maintain that phenomenology is a kind of science of human experience, something that reveals essences and perhaps even fundamental understandings of being itself. Under this view, it is sometimes held that if phenomenological ideas are taken up within wider activist work applied to specific practical problems, then that work, as such, is no longer a form of phenomenology. I have also encountered some who hold the opposite view; phenomenology is necessarily an engaged, critical, and even activist philosophical perspective. Under this second view, it is sometimes held that movements such as 'critical phenomenology', while laudable, are also redundant.[1] How should we navigate these disagreements, especially those of us convinced that these ideas are crucial, or at least potentially useful, for making the world safer, healthier, more sustainable, and more just? And how do these disagreements reverberate through contemporary work in the phenomenology of technology?

In particular, I would like to explore the implications of these disagreements for the 'postphenomenological' perspective. Work in

---

1   For more on critical phenomenology, see Weiss, Salamon, & Murphy (2020); and also the journal *Puncta*: https://journals.oregondigital.org/index.php/pjcp/index

postphenomenology brings anti-essentialist and anti-foundationalist commitments of American pragmatism, as well as other postmodern ideas, to the development of a distinctive phenomenological account of human-technology relations. Building on the work of the grandfather figure of this school of thought, Don Ihde, postphenomenology offers a kind of toolkit for exploring the uses, design, and implications of technology (e.g., Ihde, 2009; Verbeek, 2011; Rosenberger & Verbeek, 2015; Wellner, 2015; Irwin, 2016; Rosenberger, 2017a; Van Den Eede et al., 2017; Aagaard et al., 2018; Hasse, 2020; de Boer, 2020; Fried & Rosenberger, 2021; Kudina, 2023; Rosenberger, 2024).[2] Despite the practical orientation of postphenomenology, there are tensions within this international and interdisciplinary collective of researchers about whether and exactly how these ideas should be taken up as a part of politically activist projects.

After reviewing some of the basics of postphenomenology, as well as some of its internal tensions and external critiques, I outline three avenues within this perspective that show potential for direct applications to activist political criticism: (1) the politics of co-constitution; (2) multistability and the politics of our devices; and (3) the political biases that can become embedded within our technologically-mediated perceptual habituation.

1. Postphenomenology and Political Criticism

Postphenomenology, as a school of thought that continues to grow and change, can perhaps be defined in terms of a number of ideas and commitments that overlap in a family-resemblance-style patchwork. While the work of postphenomenologists differs greatly from one practitioner to the next, one main philosophical idea that appears

---

2   What makes postphenomenology an example of postmodernism? I have in mind Ihde's explicit integration of anti-essentialist and anti-foundationalist commitments into phenomenology, which he pulls from Foucault, Dewey, Hickman, and especially Rorty, among others. By 1993, he's referring to this perspective as 'postphenomenology', and casting it as a postmodern one. He writes, 'What all the postmodern captures is the sense of transition, of a proliferating pluralism, and—for the nostalgic—a "loss of centers" or "foundations" [...] I have previously called this style of phenomenology I have practiced a "nonfoundational" phenomenology. [Ihde, 1986] Postphenomenology is just another way of characterizing it as a different form, but owing to its ancestry' (Ihde, 1993, p. 1).

across many of these works is a commitment to a kind of situatedness, non-foundationalism, and a practical orientation. That is, rather than arguing for context-free essentialisms, postphenomenology specializes in the deep description of human relationships with technology in all their patterns and diversity, and in relation to people's concrete projects and problems. As Ihde put it back in the 1980s, 'what the philosopher is doing, if you will, is not doing foundational philosophy, but is doing a kind of critical reflection upon what has happened to our 'episteme', our perception of the time' (Ihde 1986, p. 25). In many ways, the various ideas of the postphenomenological framework (e.g., Ihde's four human-technology relations, the notion of multistability, the work on co-constitution and technological mediation theory, etc.) are useful for drawing out and articulating the concreteness and variability of human relationships with technology. Often, these investigations are approached in terms of the technologically 'mediated' character of human-technology relations in which humans and their world are co-constituted through technological mediation (e.g., Verbeek, 2011; de Boer, 2020; Kudina, 2023). Sometimes this situatedness is addressed and defended directly (e.g., Rosenberger, 2017b). However, most often, postphenomenological research is simply conducted in a manner consistent with these commitments, building from the starting point of human-technology relations, and continuing through interdisciplinary investigation.

If postphenomenology is thus strongly positioned to provide useful insights into the concrete situatedness of our relationships with technologies, then what does this mean for its potential for contributing to activist political critique? If by 'politics' we refer generally to structures of power people have over and in relation to one another (including everything from issues of governance, to patterns of racism and prejudice, to questions of rights and justice), and if by 'activism' we refer to engagement with real-world problems, then how can and should postphenomenology be politically activist?

These issues are unsettled. Ihde himself has often appeared hesitant to take up postphenomenological insights in explicit criticism of technological trends. While his corpus is peppered with case-specific critical comments here and there, Ihde has been at times dismissive of the critical work of others, often rejecting it as totalizing, or essentializing, or overgeneralizing, or as something that fails to recognize technology's multistability. For example, as Albert Borgmann summarizes, 'in his later work, Ihde rounded out his pioneering distinctions into a pluralist and essentially affirmative view of technology, an outlook he festooned with deflationary attacks on unified theories and nostalgic laments' (2005).[3]

This rings in tune with some of the criticisms of postphenomenology that have begun to accumulate. For example, one influential line of critique takes issue with the pragmatism and anti-essentialism of postphenomenology. (For a few of the best of these, see: Rao et al., 2015; Smith, 2015; Zwier, Blok, & Lemmens, 2016; Ritter, 2021; Scharff, 2022.)[4] Oftentimes these critiques are levelled in terms of issues of intelligibility or completeness. That is, it has sometimes been alleged that in eschewing essentialist metaphysics, postphenomenology is missing out on something important. In my view, these critiques take

---

3   In tune with this, Ihde has recently written that, 'all technologies are "multistable", not restricted to single uses. If this is the case, it does not take much to see that dealings with technologies pose problems for both prediction and ethics' (2022, p. 121).

4   Sometimes these criticisms are levelled against postphenomenology as an exemplar of the 'empirical turn', a conception of the field of philosophy of technology in which the investigation of concrete problems and devices should serve as the jumping off points for philosophical investigation, as opposed to starting with large-scale generalizations or foundational claims (see, e.g., Achterhuis, 2001; Kroes & Meijers, 2001). Frankly, I never cared much for the empirical turn as a terminology, and I care even less about the critiques of it. As a practicing postphenomenologist of my generation, I've simply inherited this fraught conception of the field. On the one hand, I do very much identify with the common concerns identified across the work of the 'empirical turn' generation as Hans Achterhuis has identified them, i.e., Donna Haraway, Langdon Winner, Hubert Dreyfus, Albert Borgmann, Don Ihde's postphenomenology, and Andrew Feenberg's critical constructivism. On the other, I was never convinced they had all so strongly 'turned away' from their predecessors as both the proponents and the detractors of the empirical turn claim. Still, there is important philosophy to do on exactly these issues. For example, there are important questions raised in these discussions over the proper role in the philosophy of technology for transcendental argumentation and conditions of possibility. While I may not care much for the empirical turn qua characterization of the field (either as one to ascribe to, or one to rebel against), I do very much care about the non-foundationalism, anti-essentialism, and epistemological situatedness of postphenomenology. And where these pragmatic anti-essentialist and situated commitments of postphenomenology led Ihde himself to a hesitation toward ethical and political pronouncements regarding technology, I instead believe these same commitments should lead us exactly toward them. For further discussion, see footnote 11, below.

on a special bite in the occasional times they attempt to show that postphenomenology is limited specifically in terms of contributing to political critique. For example, as Jochem Zwier and colleagues suggest, 'postphenomenological analyses of technologies generally concern how technologies understood as human-technology relations help constitute a world. Yet our present ecological situation indicates something that resists incorporation in our meaningful worlds' (2016, p. 331). Does postphenomenology's anti-essentialism place limits on its potential for contributing to political work, or, in this case the politics of global climate catastrophe? (We can note that there has been at least some work done by postphenomenologists on issues of climate change, e.g., Goeminne, 2011; Botin, 2019; Fried, 2023).

For their part, many who consider themselves to be doing postphenomenology do *not* conceive of this perspective as a theory of everything, whatever that might mean. That is, two things can be simultaneously true: (1) this perspective, with its specialization in the deep description of human-technology relations, can make useful contributions to many far-reaching projects, and (2) postphenomenology by itself cannot provide any kind of comprehensive account of humanity and the world (again, whatever that even means). In particular, postphenomenology does not purport to be a political or ethical or social theory. (For example, postphenomenology does not include within itself, say, an account of democracy, or rights, or capitalism.) Nevertheless, this perspective can make valuable, and perhaps distinctive, contributions to this kind of work.

A number of postphenomenologists participate in explicitly politically-engaged projects (e.g., Goeminne, 2011; Warfield, 2017; Wittkower, 2017; Rosenberger, 2017a; Botin, 2019; Botin, de Boer, & Børsen, 2020; Verbeek, 2020; Romele, 2021; Baş, 2022; Fried, 2023; Romele, 2024; Rosenberger, 2024). One major way that this kind of work has been accomplished is through the strategic combination of postphenomenological insights with other social and political frameworks, such as actor-network theory and other science and technology studies accounts (e.g., Verbeek, 2011; Rosenberger, 2014; Rosenberger, 2017a; Arzroomchilar, 2022), Bourdieusian social theory (Romele, 2021; 2024), Arendtian political theory (Baş, 2022), and Feenbergian Critical Constructivism (e.g., Rosenberger, 2017a; Botin, de Boer, & Børsen, 2020; Keymolen,

2021).[5] In these cases, the distinction between this perspective's internal developers and at least some of its external critics may be somewhat arbitrary, really just a matter of style. Those within postphenomenology who are developing links with other perspectives are implicitly or explicitly engaging in the critique of the limits of this perspective, but in a non-dismissive manner. In any case, in these various lines of work it is understood that postphenomenology has something useful—and perhaps even crucial—to offer to activist political projects.

For my own part, I am strongly convinced that postphenomenology has the potential to make significant contributions to activist political critique. My view is that, in fact, the pragmatism of postphenomenology obligates those working within this perspective to be engaged in practical political and ethical action. I see this as a yet unmet challenge for postphenomenology, one that stems from its own bottommost philosophical commitments. While not already a political or ethical theory, and while—like any perspective—it is already always implicated in politics and ethics, the postphenomenological toolkit can be put toward the identification of patterns of discrimination, the revealing of harms, the articulation of more egalitarian practices, and the criticism of injustice.

In what follows, I review three specific places within the postphenomenological framework that are proving to be especially fruitful for the development of politically activist lines of study.

2. The Politics of Co-Constitution

Donna Haraway writes, 'Beings do not preexist their relatings [...] There are no pre-constituted subjects and objects, no single sources, unitary actors, or final ends' (2003, p. 6). Karen Barad similarly follows with the claim that, 'relata do not preexist relations; rather relata-within-phenomena emerge through specific intra-actions' (2003, p. 815). These statements reflect a posthumanist sentiment within many important lines of feminist work, including feminist new materialism, which conceives of humans and the world and their technologies in terms of an ontology

---

5   See especially the 2020, 24 (1&2) special issue of the journal *Techné* on the topic of the intersection between Feenberg's critical constructivism and postphenomenology.

of relations.⁶ Postphenomenology has always been a fellow traveller in terms of these commitments. For example, Peter-Paul Verbeek, the leading light in following out the implications of these ideas for the philosophy of technology, writes, 'human-world relationships should not be seen as relations between preexisting subjects who perceive and act upon a preexisting world of objects' (2011, p. 15). To explore the ways that posthuman commitments to a relational ontology play out within postphenomenology, and to consider their implications for political activism, we should turn to the notion of technological mediation.

The notion of mediation is a central idea within work on postphenomenology. Technologies are understood to be more than merely one of the things that a person might encounter in the world, one of the things they might perceive and interpret, one of the things they might act upon in some way. Technologies are instead mediators that come between this person and those things of the world, mediating their relationship and transforming the encounter, changing how a person may perceive, and interpret, and act. Crucially, this technological mediation is understood not only to change what a user can do, but to reshape the entire technological situation.⁷ As Bas de Boer explains,

---

6   We can distinguish this kind of feminist posthumanism (with which postphenomenology shares a relational ontology) with the posthumanism of transhumanists that push a utopian view that technological developments will solve our problems. The latter often comes under criticism by postphenomenologists (e.g., Ihde, 2008).

7   It can be noted that postphenomenologists often have it both ways in their use of language to describe co-constitution and human-technology relations. That is, sometimes entities are discussed as if they are pre-constituted, for example when technologies are described to come 'in between' the user and the world as if all three are pre-existing as such. For example, this is the case when, following Ihde, postphenomenologists use a kind of 'I – technology – world' formula to describe human-technology relations. Even the term 'human-technology relations' implies that there are pre-existing humans and technologies to relate to one another. Of course, postphenomenologists insist at the same time that all of these entities are continuously co-constituting one another, and that none of these entities are what they are in separation from the others. Commenters disagree about how much of a problem this may be. In my view, on the one hand we should remain on guard for moments where this kind of slippage or sloppiness in terminology can lead to confusion or inaccuracy. And yet also on the other hand we can remain generous and recognize that a language of 'in between-ness' and I-technology-world formulations are offered as provisional, as a way to describe things in normal language while at the same time still understanding all parts to be co-constituted. The question of how best to approach these issues of co-constitution is a cutting-edge area of investigation, with, for example, innovative formations of the

'reality comes into being in the relations between human beings and technologies. A central idea within postphenomenology is that technologies mediate the relationship between humans and the world, thereby co-constituting specific experiences and understandings of reality' (2020, p. 22). It is through technological mediation that users of technologies become who they are. And it is through technological mediation that the world encountered by those users becomes what it is. Postphenomenologists have developed these insights into a kind of mediation theory (combining them with work from feminist new materialism, actor-network theory, and other related perspectives), and have applied these ideas to everything from education, design, laboratory instrumentation, and pioneering work in technological ethics (e.g., Verbeek, 2011; Hauser et al., 2018; Hasse, 2020; de Boer, 2020; Lewis, 2021; Wakkary, 2021; de Boer & Kudina, 2022; Kudina, 2023; Rosenberger, 2024).

Verbeek has influentially argued that our moral situation is substantially informed by technological mediation. He writes that 'there is a complex interplay between humans and technologies within which neither technological development nor humans has autonomy. Human beings are products of technology, just like technology is a product of human beings' (Verbeek, 2011, p. 115). Technological mediation thus informs everything from what it means for us to be moral actors, to who maintains moral authority (e.g., nurses and doctors within hospitals), to what options are available in our moral decision-making, as well as to what decisions must be made in the first place. Take, for example, the potential for machine learning algorithms to be used in making medical diagnoses. Bas de Boer and Olya Kudina explore the possible ways that these technologies could reshape the moral decision-making landscape. They write that, 'Through the presence of ML [machine learning], medical professionals, patients, and the relationships between them are co-constituted in new ways', and these new co-constitutions have considerable moral implications (de Boer & Kudina, 2021, p. 250). The use of machine learning predictive algorithms has the potential to reshape the nature of medical objectivity and judgement. This could bring about substantial changes to multiple aspects of medical decision making,

---

I-technology-world formula under development that stress the co-constitution of its parts through various arching arrows (e.g., Hauser et al., 2018; Kudina, 2023).

including what data are important to diagnoses (with a potential bias toward what can be fed into the algorithm), what diagnostic challenges physicians face (such as navigating the opacity of machine learning processes), and what medical 'responsibility' even means as duties are delegated to these devices.

This line of thinking on the co-constitution of technological mediation can be refined into a useful toolkit for the analysis of our political situation. Verbeek has been leading this push, arguing that, 'The postphenomenological approach can expand this neo-Deweyian interpretation of politics as issue formation: from the perspective of human-world relations, both the formation of publics and the rise of issues are in fact technologically mediated processes [...] technologies help to shape the issues around which publics can form themselves: they reveal how technologies are involved in representations of the world, and therefore in the concerns that people have' (2020, p. 151). Just as we've seen in work on the technological mediation of ethics, our politics can be usefully reconceived in terms of how it is co-constituted by our devices. Technological mediation contributes to the co-shaping of political decision-making into what it is, what the decision points are, how we as political decision-makers are variously situated, what options are available, and how authority is secured.

One example can be seen in my own line of critique of the use of frog dissection in grade-school education. (For the most recent iteration of these criticisms, which leans heavily on technological mediation theory, see: Rosenberger, forthcoming.) The practice of having children dissect frog corpses as a part of the public-school biology curriculum is commonplace in countries such as Canada and the United States. Because this raises both ethical (in terms of animal treatment) and ecological (in terms of specimen sourcing) concerns, many have raised objections. These objections include the push for 'student choice' laws in which states require schools to allow students to engage in an alternative assignment if they choose.

I argue that the practice of corpse dissection should be understood as a form of technological mediation within the classroom. (I like to refer to the practice as 'corpse dissection', rather than frog dissection, to emphasize the artefactual elements of this educational situation. Students in the classroom do not merely encounter 'real' frogs. They encounter already captured, already transported, already killed, already pre-prepared corpses-for-dissection.) *The technology of the frog corpse itself is the key mediating technology in this story.* It is the frog corpse itself—the frog body preserved with formaldehyde and prepared for use as an educational activity—that sets up the surrounding circumstances, including the details of the digital alternatives (which tend to mimic that non-digital corpse), as well as the activist push for student choice laws. The existence of this technology, as well as its status as commonplace, deeply co-constitute both the political context and the political actors of this situation.

Frog corpse dissection is established in these parts of the world as a kind of educational ideal. This is the status quo. Other options, such as computer simulations, are thus constituted as mere 'alternatives'. These computer simulations are thus setup to attempt to reproduce the experience of frog dissection (e.g., with a digital scalpel and dead-looking frog onscreen). And students in this scenario are thus plunged into the situation of choosing between either complicity or taking up action as a conscientious objector. The debate over these issues is constituted by the mediating technology of frog corpse dissection as one between the (allegedly) best education for our children on the one hand, and a concern for ethics and the environment on the other. I suggest that the notion of technological mediation is useful in this case for drawing out all these dynamics and subjecting them to critical reflection. There is the potential here for contribution to this specific political debate, one with ecological, ethical, educational, and policy implications, as well as implications for computer simulation design. My argument is that this entire co-constituted dynamic—including the assumed status of corpse dissection as an educational ideal, as well as the corresponding assumption that simulated alternatives are obligated to mimic corpse dissection—must be overturned.

3. The Politics of Technological Multistability

Another central idea within the postphenomenological framework is the notion of multistability. Ihde first developed this notion to articulate the multiplicity possible for human visual perception (1977). He has since expanded this idea to help articulate the variability of human-technology relations (e.g., Ihde, 1986; 1990; 2009). The term 'multistability' has come to refer to the always multiple—though not unlimited—ways that a given technology can mediate a user's relationship with the world. Multistability thus points to the various dimensions across which the same technology may transform a user's experience differently in different circumstances. A given device may be differently meaningful to different users, may fit differently into various contexts, may advance differently along different lines of development, or may be put to different purposes. At the same time, the notion of multistability additionally refers to the limitations of a given technology in mediating user experience; while a technology may be put to multiple uses, it is also the case that its specificity restrains it from merely being used for any purpose. For example, a pen can be used for writing, and this was likely the purpose for which the pen in your hand was designed and manufactured and purchased. But that same pen could also be used for stabbing another person (like they do all the time in movies).[8] Or the tube of the pen could be used to perform an emergency tracheotomy (although there appears to be some disagreement over its actual suitability for this contingency).[9] And yet the pen cannot be used to do simply anything, or come to mean simply anything. Under this terminology, human-technology relations are limited to particular 'stabilities' (or 'variations').

Contemporary work in postphenomenology has significantly expanded the conceptual and methodological framework around the notion of multistability (e.g., Rosenberger, 2014; Whyte, 2015; Aagaard, 2018; Wiltse, 2020; Keymolen, 2021; de Boer, 2023; Rosenberger, 2023). Many of these new ideas have the effect of emphasizing the situated details of human-technology relations. For example, Heather Wiltse explores the ways that multistable technologies themselves can at times adjust and adapt to the user, becoming different objects in the process,

---

8   O. Rutigliano (2021, November 18). Ten murders-by-pen in movies. *CrimeReads*, https://crimereads.com/ten-murders-by-pen-in-movies/

9   A. M. Seaman (2016, April 28). Forget about saving a life by plunging a pen through the neck. *Reuters*, https://www.reuters.com/article/us-health-breathing-pen/forget-about-saving-a-life-by-plunging-a-pen-through-the-neck-idUSKCN0XP32Q; Editorial Staff (2016, July 24). Tracheotomy: Does TV get it right?. *American Lung Association*, https://www.lung.org/blog/tracheotomy-does-tv-get-right

amounting to a kind of 'multi-instability' (e.g., 2020). Under Wiltse's account, digital technologies are case-in-point examples of technologies that may exhibit this kind of multi-instability, such as voice-interactive systems that adjust to a user's particular vocalizations, or predictive algorithms that learn a user's preferences.

In addition, several lines of work investigate what goes into the establishment of a human-technology relation in terms of one stability rather than another.

On one side, this includes specificities emerging from the position of the user. I have described a user as bringing a particular 'relational strategy' to their encounter with technology, i.e., a bodily and interpretive approach toward a particular stability of a technology (e.g., Rosenberger, 2014; 2023). For example, a person brings a particular set of understandings and bodily comportments to use a pen for writing compared to, say, wielding it as a stabbing weapon. A user's individual history of experience can become sedimented in perceptual habituation. After a lifetime of using the pen for writing, each new pen you see will simply be encountered immediately in terms of its pen-as-writing-implement stability.

On the other side, several postphenomenologists explore how best to conceive of the way that the specificities of the world—including both the design of the device itself as well as its larger context—afford particular possibilities for action and thus incline particular stabilities for human-technology relations (e.g., Aagaard, 2018; de Boer, 2023; Rosenberger, 2023; Romele, 2024; Mykhailov & Liberati, forthcoming). As Cathrine Hasse puts it, 'A multistable technology is a structure that follows different stable trajectories that lead to variations in the artefact as it is embedded in what is termed 'life worlds' in post-phenomenology 'collective activities' in cultural-historical theory' (2013, p. 87). Bas de Boer explains that a central reason that a technology affords one particular stability rather than another is precisely because of the context of 'normativity' within which that human-technology relation takes place (2023). As he puts it, 'the form of life within which technologies are immersed influences the affordances a technology is perceived to offer' (de Boer, 2023, p. 2275). In addition to an individual user's approach to the pen, this device is set within a context of culture within which the pen-as-writing-implement stability dominates; pens are mass produced and sold for this purpose.

I have come to use the term 'dominant stability' to refer to the one that has become the most prevalent—the main stability that tends to be taken up by users, the one that has become established within a network of other related things.

There are clear political dimensions to technological multistability. The dominance of one stability over alternatives is politically non-neutral. As Lars Botin writes, 'the ethical and political dimensions of technology are multiple and multistable, and we need to take this multiplicity and multistability seriously in order to be able to foresee and engage in the political debate and discussion of sustainable futures' (2019, p. 160). One place where issues of technological multistability intersect with politics is in terms of what could be called the 'closure' and 'opening' of stabilities (e.g., Rosenberger, 2017a; 2023). Alterations will at times be made to devices with the effect of specifically closing off a particular stability, or, contrariwise, keeping a stability accessible. Politics are present in cases in which stabilities are contested; a stability may come to dominate despite objections, or it may come to dominate in ways that advantage one group over another. Such enforcements of the dominant stabilities of technologies can function as a part of larger political agendas, potentially reinforcing the usages preferred by the already powerful, and doing so at the expense of the already marginalized. If someone were to take up the alternative usage in such a case, then it could constitute an act of political resistance.

For example, one domain where these ideas have proven useful is the analysis of the politics of the objects of public spaces, where different groups with varying levels of privilege and power use space in different ways. Studies include investigations into the politics of the multistability of bicycle lanes (Appleton, 2021), skateboarding (Giamarino et al., 2023), fire hydrants (Rosenberger, 2017c), and issues of disability (Mitchell, 2021). (Of course, here is a place where we see the importance of the connections that some postphenomenological researchers are making to theoretical and investigative frameworks that extend out beyond individual human-technology relations and out into larger social and political structures, such as actor-networks, the Bourdieusian habitus, Coeckelberghian narratives, Akrichian scripts, etc.—e.g., Verbeek, 2011; Rosenberger, 2017a; Coeckelbergh, 2017; Romele, 2024.)

The notion of dominant strategies is intended to highlight some of these political dynamics. There is a necessary relativity to the term; what is dominant for one community may not be the same for another. Thinking about dominant stabilities should prompt political questions, such as: dominant for whom? And: dominant over whom?

In my own work, I have investigated the political ramifications of multistability in terms of the problem of homelessness (e.g., Rosenberger, 2017a; Rosenberger, 2023). My way into this topic is the design of public spaces, and what is sometimes called 'hostile design' or 'hostile architecture'. That is, I have been analyzing how the objects of public spaces are sometimes redesigned in ways that are hostile to those living unhoused. This has included investigation into the multistability of a wide variety of objects and spaces. And more, it has included the study of how the stabilities of objects and spaces that are taken up by those who are living unhoused are often closed off through design. For example, benches that could be used as a place to sleep are sometimes closed off such that they can only be used as a place to sit (e.g., through the addition of things like armrests or seat dividers). Garbage cans that could be used as a place to find discarded food or recyclables are sometimes closed off such that they can only be used to deposit trash. Any number of public spaces that could be used as sleeping or living areas (e.g., parks, sidewalks, underpasses, plazas, alleyways, etc.) are sometimes closed off from these usages through any number of means (e.g., obstructions, surveillance systems, loud sound devices, water sprinklers, etc.). I have worked to criticize these discriminatory design strategies which I claim function as a small part of a larger anti-homeless agenda (which includes anti-homeless laws, among other things) that is focused on pushing the unhoused out of shared public spaces above all else.

4. The Politics of Perceptual Habituation

One further area where postphenomenology may be able to make distinctive contributions is on questions of the political embeddedness of technologically-mediated perception itself. As users become accustomed to their devices and spaces, how do associated politics become incorporated into a person's habits of perception? As a user develops everyday relationships with the technologies they often use in their everyday life, how might this everydayness itself become implicated in the larger political agendas of others?

My suggestion is that one way to help draw out and critically analyze this potential site for politics is through the strategic combination of insights from postphenomenology and perspectives that specialize in issues of political epistemology. Some examples include critical and feminist phenomenology, epistemologies of ignorance, work on technological imaginaries and narratives, epistemic injustice, and critical constructivism, among others. However, my preferred point of connection is work coming out of feminist philosophy of science on standpoint theory and situated knowledges.[10]

The tradition of feminist standpoint theory emphasizes the way that knowledge is not free-floating and abstract; it is something generated and possessed by actual human beings. This means that to understand knowledge, we must recognize people as knowers (e.g., Smith, 1987; Haraway, 1988; Collins, 1990; Harding, 1991; Hartsock, 1998; Harding, 2003). Knowledge is thus something held by individuals, individuals with their own histories of experience and who encounter the world through their own limited perspectives. This introduces an inherent politics to epistemology, one that follows from the situatedness of knowers and the groups to which they belong, and the power differentials between those groups. Or, as Haraway notes, 'All knowledge is a condensed node in an agonistic power field' (1988, p. 577).

My own go-to figure in this philosophical tradition is Sandra Harding, who brings these ideas to the philosophy of science. Harding conceives of the inherent epistemological limitations of individuals, as well as their associated groups, in terms of bias. As she puts it, 'the assertion is that human activity, or "material life", not only structures but sets limits on human understanding: what we do shapes and constrains what we can know' (Harding, 1991, p. 120). There is a political dimension to these biases because, while any group will always have them, those in powerful groups will be particularly ill

---

10   And it should be recognized that while there is a lot of work to do to follow out these connections between postphenomenology and feminist epistemology, these resonances have always been present; Ihde has noted these points of contact throughout his corpus (see, e.g., 1993, ch. 9; 1998, ch. 11, for early examples), and these resonances continue through the contemporary connections between postphenomenology and feminist new materialism made in the work of Hasse, Verbeek, and others.

equipped to recognize those biases that support their own position of power. Meanwhile, those in marginalized societal positions will have a special vantage point on the biases of the powerful because those biases contribute to their marginalization. According to Harding, these biases can be routed out only by taking onboard others into the knowledge-making process and taking seriously the everyday lives of those with less power and influence. That is, it is only through combining perspectives that biases can be exposed and eliminated. And she argues that even science itself is not immune to these effects. Harding writes that, 'In a hierarchically organized society, objectivity cannot be defined as requiring (or even desiring) value neutrality' (1991, p. 134).

The postphenomenological philosophical perspective works in accord with these commitments to embodied, situated, and mediated subjects.[11]

---

11 It is this commitment to situatedness that many critics of postphenomenology specifically, and critics of the empirical turn more generally, appear to me to fail to appreciate. It is not merely, as some caricaturize, that postphenomenology only focuses on specific devices; it is that postphenomenology recognizes that all knowledge claims are levelled from situated standpoints. This includes not only people in their daily lives and scientists in their labs, but also philosophers of technology. This is one major reason that postphenomenologists are often uncomfortable with essentialisms, overgeneralizations, totalizing claims, and stories about Technology with a capital T, etc. Such claims appear to be reinstating the 'god trick' criticized by Haraway. This also helps to explain postphenomenology's affinity for perspectives that remain consistent with themes of situated knowledge, such as critical constructivism, standpoint theory, new materialism, and actor-network theory.

So, for example, despite the rhetoric sometimes espoused by Ihde and Verbeek, postphenomenological investigations *can and perhaps should* at times include transcendental argumentation that seeks out conditions of possibility. (For an in depth discussion on these issues, including multiple critiques of postphenomenology, as well as several defences consistent with my formulation here, see *Foundations of Science*, 2022, volume 27, issues 1–4). At the same time, those transcendental postphenomenological investigations cannot result in fixed essences or the discovery of some ontological dimension if that implies a non-situated perspective; the results must be limited to spheres of investigation, and remain contextual and situated.

An example here is work on climate catastrophe. We all share the same planet, and human technological development is changing the environment in dangerous ways. However, this should not imply that everyone on the planet faces the same dangers in the same ways, and neither does it imply that these ecological dangers must somehow be the result of some essential and identical way that the world is revealed to all of us today. These are urgent political problems, and the philosophy

My suggestion is that important contributions to political criticism based in the philosophy of technology can be made by following out connections between postphenomenology and feminist epistemology. We can work to describe with greater precision how the particularities of technologically-mediated experience are shaped by a user's situated perspective on the world. In particular, we can bring together a standpoint conception of epistemological situatedness with work in postphenomenology on the field of awareness. That is, we can explore how human epistemological limitations inform our technologically-mediated experience, and how those experiences become set within sedimented contexts of pre-perceptual expectation. (For more on these themes, see: Rosenberger, 2017a, chapter 5; Rosenberger, 2021; Wellner, forthcoming.)

These explorations have the potential to connect as well to related work in feminist phenomenology and queer studies. For example, Sara Ahmed writes that what the 'flow of perception tells is the partiality of absence as well as presence: what we do not see (say, the back or side of the object) is hidden from view and can only be intended. We single out this object only by pushing other objects to the edges or "fringes" of vision' (2010, p. 239). This is to say that there is a politics to what we fail to notice. And there is potential for postphenomenology to make distinctive contributions to political criticism regarding our technologically-mediated perception.

An example is the various relationships people have with public-space surveillance equipment. For many, surveillance technologies like security cameras are simply a part of the normally largely unnoticed background of the built environment, objects that perch within the edges or fringes of vision, as Ahmed says.[12] However, we can imagine some people with particular jobs or interests that maintain a different experiential relationship to these things, people for whom security

---

of technology can be a contributor to the understanding of these dangers, to the criticism of the large-scale institutions responsible, as well as to the creation of solutions. There is a distinctive role to play for postmodern perspectives, including postphenomenology among others, that recognize the differences in the embodied standpoints of the different people and groups and populations of the planet.

12 Of course there is a whole field of surveillance studies dedicated to the study of these issues. For more on the phenomenology of security cameras in particular, see, e.g., Friesen et al. (2009); Rosenberger (2020).

cameras often stand forward as important or noticeable. Perhaps someone who designs, or sells, or installs these kinds of devices will be more inclined to take notice of them. Or perhaps a privacy advocate will be more inclined to take note of the security apparatus around them.

Relevant here, it is also possible that differences in privilege and power will lead to different levels of awareness of surveillance systems. For example, if you are a poor or unhoused person who is targeted by some of the laws of a public space (laws against things like loitering, panhandling, or sleeping in public), then you may be more aware of the security cameras used by those in authority to help in their efforts to enforce those laws. Or, for example, if you are someone against whom facial recognition systems tend to discriminate, then you may learn to be more aware of the surveillance machinery that runs those systems. In this way, the act of not noticing surveillance systems is related to one's status as part of the groups that are not targeted by the systems of harassment that can accompany being the subject of surveillance. The 'unnoticed' and transparent 'backgrounded' status that surveillance cameras maintain for many people is thus the result of, among other things, a kind of political privilege, and one built into learned perceptual habituation.

5. Towards a Politically Activist Postphenomenology

There is room to take advantage of postphenomenology's distinctive insights into human-technology relations for contribution to political critique. As an engaged philosophical perspective focused on the concreteness of human experiences and technological designs, as one with a track record of original contributions to technological ethics, and as one associated with pragmatist philosophy and feminist epistemology, I suggest that it is an imperative for postphenomenology to strive toward making contributions to activist political discourse. And we can see that some work in this perspective has been underway on fraught political topics such as satellite imaging, discriminatory design, unsustainable practices, traffic policy, bicycle lane policy, and anti-homeless designs in public-spaces (e.g., Goeminne, 2011; Rosenberger, 2017a; Wittkower, 2017; Botin, 2019; Fried, 2023; Appleton, 2021; Rosenberger, 2024).

But there are headwinds. Work on the application of postphenomenological insights to larger political critique is done despite several things, including a conspicuous lack of political engagement in the history of this perspective, criticisms from others about an alleged lack of suitability of these ideas for political work, as well as Ihde's own misgivings. In my own experience at least, I have not found any of these to present insurmountable obstacles to doing postphenomenologically-informed activist work.

Above, I have articulated three places in the postphenomenological framework that I believe are showing strong potential for application to political work: the co-constitution of technology mediation; the dynamics of technological multistability; and the sedimentation of our technologically-mediated habits of perception. What can be noted about these ideas is that they are all central features of the postphenomenological framework. This implies that much of the postphenomenological framework of concepts has the potential for application to activist political critique.

References

Aagaard, J. (2018). Magnetic and multistable: Reinterpreting the affordances of educational technology. *International Journal of Educational Technology in Higher Education, 15*(4), https://doi.org/10.1186/s41239-017-0088-4

Aagaard, J., Friis, J. K. B., Sorensen, J., Tafdrup, O., & Hasse, C. (Eds). (2018). *Postphenomenological methodologies: New ways in mediating techno-human relationships*. Lexington Books.

Achterhuis, H. (Ed.). (2001). *American philosophy of technology: The empirical turn* (R. P. Crease, Trans.). Indiana University Press.

Ahmed, S. (2010). Orientations matter. In D. Coole & S. Frost (Eds), *New materialisms: Ontology, agency and politics* (pp. 234–257). Duke University Press.

Appleton, C. (2021). Exploitable multistability: The view from the bike lane. In L. Botin & I. B. Hyams (Eds), *Postphenomenology and architecture: Human technology relations in the built environment* (pp. 45–69). Lexington Books.

Arzroomchilar, E. (2022). Some suggestions to improve postphenomenology. *Human Studies, 45,* 65–92, https://doi.org/10.1007/s10746-021-09615-1

Barad, K. (2003). Posthumanist performativity: Toward an understanding of how matter comes to matter. *Signs, 28*(3), 801–831, https://doi.org/10.1086/345321

Baş, Melis. (2022). *Technological mediation of politics: An Arendtian critique of political philosophy of technology* [Doctoral dissertation, University of Twente], https://doi.org/10.3990/1.9789036553667

Borgmann, A. (2005, January 8). Review of *What Things Do*. Notre Dame Review of Books, https://ndpr.nd.edu/reviews/what-things-do-philosophical-reflections-on-technology-agency-and-design/

Botin, L. (2019). Sustainable futures: Ethico-politico dimensions of technology. In R. Lally (Ed.), *Sustainability in the Anthropocene age: Philosophical essays on renewable technologies* (pp. 153–70). Lexington Books.

Botin, L., de Boer, B., & Børsen, T. (2020). Technology in between the individual and the political: Postphenomenology and critical constructivism. *Techné: Research in Philosophy and Technology, 24*(1/2), 1–14, https://doi.org/10.5840/techne2020241

de Boer, B. (2020). *How scientific instruments speak: Postphenomenology and technological mediations in neuroscientific practice*. Lexington Books.

de Boer, B. (2023). Explaining multistability: Postphenomenology and affordances of technologies. *AI & Society, 38*, 2267–2277, https://doi.org/10.1007/s00146-021-01272-3

de Boer, B., & Kudina, O. (2021). What is morally at stake when using algorithms to make medical diagnoses? Expanding the discussion beyond risks and harms. *Theoretical Medicine and Bioethics, 42*(5–6), 245–266, https://doi.org/10.1007/s11017-021-09553-0

Coeckelbergh, M. (2017). *Using words and things: Language and the philosophy of technology*. Routledge.

Collins, P. H. (1990). *Black feminist thought: Knowledge, consciousness, and the politics of empowerment*. Unwin Hyman.

Fried, S. J. (2023). Satellites, war, climate change, and the environment: Are we at risk for environmental deskilling? *AI & Society, 38*, 2305–2313, https://doi.org/10.1007/s00146-020-01047-2

Fried, S. J., & Rosenberger, R. (Eds). (2021). *Postphenomenology and imaging: How to read technology*. Lexington Books.

Friesen, N., Feenberg, A., & Smith, G. (2009). Phenomenology and surveillance studies: Returning to the things themselves. *The Information Society, 25*, 84–90. https://doi.org/10.1080/01972240802701585

Giamariano, C., O'Connor, P., & Willing, I. (2023). The impacts of hostile designs on skateboarding as a form of active transportation and recreation: Comparing perspectives from public universities in Australia, the United Kingdom, and the United States. *Cities and Health, 7*(3), 416–432. https://doi.org/10.1080/23748834.2022.2158769

Goeminne, G. (2011). Postphenomenology and the politics of sustainable technology. *Foundations of Science, 16*(2–3), 173–194, https://doi.org/10.1007/s10699-010-9196-5

Haraway, D. (1988). Situated knowledges: The science question in feminism and the privilege of partial perspective. *Feminist Studies, 14*(3), 575–599.

Haraway, D. (2003). *The companion species manifesto: Dogs, people, and significant otherness*. Prickly Paradigm Press.

Harding, S. (1991). *Whose science? Whose knowledge?* Cornell University Press.

Harding, S. (Ed.). (2003). *The feminist standpoint theory reader: Intellectual and political controversies*. Routledge.

Hartsock, N. C. M. (1998). *The feminist standpoint revisited and other essays*. Westview Press.

Hasse, C. (2013). Artifacts that talk: Mediating technologies as multistable signs and tools. *Subjectivity, 6*(1), 79–100, https://doi.org/10.1057/sub.2021.29

Hasse, C. (2020). *Posthumanist learning: What robots and cyborgs teach us about being ultra-social*. Routledge.

Hauser, S., Oogjes, D., Wakkary, R., & Verbeek, P.-P. (2018, June 8). An annotated portfolio on doing postphenomenology through research products. DIS '18: Proceedings of the 2018 Designing Interactive Systems Conference, Hong Kong. *ACM*, 459–471, https://doi.org/10.1145/3196709.3196745

Ihde, D. (1977). *Experimental phenomenology*. Putnam.

Ihde, D. (1986). *On non-foundational phenomenology*. Fenomenografiska notiser 3 (S. Chaiklin, Ed.). Institutionen för pedagogik: Göteborgs Universitet.

Ihde, D. (1990). *Technology and the lifeworld: From garden to earth*. Indiana University Press.

Ihde, D. (1993). *Postphenomenology: Essays in the postmodern context*. Northwestern University Press.

Ihde, D. (1998). *Expanding hermeneutics: Visualism in science*. Northwestern University Press.

Ihde, D. (2008). *Ironic technics*. VIP/Automatic Press.

Ihde, D. (2009). *Postphenomenology and technoscience: The Peking University lectures*. State University of New York Press.

Ihde, D. (2022). *Material hermeneutics: Reversing the linguistic turn*. Routledge.

Irwin, S. O. (2016). *Digital media: Human-technology connection*. Lexington Books.

Keymolen, E. (2021). In search of friction: A new postphenomenological lens to analyze human-smartphone interactions. *Techné: Research in Philosophy and Technology, 23*(3), 354–378, https://doi.org/10.5840/techne20211124150

Kroes, P., & Meijers, A. (Eds). (2001). *The empirical turn in the philosophy of technology*. JAI Press.

Kudina, O. (2023). *Moral hermeneutics and technology: Making moral sense through human-technology-world relations*. Lexington Books.

Lewis, R. S. (2021). *Situating media literacy: A posthumanist approach*. Open Book Publishers, https://doi.org/10.11647/obp.0253

Mitchell, J. P. (2021). Unsafe ground: Technology, habit, and the enactment of disability. *Women, Gender & Research, 2*, 24–39, https://doi.org/10.7146/kkf.v31i2.127873

Mykhailov, D., & Liberati, N. (2023). Back to the technologies themselves: Phenomenological turn within postphenomenology. *Phenomenology and the Cognitive Sciences*, https://doi.org/10.1007/s11097-023-09905-2

Rao, M.B., Jongerden, J., Lemmens, P., & Ruivenkamp, G. (2015). Technological mediation and power: Postphenomenology, critical theory, and autonomist Marxism. *Philosophy & Technology, 28*, 449–474, https://doi.org/10.1007/s13347-015-0190-2

Ritter, M. (2021). Philosophical potencies of postphenomenology. *Philosophy & Technology, 34*, 1501–1519, https://doi.org/10.1007/s13347-021-00469-0

Romele, A. (2021). Technological capital: Bourdieu, postphenomenology, and the philosophy of technology beyond the empirical turn. *Philosophy & Technology, 34*(3), 483–505, https://doi.org/10.1007/s13347-020-00398-4

Romele, A. (2024). *Digital habitus: A critique of the imaginaries of artificial intelligence*. Routledge.

Rosenberger, R. (2014). Multistability and the agency of mundane artifacts: From speed bumps to subway benches. *Human Studies, 37*, 369–392, https://doi.org/10.1007/s10746-014-9317-1

Rosenberger, R. (2017a). *Callous objects: Designs against the homeless*. University of Minnesota Press.

Rosenberger, R. (2017b). Notes on a nonfoundational phenomenology of technology. *Foundations of Science, 22*, 471–494, https://doi.org/10.1007/s10699-015-9480-5

Rosenberger, R. (2017c). On the hermeneutics of everyday things: Or, the philosophy of fire hydrants. *AI & Society, 32*, 233–241, https://doi.org/10.1007/s00146-016-0674-3

Rosenberger, R. (2020). Hostile design and the materiality of surveillance. In H. Wiltse (Ed.), *Relating to things: Technology and the artificial* (pp. 135–150). Bloomsbury.

Rosenberger, Robert. (2021, September 16). The politics of the passive subject. *Social Epistemology Review and Reply Collective*, https://social-epistemology.com/2021/09/16/the-politics-of-the-passive-subject-robert-rosenberger/

Rosenberger, R. (2023). On variational cross-examination: A method for postphenomenological multistability. *AI & Society, 38*, 2229–2242, https://doi.org/10.1007/s00146-020-01050-7

Rosenberger, R. (2024). *Distracted: The philosophy of cars and phones*. University of Minnesota Press.

Rosenberger, R. (forthcoming). A note on the materiality of educational frog dissection. In P. Briel & M. Bohlmann (Eds), *Postphenomenology and technologies within educational settings*. Lexington Books.

Rosenberger, R., & Verbeek, P.-P. (Eds). (2015). *Postphenomenological investigations: Essays on human-technology relations*. Lexington Books.

Scharff, R. C. (2022). On making phenomenologies more phenomenological. *Philosophy & Technology, 35*, 62, https://doi.org/10.1007/s13347-022-00544-0

Smith, D. E. (1974). Women's perspective as a radical critique of sociology. *Sociological Inquiry, 44*(1), 7–13.

Smith, D. (2015). Rewriting the constitution: A critique of 'postphenomenology'. *Philosophy & Technology, 28*(4), 533–51, https://doi.org/10.1007/s13347-014-0175-6

Van Den Eede, Y, Irwin, S. O., & Wellner, G. (Eds). (2017). *Postphenomenology and media*. Lexington Books.

Verbeek, P.-P. (2005). *What things do: Philosophical reflections on technology, agency, and design*. Pennsylvania University Press.

Verbeek, P.-P. (2011). *Moralizing technology*. University of Chicago Press.

Verbeek, P.-P. (2020). Politicizing postphenomenology. In G. Miller & A. Shew (Eds), *Reimagining philosophy of technology, reinventing Ihde* (pp. 141–155). Springer.

Wakkery, R. (2021). *Things we could design: In more than human-centered worlds*. MIT Press.

Warfield, K. (2017). MirrorCameraRoom: The gendered multi-(in)stabilities of the selfie. *Feminist Media Studies, 17*(1), 77–92, https://doi.org/10.1080/14680777.2017.1261843

Weiss, G., Murphy, A. V., & Salamon, G. (2020). *50 concepts for a critical phenomenology*. Northwestern University Press.

Wellner, G. (2016). *A postphenomenological inquiry of cell phones: Genealogies, meanings, and becoming*. Lexington Books.

Wellner, G. (forthcoming). Fighting gender bias in AI by transforming background relations into alterity relations. In G. Wellner, L. Friedman, & R. Rosenberger (Eds), *Postphenomenology and feminist theory*. Lexington Books.

Whyte, K. P. (2015). What is multistability? A theory of the keystone concept of postphenomenological research. In J. K. B. O. Friis & R. P. Crease (Eds), *Technoscience and postphenomenology: The Manhattan papers* (pp. 69–81). Lexington Books.

Wiltse, H. (2020). Revealing relations of fluid assemblages. In H. Wiltse (Ed.), *Relating to things: Design, technology, and the artificial* (pp. 239–253). Bloomsbury.

Wittkower, D. E. (2017). Discrimination. In J. C. Pitt & A. Shew (Eds), *Spaces for the future: A companion to the philosophy of technology* (pp. 14–28). Routledge.

Zwier, J., Blok, V., & Lemmens, P. (2016). Phenomenology and the empirical turn: A phenomenological analysis of postphenomenology. *Philosophy & Technology, 29*, 313–333, https://doi.org/10.1007/s13347-016-0221-7

5. Technological Mediation without Empirical Borders

Martin Ritter

Introduction

Postphenomenology is often seen as *the* approach elucidating how technology transforms experience. Phenomenologically speaking, it promises to show how technology conditions the appearance of phenomena. In this chapter, I evaluate its ability to fulfil this task. I intend to demonstrate how, to bring out its full potential, postphenomenology must revisit its basic concepts and adjust its method. The chapter is divided into two main parts: first, I critically analyze the shortcomings of postphenomenology, and second, I suggest modifications to it. In the first, longer part, after briefly recalling the hallmarks of postphenomenology, I focus on its (missing) concept of technology, its theory of technological mediation, and its method. I assess the soundness of these elements and expose their limits.[1] Based on these critical reflections, in the second part I outline the basic contours of a modified, phenomenological postphenomenology.

1. The Basics

Postphenomenology is inseparably linked with the name of Don Ihde, its founder, who used this label in 1993 to designate the method he had been practicing already for two decades (Ihde, 1993). In 2006,

---

[1] My inevitably schematic reflections cannot do justice to all the meritorious work done by postphenomenologists. Their aim is to identify the limits we must transcend to elucidate the technological mediation of experience.

he identified three distinctive characteristics of postphenomenology (Ihde, 2009, pp. 9–23). First, it is a phenomenological approach, yet quite radically transformed by pragmatism. Whereas Edmund Husserl drew heavily on early modern epistemology, and hence succumbed to subjectivism, John Dewey overcame psychologism by basing his analyses on an organism/environment model rather than a subject/object model. In Ihde's eyes, we need this pragmatic ontological framework to adequately understand experience. On the other side, postphenomenology takes some useful concepts from phenomenology, especially those of variational theory, embodiment, and lifeworld. In the case of variational theory, Ihde draws exclusively on Husserl, whereas he acknowledges the concepts of embodiment and lifeworld as significantly enriched by Martin Heidegger and Maurice Merleau-Ponty. Thanks to pragmatism, we understand that there is no purely subjective consciousness: (subjective) experience is always physically, materially, and socio-culturally embedded. Thanks to phenomenology, we can analyze experience using variational theory while acknowledging the role of embodiment and situating our life in a specific lifeworld. The third characteristic, which makes postphenomenology fully contemporary, is the inclusion of technoscience studies. Ihde fully embraces the so-called empirical turn in the philosophy of technology: we need to stay away from abstract generalizations about technology and focus instead on concrete technologies in their particularities.

In *A Field Guide to Postphenomenology* (2015), Robert Rosenberger and Peter-Paul Verbeek specify the *modus operandi* of postphenomenology. Due to its 'practical and material orientation, postphenomenology always takes the study of human-technology relations as its starting point' (Rosenberger & Verbeek, 2015, p. 31). Accordingly, it analyzes various roles that technologies play in human-world relations and aims at elucidating '*how, in the relations that arise around a technology, a specific "world" is constituted, as well as a specific "subject"*' (Rosenberger & Verbeek, 2015, p. 31, emphasis in the original). Crucially, such a philosophical reflection always presupposes empirical work as its basis, usually in the form of case studies. This empirical starting point has its counterpart in a pragmatic outcome of the analysis: '*postphenomenological studies typically make a conceptual analysis of the implications of technologies* for one or more specific dimensions of human-world relations—which can be epistemological, political, aesthetic, ethical, metaphysical, et cetera' (Rosenberger & Verbeek, 2015, p. 31, emphasis in the original). It is not enough to describe how technologies change our experience: we must critically assess the consequences of these mediations.

Regarding these consequences, postphenomenology emphasizes the possibility of (re)designing how technologies shape our lives. This emphasis is partially responsible for the impression that its approach is techno-optimistic in contrast to older, predominantly pessimistic conceptualizations of technology. According to postphenomenology, we must focus on particular technologies as it is the only way to both realistically appreciate their impact and pragmatically influence it. This is nicely captured by the subtitle of Verbeek's book *Moralizing Technology* (2011): 'Understanding and Designing the Morality of Things'. Technologies do shape our actions, but we should not focus— negatively—on protecting humans from the detrimental effects of new technology. Rather, we need to 'accompany' technologies (Verbeek, 2010) while engaging with designers to make technologies—positively— not only morally but also politically beneficial. Yet even without taking designers into consideration, as soon as we base our research empirically, and hence pay attention to concrete technologies and the possibilities they unlock, we become able to see that technologies can be 'the source of new forms of social agency and self-awareness' and open up 'new political spaces' (Verbeek, 2017, p. 303). Postphenomenology is eminently interested in the new possibilities of human experiencing and acting created by technologies, and takes heed of them from the perspective of design ethics (Verbeek, 2006).

2. Up-to-Date Postphenomenology

Having briefly summarized the distinctive traits of postphenomenology, let me scrutinize three closely connected elements or dimensions of its approach. First, how does postphenomenology conceptualize technology? Second, how does it apprehend the mediation of experience by technology? Third, how does it analyze this mediation and base its findings?

I focus on these three questions for two reasons. On the one hand, the dimensions addressed by them constitute the fundamentals of the postphenomenological approach. On the other hand, by analyzing them one by one, I hope to offer not only a comprehensive but also a comprehensible explication of the limits of postphenomenology.

2.1 Technology

Postphenomenologists do *not* define technology. They prefer material technologies to immaterial concepts when doing their analyses. Or, they base their conclusions on analyzing specific relations with concrete technologies. Such an approach should prevent not only thinking of technology too abstractly but also turning it into a sort of substance or an autonomous force capable of subjugating humans. Simply put, we risk essentialism the moment we try to formulate what technology *is*, and there is no such risk if we turn to what is used *as* technologies. However, postphenomenologists inevitably *do* apply some concept of technology when doing their research, i.e., when analyzing particular things *as* technologies. As I intend to show in this section, they should make their concept of what makes a thing or a process technological explicit and sound. Just as importantly, they must be able to demonstrate that technology has a significant, noteworthy impact on our lifeworld. To accomplish these tasks, postphenomenologists cannot but transcend the sphere of particular technologies: they need a concept of technology (as) significantly mediating human experience. To be sure, such a concept will not be independent of particular technologies. Yet, as soon as we ask the question of what makes technology able to condition the appearing of other phenomena, our dealing with particular technologies evokes questions that necessitate transcending the very sphere of particularities. This section seeks to demonstrate this by proceeding from more specific (and tangible) phenomena to more general ones.

Allow me to begin with quite an obvious fact: the empirical turn as realized by postphenomenology is a turn to technological *artefacts* (Coeckelbergh, 2022, p. 259). But this triviality evokes an arguably essential question: how do postphenomenologists *select* a technology that they turn to? What is the criterion of their choice? To indicate why this question must be addressed, let me discuss some possible answers to it. First, since postphenomenology seeks to be fully contemporary (Ihde, 2009, p. 19), one can suggest turning to the most *recent* technologies. But is there any reason to think that they have the most significant impact on human experience? If not, why prefer them? Pieter Lemmens speaks in this context about the 'myopic fascination with empirically describing the effects of the most recent technocommodities on a consumer-subject that is not in any way problematized' (Lemmens, 2017, p. 308), which may sound a bit harsh, but it rightly indicates the problematic nature of this criterion. Second, one might argue that we should focus on the technologies with the most *transformative* impact on experience. But how can we say in advance, i.e., before analyzing a particular technology, how radical its impact is? Our presumptions may quite easily be misleading, contingent on prevailing views. Third, we could take *societal needs* as the decisive criterion. But they are far from being obvious. Society never gives equal space to all its members to express their concerns. In our representative democracies, politicians are supposed to give voice to the people. Yet even in the best possible scenario, philosophers cannot unquestioningly rely on how politicians specify the priorities of, for example, government-supported research.

Obviously, this is not a list of all conceivable criteria. And, admittedly, all the criteria just mentioned *are* relevant. It is reasonable to pay attention to new and/or widely used technologies as they may lead to significant transformations. Such a focus is socially responsible. Novelty itself, however, is no criterion, while the other two criteria necessitate further discussion. Besides, non-postphenomenological philosophers of technology, such as those inspired by the so-called critical theory of technology, can argue that their approaches are better equipped to identify the technologies in need of being addressed by society. To make their approach compelling, postphenomenologists *must justify* why their focus on this or that technology is philosophically relevant. And such a justification cannot be made simply and only *ad hoc*. They must offer a more *general reasoning*. This is desirable also because turning to something always means turning away from something else. Without some guideline directing their focus, postphenomenologists risk missing crucial cases of technological mediation.

Taking one step back, there is another pressing question regarding the postphenomenological turn to technology realized as a turn to artefacts.

Should we principally address *all* the artefacts or just the *technological* ones? And what about the things not artificially made by humans? Can they technologically mediate experience? Postphenomenologists sometimes seem to propose a turn to objects as such (Verbeek, 2005, p. 2), yet they do limit their focus to technologies, and technologies are never—according to postphenomenologists—the objects in themselves. A thing rather *becomes* technology as a part of a human pragmatic context. But on what basis do we identify something as technology? Not all entities entering human pragmatic contexts are considered technologies. Or, in case we do take all the parts of these contexts as technologies, postphenomenology needs to be conceptualized in a more inclusive way. Such an approach is implied by Yoni Van Den Eede (2022). Seeking to bridge the gap between the empirically and transcendentally oriented approaches in the philosophy of technology (I will address this duality later), he takes inspiration from Graham Harman's object-oriented-ontology and points to a universal thing-transcendentality. By this, he means that each thing transcends any possible relation to it, and understanding of it, while remaining a reservoir for unforeseeable transformative processes. Elaborating on Van Den Eede, we could imagine a more inclusive kind of postphenomenology focusing not only on *technological* mediation but more broadly on mediation by *any* object.

Yet, instead of promoting such an approach, I want to underline that postphenomenology, precisely because of its focus on technology, cannot avoid addressing not only the question of why to turn to this or that technology but also the question of why to turn to technology at all. The just-mentioned theory of not-only-technological mediation is fully possible, but the theory of *technological* mediation is arguably even more needed. It is needed exactly because—and as far as—our experience is *fundamentally* mediated by technology. Postphenomenologists are rather hesitant about the universality of technological mediation. They do not claim, at least not categorically, that technology mediates human experience *in toto*. This seems quite understandable: who would dare to claim that *all* experiences are mediated by technological artefacts? But to claim that experience is fundamentally mediated by technology is not the same as claiming that each and every experience is mediated by some technological artefact. To swiftly clarify my point, allow me to point to Ihde's famous analysis of the telescope (Ihde, 2011; 2016): with the introduction of this technology, humans started to experience the world differently, and they do so till today. Or, the existence of a home—which is a technology making human homeliness (and homesickness, too) possible—is a fundamental condition of our experience. In other words, technology can change not (only) particular experiences but the lifeworld as such, namely the basic framework of human experience. I argue that postphenomenology should focus on *such* transformative processes. And to be able to do that, it must deal with the questions formulated in the previous paragraphs.

2.2 Mediation

Postphenomenology focuses on human interactions with technological artefacts, yet it does *not* concentrate on the technological things *themselves*. As stated by Rosenberger and Verbeek and quoted above also, it takes 'the study of human-technology relations as its starting point' and elucidates '*how, in the relations that arise around a technology, a specific "world" is constituted, as well as a specific "subject"*' (Rosenberger & Verbeek, 2015, p. 31, emphasis in the original). The emphasis lies on the *relations* with and around a technology, not on the technology itself. Of course, there would be no human-technology relation without a technology. But it is not the technology itself that by itself shapes humans and the world. Rather, it partially contributes to constituting a specific world and a specific subject by making specific 'relations that arise around' it possible. Yet these relations are always already co-enacted by humans and the process of mediation takes place based on this interrelatedness. Hence, technological mediation is not, strictly speaking, generated by the technology itself but rather by the relations arising around it.

Since postphenomenologists understand technologies pragmatically, as means of our actions, they predominantly analyze technological mediation by focusing on what technologies do *when used*. I already criticized such an approach: we can either seek to fully realize what technologies do even beyond our pragmatic intentions, or reduce their mediating power to what they do as part of our practical contexts (Ritter, 2021a, pp. 586–588). Recently, Dmytro Mykhailov and Nicola Liberati developed a similar line of reasoning by drawing on Husserl's concept of passive synthesis: technologies themselves (can) have their own intentionality, or their 'inner passive activity', irreducible to and independent of our intentionality and activity. The authors rightly underline that technologies can, for example, autonomously interact with other objects while this interaction may take place outside of the subject's consciousness. 'Technological intentionality exists *before* or *outside* the mediation', claim the authors (Mykhailov & Liberati, 2023, p. 15, emphasis in the original).

I agree with these and other researchers (e.g., Aydin et al., 2019) that postphenomenology does not take *the autonomy of technology* seriously enough. This flaw affects its relational ontology, too. Despite declaring that technology is just as important a part of the human-technology-world relation as humans themselves, postphenomenologists do *not* develop a genuinely *inter*-relational ontology. This becomes visible, I believe, in how Rosenberger and Verbeek distinguish their approach from that of actor-network theory (ANT). In contrast to ANT, postphenomenology does not abandon the distinction between subjects and objects. It insists on this dichotomy to 'do justice to human experiences of being subjectively "in" a word' while analyzing 'engaged human-world relations, and their technologically mediated character, from a first-person perspective' (Rosenberger & Verbeek, 2015, p. 20). In fact, the traditional subject-object dichotomy is not necessary to do justice to human experiencing in the world, or to enable analysis of it from a first-person perspective. To put it more concretely, there is no need to dichotomize (intentional) humans as subjective agents in contrast to merely functioning (non-intentional) objects in order to phenomenologically analyze human experience.[2] Postphenomenology inclines to such a dichotomization, which has as its consequence—as Bruno Latour puts it regarding phenomenology—an 'excessive stress given by phenomenologists to human sources of agency' (Latour, 2005, p. 61, n. 67). I agree with Verbeek that 'the postphenomenological perspective and Latour's actor-network theory are not as incompatible as Latour himself supposes' (Verbeek, 2005, p. 168), but making them

---

2   I cannot discuss here the different ontologies of phenomenology and ANT. Even less do I intend to discuss ontology as such. My point is that the (non-)acceptance of the subject-object dichotomy has no direct impact on the possibility of analyzing human experience.

compatible implies making postphenomenology less subjectivist. Specifically, we have to pay as much attention to objects and their agencies as to human agency while acknowledging that experience cannot be fully accounted for from a first-person perspective only.

Generally put, postphenomenology usually does *not* focus on human-technology-world relations *in toto* but rather on *human relating to* technology. As is very well known, Ihde (1990) distinguished four basic forms of human-technology-world relations, and other postphenomenologists, especially Verbeek (2008), added more. Taking into consideration this (still expanding) list, I can formulate the problem of insufficient inter-relationality, and of the undervaluation of technology, from a different angle. In the schematic depictions of human-technology relations, the arrow is never directed from the right to the left, i.e., from 'world' to 'technology' or from 'technology' to 'human' (e.g., Verbeek, 2008, p. 389, p. 391, p. 393). This indicates that, whatever the relations 'arising around a technology' may be, these relations remain induced by humans. The 'inter-relation' is about *our* relating to the world (and to fellow humans) through technologies. What is missing in these schemes is the possibility of the arrow pointing in the opposite direction.[3] Or, to express the very same problem otherwise: there seems to be no possibility of putting 'technology' on the left, thus effectively making the scheme 'technology-human-world'.

To be clear: I do not call for thinking of technology as using humans. What I do claim is that, to fully realize the contribution of technologies to technological mediation, we should aspire to take as our *starting point* not only 'the study of human-technology relations' (Rosenberger & Verbeek, 2015, p. 31) but the study of both *these* relations *and* technology-human relations. Admittedly, it is a difficult task to conceptualize the (non-intentional) relational agency of technologies, yet only on such a basis can we fully realize '*the relations that arise around a technology*' (Rosenberger & Verbeek, 2015, p. 31, emphasis in the original) as conditioned by both humans and the technologies themselves. In other words, if we want to elucidate how technologies influence our experience, we cannot do

---

3   Lately, Bas de Boer and Peter-Paul Verbeek have attempted to conceptualize the reciprocal character of human-technology relations (cf. de Boer & Verbeek, 2022). See also Aydin et al. (2019, p. 328) for an attempt to think of technology as a part of the world itself.

so by focusing solely on the relations *we have* with them, thus reducing technological mediation to how *our relating* to technologies influences our experience. The postphenomenological approach to human-technology relations is unnecessarily humancentric, and this bias originates from its pragmatic, not phenomenological, roots: it is conditioned by the implicit identification of technology with something we pragmatically relate to. Yet to overcome this limit, we must do more than acknowledging the 'inner passive activity' of technologies. For the question is: how does this intentionality contribute to technological mediation? And, indeed, how does *our* intentionality contribute to it?

The process of technological mediation cannot be reduced to human or technological intentionality. Rather, it seems to be produced by the intertwining of these intentionalities. However, the situation is even more complicated because the contribution of both technologies *and* humans to the process of technological mediation can be non-intentional and/or non-intended. In fact, there is *an essential difference* between the process by which the technologies themselves intentionally relate (whether to their environment or to us) and the process by which these technologies affect our relating to the world, i.e., technologically mediate. Similarly, there is *an essential difference* between the process of our intentional relating to the world through technologies and the process by which this intentional using of technologies affects our relating to the world, i.e., contributes to technological mediation. This indicates that it is extremely difficult, if not impossible, to determine where exactly, and when exactly too, the process of technological mediation takes place. But perhaps we are looking in the wrong place when trying to capture technological mediation as an empirically observable (inter)relational process. I will return to this question.

2.3 The Case of Empiricism

In the previous two sections, I focused on what postphenomenology analyzes and why. Accordingly, I examined its concepts of technology and technological mediation. In this section, I concentrate on *how* postphenomenology analyzes the influence of technology on human experience. Of course, this methodological question is not independent of the previous ones. On the contrary, the way we analyze something affects the thing itself, namely what we see as technology and how we understand technological mediation. Hence, in the previous two sections I have already addressed, implicitly, the empirical turn as realized by postphenomenology. This section complements the aforesaid.

As I have explained elsewhere (Ritter, 2021b, pp. 1503–1505, pp. 1512–1515), Ihde's philosophy of technology is not limited to the analysis of human individual engagements with technology. In *Technology and the Lifeworld* (1990, p. 161), he distinguishes three programs: in addition to (1) 'a phenomenology of technics', Ihde outlined (2) 'cultural hermeneutics' and (3) a 'final program' (with no formalized title) revealing the 'curvatures of the contemporary lifeworld'. In its continuing development, however, postphenomenology has tended to focus on the first program only: a phenomenology of technics is usually carried out when postphenomenologists study human-technology relations. Even Ihde himself has lately leaned toward reducing his philosophy to such a 'praxis-oriented analysis' (cf. Ihde, 2015, p. xii). Generally, postphenomenology seems to have developed from a more broadly, and perhaps more vaguely, designed approach to one focusing exclusively on human-technology relations. And this transformation, I believe, is closely related to the intent of postphenomenologists to promote their approach as a form of 'empirical philosophy' (Rosenberger & Verbeek, 2015, p. 30). Postphenomenology wants to stay close to 'actual technological practices and artifacts' (Rosenberger & Verbeek, 2015, p. 30), which is not easily compatible with formulating general theses about the global characteristics of our lifeworld.

As empirical philosophy, postphenomenology focuses on case studies, or more precisely on *user* cases: on the experiences of human beings using technologies. This method has several pitfalls. First, there is a danger of focusing on a technology just and only when it is being used. But technologies can transform our experience without being used, as well (cf. Kiran, 2012, pp. 83–84). For example, even when we do not use airplanes (or spacecrafts), we experience the world 'through' them as something we can travel the length and breadth of. Second, in its intent to stay close to actual practices and artefacts, postphenomenology tends to analyze human-technology relations as the relations between an individual and a technology, without being sufficiently sensitive to the fact that a human being is never a self-dependent atom but always already a social—i.e., in a sense non-individual—entity (cf. Romele, 2021; Arzroomchilar, 2022, pp. 76–78). The same is true about any technology: it is not just an individual thing but is permeated with non-particular characteristics. Simply, there is *no* truly, or rather merely, individual human-technology relation. Third, how can we generalize the findings based on particular cases of human-technology relations? The aim of case studies is *not* to elucidate particular cases themselves. Rather, the cases should be exemplary: they are supposed to be the cases of something non-particular. Is postphenomenology (1) willing and (2) able to conceptualize this? To what degree can it take the non-particular as something (temporarily) stable, given the postphenomenological idea of the principal multistability of technologies (e.g., de Boer, 2021)?

All the issues mentioned in the previous paragraph concern the *object* of inquiry. Yet, any case study has its *subjective* side as well: how is a researcher supposed to proceed to bring forth a *valid* case study? As underlined by Mariska Thalitha Bosschaert and Vincent Blok, to diminish the risk of investigator bias, case studies need to follow a clearly defined methodology: if a case study does not meet this requirement, it should be labelled 'an *impressionistic* case-study in contrast to a *methodological* case-study' (Bosschaert & Blok, 2023, p. 794, emphasis in the original). Postphenomenologists have been trying to make their approach scientifically founded and hence less 'impressionistic' (cf. Verbeek, 2016; Aagaard et al., 2018). But what all these efforts primarily expose is that, even when grounding our findings in 'the empirical', we cannot do without developing a conceptual framework making empirically oriented research methodically sound. For (not only) this very reason, I agree with Bosschaert and Blok that 'the empirical and the structural are both inevitable in a philosophical understanding of technologies, and interrelated' (2023, p. 799). To put it a bit bluntly, what we see as (empirically) given depends on our theories (cf. Misa, 2009).

Bosschaert and Blok speak about 'a bias toward describing the concrete' of the empirically oriented philosophers of technology (2023, p. 797) and question the assumption 'that structural issues can be resolved by means of studies of concrete technologies' (2023, p. 798). I do consider it possible to disclose 'structural issues' through studying concrete technologies. But we cannot achieve this by *basing* our analysis on the experiences of humans using technologies. Such an analysis must already be informed by the above-mentioned reflections, namely by taking into account—explicitly and methodically—that our individual human-technology relations are always already trans-individual and that technologies are never merely individual but always already systemic, i.e., parts of larger technological systems. Taking these dimensions into consideration, we can no more take 'empirical' particularities as our starting point—or, to formulate it positively, we can explicitly acknowledge the empirical in its truth not as a positivist givenness but as a givenness *achieved* by theoretical effort. By developing such an approach, we can make it possible to deal with 'structural issues' and even to formulate general theses about the global, yet historically conditioned, characteristics of our lifeworld.

3. Contours of Phenomenological Postphenomenology

In his 'program for postphenomenological research', Verbeek (2016) distinguishes three lines of inquiry: epistemological, ethical, and metaphysical. Postphenomenology should study how technological mediation shapes our knowledge, morality, and metaphysical frameworks. The third, metaphysical, line of inquiry should analyze the mediated character of metaphysics but also 'develop a metaphysical framework for understanding the phenomenon of technological mediation itself' (Verbeek, 2016, p. 199). This is a remarkable suggestion, especially considering the disinclination of postphenomenologists to develop theories separate from empirical cases: a 'metaphysics of mediation' seems to transcend a research field investigating 'the role played by specific technologies in specific contexts' (Verbeek, 2005, p. 7). In other words, it transcends particularities to offer a general theory. I do agree that such a reflection must be an inseparable, indeed vital, component of postphenomenology if it aspires to be a philosophical endeavour, not an empirical science. In a similar vein, I have sought to indicate some elements, so far rather negatively, of what I would prefer to call a phenomenology, and not a metaphysics, of mediation. Before sketching some of its basic lines, allow me to take a very brief look at the recent 'empirical-transcendental debate' in the philosophy of technology (Lemmens & Van Den Eede, 2022).

I agree with Alberto Romele that postphenomenology has always perceived technology in a sense transcendentally, namely 'as a condition of possibility for a specific relationship with the world' (2022, p. 977). However, the empirical turn philosophers have a narrow concept of the transcendental. They connect the term with the conditions of possibility of technology and conclude that, if we focus on such conditions, we do not pay enough attention to the technologies themselves (e.g., Achterhuis, 2001, p. 3; Verbeek, 2005, p. 7). But such a conclusion is too hasty. It is fully possible to pay attention to *both* the conditions of possibility of technology *and* to the technologies themselves. In fact, although it is questionable if in postphenomenology 'technology itself is understood within two of its own conditions of possibility—humans and the world' (Romele, 2022, p. 977), there seems to be no specific reason why postphenomenology could not take these two conditions into account. But whether we pay attention to them or not, we still can think of technologies as having a transcendental function, i.e., as making possible a specific givenness of the world. Hence, as Lemmens puts it, we need to 'technologize the transcendental': instead of emphasizing the non-technological condition of technology, we must 'recognize technology itself as the transcendental operator' (2022, p. 1307).

If we take the transcendental as referring to what conditions human experience without necessarily transcending it, we can claim that postphenomenology cannot but take the transcendental into account. The mediating is itself the transcendental. Hence the three questions raised above can be reformulated thus: how to conceive of the mediating/transcendental itself? How to conceptualize the mediating process? And how to analyze it? By answering these questions, I seek to outline the basic tenets, and nothing more than such abstract principles, of modified postphenomenology.

3.1 What is Essential is Invisible to the Eyes

I have argued that postphenomenology needs a concept of technology (as) significantly mediating experience. Postphenomenologists doubt this need and directly analyze things used *as* technologies. But to justify their turning to this or that technology, and not to another one, they have to give reasons why they consider it as significantly transforming our experience. Even more elementarily, they have to justify their belief that it is technology, and not non-technological things or processes, that has such an impact. Only on such a theoretical basis can postphenomenology be seen as a philosophical endeavour.

Once we open this line of inquiry, we can no longer be satisfied with particularities. Or, more precisely, we cannot be satisfied with particularities *as* particularities. Technologies are worthy of attention not due to their particularity but because their specific technological characteristics, which can be shared with other technological particularities, are capable of significantly transforming human experience. To use a somewhat banal example, we cannot be satisfied with analyzing human interactions with smartphones but are led to focus on the digital technology in its digitality. This implies that we become able to see technology both *otherwise* and *elsewhere* than usual. Digital technology is not identifiable with this or that particular smartphone; in a certain sense, digitality is not an object at all, i.e., not a thing we directly interact with. This example indicates that it may be misleading to think of technology in an objectivist way. Accordingly, it is fully justified to think of technology, in its very materiality, not as something standing in front of us but rather as something we already are a part of (cf. Aydin et al., 2019). Paradoxically, a philosophical approach that goes beyond the limited focus on artefacts as things we interact with is compatible with object-oriented ontology, provided we understand technologies not 'from our ingrained Cartesian worldview, but more as in line with McLuhanist environments' (Van Den Eede, 2022, p. 238).

I would suggest even one step forward, or perhaps backward. Acknowledging that *the* phenomenon for postphenomenology is technology, I would cite, by way of analogy, Heidegger's famous description of the phenomenological method in *Being and Time*: technology is '*necessarily* the theme' because it 'lies *hidden*, in contrast to that which proximally and for the most part does show itself; but at the same time it is something that belongs to what thus shows itself, and it belongs to it so essentially as to constitute its meaning and its ground' (Heidegger, 2001, p. 59, emphasis in the original). Technology may not ground and constitute the meaning of all phenomena, yet we must *explicitly* ask the question of how decisive its impact is, and we cannot do so without thinking of technology as something *hidden* in technologies as well.

3.2 Mediation is No Relation

According to postphenomenology, technological mediation is 'generated' by relations around a technology, which usually means by the processes arising from human relating to technology. I have sought to demonstrate that such an approach is not inter-relational enough and effectively downplays the role of technology itself (and probably of the world, too). Yet its most essential weakness, which paradoxically is its strength as well, consists in the very idea that technological mediation can be explained by, and hence reduced to, relations.

Postphenomenologists emphasize that 'humans and technologies should not be seen as two 'poles' between which there is an interaction; rather, they are the result of this interaction' (Verbeek, 2015, p. 28) and that postphenomenology 'does away with the idea that there is a pre-given subject in a pre-given world of objects, with a mediating entity between them. [...] Intentionality is not a bridge between subject and object but a fountain from which the two of them emerge' (Rosenberger & Verbeek, 2015, p. 12). I fully agree that intentionality does not connect the already established entities but rather makes their appearing possible. However, postphenomenologists *do* base their analyses on the 'inputs' of humans and technologies. They analyze how humans relate to technologies and how these technologies influence, when being used, humans in their relating to the world. When Rosenberger and Verbeek speak about 'mediation and mutual constitution' (2015, p. 12), the emphasis lies, in concord with their relational approach, on mutuality. They effectively reduce technological mediality to this mutuality. Instead of elucidating technological mediation as preceding subjects and objects, postphenomenology identifies mediation with, and analyzes it as, a mutual process of co-determining or co-constituting of subjectivity, technology, and objectivity.

Rosenberger and Verbeek rightly claim that we cannot think of intentionality as a bridge but rather as a 'fountain'. But how to do that? From the methodological point of view, the postphenomenological focus on relations is appealing because it can work with empirically given entities. Yet, we must seek to analyze intentionality, in its being technologically mediated, as 'something' neither subjective nor objective, and in this sense non-empirical. Ihde claims that 'the *interrelational ontology* [was] implied by Husserl's "intentionality" and Heidegger's "being-in-the-world"' (2015, p. xii, emphasis in the original). But neither Husserl nor Heidegger envisioned interrelational ontology. In fact, there is no natural affinity between phenomenology and such ontology. Moreover, Heidegger's concept of 'being-in-the-world' radically transformed, both ontologically and methodologically, Husserl's concept of intentionality. The same can be said about Merleau-Ponty in relation to his predecessors. Phenomenology has its own inspiring history in the course of which it has developed various methods of approaching human experience.

I suggest that, instead of relying on an interrelational, pragmatically grounded and empirically oriented philosophy of technology, we can reach for phenomenological, i.e., non-interrelational, concepts to think of 'intentionality', or 'being-in-the-world', or whatever other term we prefer to call our existence, in its being conditioned by technology. For example, we can draw on the theory of intersubjectivity (in its various versions), which offers a different concept of the relations between humans and the world than the pragmatic one. Or, we can explicitly take into consideration the fundamental notion of appearing. This could shed new light on the arguably crucial concept of lifeworld. Let me be clear: these and other concepts do not urge us to forget about relations between subjects, technologies, and the world. Quite to the contrary. Yet they can help us to fully appreciate that these relations are not all there is. If we want to elucidate technological mediation, we cannot do it by combining several relations as if they were pieces of a puzzle. Technological mediation of intentionality is irreducible to human-world relating through technology and cannot be explained by analyzing, one by one, the human-technology, and technology-human, and (perhaps) world-technology, and technology-world, etc., relations.

3.3 The Task of Thinking

The empirical orientation of postphenomenology does not make it methodologically bulletproof. The study of empirically accessible human interactions with technologies is in danger of approaching both humans and technologies (and their interactions as well) in a too atomistic, and hence reductive, way (cf. Ritter, 2021b, pp. 1505–1506).

Besides, postphenomenological analyses do not follow an unquestionable empirical method. Yet, I do not suggest buttressing postphenomenology with an objectivist methodology. One cannot substitute the effort to understand phenomena with following a strictly defined method (cf. Scharff, 2022, p. 12).

'The term "phenomenology" expresses a maxim which can be formulated as "To the things themselves!" It is opposed to all free-floating constructions and accidental findings; it is opposed to taking over any conceptions which only seem to have been demonstrated', writes Heidegger in *Being and Time* (2001, p. 50). The problem is, however, with how to *find* the things themselves, to avoid artificial constructions and fabricated conceptions. One can also put it this way: the problem is how to do justice to our concrete experience. (Post)phenomenology seeks to lay our experience bare, and this effort is remarkable, or valuable, because it shows us something we were unaware of before. Through such an analysis, not only can we see how our experience is conditioned, but we also become able to experience differently, to see things differently.

This can be done in different ways and, as is perhaps clear from my considerations up to now, I do not want here to commit myself to a specific methodology. Instead, I would like to mention a thinker not quite popular among (post)phenomenologists. In his *Minima Moralia*, Theodor W. Adorno criticizes positivism and claims that, to penetrate reality, 'to truly engage the empirical', thinking must keep its distance. 'It expresses exactly what is, precisely because what is is never quite as thought expresses it' (Adorno, 2005, p. 126). This sounded odd—and perhaps still sounds so—in the era of prevailing positivism. Yet, Adorno does not proclaim such a distance as a privilege. 'Distance is not a safety-zone but a field of tension. It is manifested [...] in delicacy and fragility of thinking' (Adorno, 2005, p. 127). Thinking can never be identical with what it thinks: any thought must aim beyond its subject 'just because it never quite reaches it, and positivism is uncritical in its confidence of doing so' (Adorno, 2005, p. 127). According to Adorno, then, 'the exaggerations of speculative metaphysics are scars of reflecting reason [...] In contrast, the immediate proviso of relativity [...] denies itself by its very caution the experience of its limit, to think which is, according to Hegel's superb insight, the same thing as to cross it' (2005, p. 128). My point is, of course, that we must not shy away from thinking beyond the given, which is tantamount to: we must dare to think. It is the only way to reveal technology as something not-only-particular, or—to put it another way—to reveal the particular in its truth.

4. Conclusion

The ability of postphenomenology to elucidate how technology transforms human experience will remain limited unless it refines its methodology. To demonstrate this, I divided my critical reflections into three sections focusing, respectively, on the postphenomenological object of inquiry, its theory of technological mediation, and its method. I identified three main shortcomings of postphenomenology: (1) by turning to technological artefacts, it does not provide a concept of technology (as) significantly mediating experience, yet it cannot do without it; (2) it reduces technological mediation to (inter)relations between humans and technology (while underrating the agency of things in these relations); and (3) the commitment of postphenomenology to the so-called empirical turn and corresponding focus on user cases makes its method theoretically lacking and substantially limits its reach. I hope to have demonstrated that scholars in the field should work to overcome these limitations. In other words, we need to cross the borders delineated by the empirical orientation of postphenomenology. To bring out the full potential of the theory of technological mediation, postphenomenology cannot immediately turn to artefacts and rely on analyzing human-technology relations, or inter-actions. Technological mediation is not simply out there, waiting to be discovered. It is not an empirical givenness. Certainly, there are humans and technologies out there, interacting and co-living in the world. But one cannot tell empirically where to look for the decisive 'cases' of technological mediation. Neither can we rely on our common sense in this matter. We undoubtedly have to document our findings in 'the empirical', but to do that, we cannot but develop concepts to make this documentation possible. In other words, to reveal the particular in its truth, we must create concepts different from what is simply given.

Seeking to outline an approach that overcomes the limits of postphenomenology, I used the collocation 'phenomenological postphenomenology'. Admittedly, it is a bit of an absurd term, yet

I find it fitting. Phenomenology is not an empirical science and postphenomenology, understood phenomenologically as something other than an empirical (e.g., psychological) science, cannot be satisfied with demonstrating how particular technologies condition particular experiences. The task is not (only) to present experiences in their being transformed, or made possible, by technologies but (rather) to demonstrate the structure of experience, i.e., the structure of our lifeworld as conditioned by technology. Or, from a different angle, (post)phenomenology analyzes not only 'subjective' experiences but, just as importantly, an 'objectively' experienced world. I put both the words 'subjective' and 'objective' in quotation marks to indicate that the experiences are not merely subjective while the lifeworld is not merely objective. The lifeworld is both 'subjective' and perfectly real: it is real correlatively to the human being living in it. And subjective experiences are never only subjective, i.e., coming from the subject, but always already 'objectively' conditioned and structured. Phenomenology aims to describe the lifeworld, i.e., the basic structure of—and for—the life of the 'subject'. Postphenomenology can do the same.[4]

References

Achterhuis, H. (Ed.). (2001). *American philosophy of technology: The empirical turn* (R. P. Crease, Trans.). Indiana University Press.

Adorno, T. W. (2005). *Minima moralia. Reflections on a damaged life* (E. F. N. Jephcott, Trans.). Verso.

Arzroomchilar, E. (2022). Some suggestions to improve postphenomenology. *Human Studies, 45*(1), 65–92, https://doi.org/10.1007/s10746-021-09615-1

Aydin, C., Woge, M. G., & Verbeek, P.-P. (2019). Technological environmentality: Conceptualizing technology as a mediating milieu. *Philosophy & Technology, 32*, 321–338, https://doi.org/10.1007/s13347-018-0309-3

de Boer, B. (2023). Explaining multistability: Postphenomenology and affordances of technologies. *AI & Society, 38*, 2267–2777, https://doi.org/10.1007/s00146-021-01272-3

---

[4] I would like to thank Bas de Boer for his stimulating comments on the first draft of this chapter. This work was supported by the European Regional Development Fund project 'Beyond Security: Role of Conflict in Resilience-Building' (reg. no. CZ.02.01.01/00/22_008/0004595), which was implemented by the project partner, the Institute of Philosophy, Czech Academy of Sciences (IP CAS).

de Boer, B., & Verbeek, P.-P. (2022). Living in the flesh: Technologically mediated chiasmic relationships (in times of a pandemic). *Human Studies, 45*, 189–208, https://doi.org/10.1007/s10746-022-09625-7

Bosschaert, M. T., & Blok, V. (2023). The 'empirical' in the empirical turn: A critical analysis. *Foundations of Science, 28*, 783–804, https://doi.org/10.1007/s10699-022-09840-6

Coeckelbergh, M. (2021). Earth, technology, language: A contribution to holistic and transcendental revisions after the artifactual turn. *Foundations of Science, 27*, 259–270, https://doi.org/10.1007/s10699-020-09730-9

Heidegger, M. (2001). *Being and time* (J. Macquarrie & E. Robinson, Trans.). Blackwell.

Ihde, D. (1990). *Technology and the lifeworld: From garden to earth*. Indiana University Press.

Ihde, D. (1993). *Postphenomenology: Essays in the postmodern context*. Northwestern University Press.

Ihde, D. (2009). *Postphenomenology and technoscience: The Peking University lectures*. State University of New York Press.

Ihde, D. (2011). Husserl's Galileo needed a telescope! *Philosophy & Technology, 24*, 69–82, https://doi.org/10.1007/s13347-010-0004-5

Ihde, D. (2016). *Husserl's missing technologies*. Fordham University Press.

Kiran, A. H. (2012). Technological presence: Actuality and potentiality in subject constitution. *Human Studies, 35*(3), 77–93, https://doi.org/10.1007/s10746-011-9208-7

Lemmens, P. (2017). Love and realism. *Foundations of Science, 22*, 305–310, https://doi.org/10.1007/s10699-015-9471-6

Lemmens, P. (2022). Technologizing the transcendental, not discarding it. *Foundations of Science, 27*, 1307–1315, https://doi.org/10.1007/s10699-020-09742-5

Lemmens, P., & Van Den Eede, Y. (2022). Rethinking technology in the Anthropocene: Guest editors' introduction. *Foundations of Science, 27*, 95–105, https://doi.org/10.1007/s10699-020-09772-z

Misa, T. J. (2009). Findings follow framings: Navigating the empirical turn. *Synthese, 168*, 357–375, https://doi.org/10.1007/s11229-008-9447-y

Mykhailov, D., & Liberati, N. (2023). Back to the technologies themselves: phenomenological turn within postphenomenology. *Phenomenology and the Cognitive Sciences*, https://doi.org/10.1007/s11097-023-09905-2

Ritter, M. (2021a). Postphenomenological method and technological things themselves. *Human Studies, 44*, 581–593, https://doi.org/10.1007/s10746-021-09603-5

Ritter, M. (2021b). Philosophical potencies of postphenomenology. *Philosophy & Technology, 34,* 1501–1516, https://doi.org/10.1007/s13347-021-00469-0

Romele, A. (2021). Technological capital: Bourdieu, postphenomenology, and the philosophy of technology beyond the empirical turn. *Philosophy & Technology, 34,* 483–505, https://doi.org/10.1007/s13347-020-00398-4

Romele, A. (2022). The transcendental of technology is said in many ways. *Foundations of Science, 27,* 975–980, https://doi.org/10.1007/s10699-020-09758-x

Rosenberger, R., & Verbeek, P.-P. (Eds). (2015). *Postphenomenological investigations: Essays on human-technology relations.* Lexington Books.

Scharff, R. C. (2022). On making phenomenologies of technology more phenomenological. *Philosophy & Technology, 35,* 62, https://doi.org/10.1007/s13347-022-00544-0

Van Den Eede, Y. (2022). Thing-transcendentality: Navigating the interval of 'technology' and 'Technology'. *Foundations of Science, 27,* 225–243, https://doi.org/10.1007/s10699-020-09749-y

Verbeek, P.-P. (2005). *What things do: Philosophical reflections on technology, agency, and design* (R. P. Crease, Trans.). Pennsylvania University Press.

Verbeek, P.-P. (2006). Materializing morality. Design ethics and technological mediation. *Science, Technology, & Human Values, 31*(3), 361–380, https://doi.org/10.1177/0162243905285847

Verbeek, P.-P. (2008). Cyborg intentionality: Rethinking the phenomenology of human-technology relations. *Phenomenology and the Cognitive Sciences, 7*(3), 387–395, https://doi.org/10.1007/s11097-008-9099-x

Verbeek, P.-P. (2010). Accompanying technology. *Techné: Research in Philosophy and Technology, 14*(1), 49–54, https://doi.org/10.5840/techne20101417

Verbeek, P.-P. (2011). *Moralizing technology: Understanding and designing the morality of things.* University of Chicago Press.

Verbeek, P.-P. (2016). Toward a theory of technological mediation: A program for postphenomenological research. In J. K. B. Friis & R. P. Crease (Eds), *Technoscience and postphenomenology: The Manhattan papers* (pp. 189–204). Lexington Books.

Verbeek, P.-P. (2017). The struggle for technology: Towards a realistic political theory of technology. *Foundations of Science, 22,* 301–304, https://doi.org/10.1007/s10699-015-9470-7

6. Seeing the Phenomenon: The Radical Disembodiment of *In Vitro* Human Reproduction

Dana S. Belu

Introduction

Human reproduction has become an integral part of the technosystem or the 'total organization of society around technologies and technical disciplines' (Feenberg, 2017, p. 119). Technological and non-sexual reproduction through IVF (*in vitro fertilization*) has become so popular that in 2021, the CDC reported a whopping 3% of children in the United States were born through IVF—the gateway form of assisted reproductive technology (ART). As of 2023, over ten million children have been born through IVF (Hart & Wijs, 2022). This procedure combines a human egg and sperm in a petri dish to form an embryo. It has enabled numerous derivative ARTs, notably preimplantation genetic testing, embryo selection, cytoplasmic transfer, and maternal spindle transfer, among many others. Most recently it has facilitated IVG (*in vitro gametogenesis*): a cutting-edge technique that promises to develop eggs and sperm from adult somatic cells. IVG renders a woman's reproductive body superfluous for conception, though gestational surrogates will still be needed to complete the pregnancy, at least until the availability of ectogenesis through the artificial womb.[1]

---

[1] Ectogenesis—a term coined by scientist J. B. S. Haldane in 1924—describes conception outside the uterus as is now possible through IVG and then linking it up with an ecto-uterus: a gestating machine, an artificial womb. The development of the artificial womb is still in its experimental stages.

In this chapter, I will combine feminist phenomenology with aspects of social constructivism to show how the use of IVF and some related ARTs, notably IVG, reveal the radical technologization of a woman's reproductive body. Following Martin Heidegger's technological theory of enframing I have coined the phrase reproductive enframing to describe this technological process. This radical technologization remains invisible if thought just phenomenologically or from the perspective of social constructivism. This is because social constructivism overemphasizes 'production' and a dialectical understanding of the exchange between nature and technology while Heidegger's phenomenological theory of technology understates the empirical exchange between nature and technology, including dominant social norms that ART reinforces. Bringing these two methods together into a flexible feminist phenomenology of technology allows me to show how the use of ART, especially IVF and IVG, frames women's bodies as neither subjects nor objects of technical action but as resources, inseparable from the technologies that absorb them.

IVG is a process whereby adult somatic cells, such as blood or skin cells from one or both parents, are reprogrammed into induced pluripotent stem cells (iPCS) and then differentiated into *in vitro* human gametes, i.e., eggs or sperm. Then, IVF picks up the process by combining the gametes in a petri dish to create an embryo for implantation and gestation. As of the writing of this chapter, scientists in Japan have already produced successful IVG in mice and have also successfully derived human gametes (Notini, Gyngell, & Savulescu, 2020, p. 123). Although it is still in its experimental stages, reproductive medicine and genetic engineering see IVG as the next frontier in scientific human reproduction meant to correct the shortcomings and contingencies of non-scientific human reproduction and to expand the limitations of some current ARTs. According to Dr Hugh Taylor, a reproductive health specialist at The Yale School of Medicine, 'it's not a matter of if this will be available for clinical practice but just a matter of when' (Stein, 2023, p. 1). Dr Peter Marks, a top Food and Drug Administration (FDA) official, states that the FDA considers IVG 'a very important technology that we are very interested to move along' (Stein, 2023, p. 3) Some notable capabilities of IVG include its therapeutic potential, its eugenic potential, its enabling same sex couples to reproduce genetically using genes from both partners, its enabling single individuals to reproduce (by) themselves and its enabling multiplex genetic parentage. However, due to substantive ethical and legal considerations, Congress continues to prohibit the FDA from considering scientific proposals that involve the genetic manipulation of human embryos. Despite this restriction, private companies are joining the race to fast track IVG technology and begin producing babies from skin cells.

It may be premature to discuss the practice and popularity of IVG but given IVF's huge popularity and the much greater ease and flexibility of IVG, it is likely that IVG will become a game changer in the scientific-technological reproduction of humans. Since IVG dispenses with the often tricky and dangerous step of IVF—i.e., the superovulation of a woman and the extraction of her eggs—it can be expected that, if successful, IVG will amplify the popularity of IVF and of ART more generally. It will also enhance the predictability and control of human reproduction. While we can't predict with certainty the future of IVG, the media already touts that, like IVF before it, it is merely a tool, a value neutral means for attaining various ends. I challenge this phenomenologically naïve view by bringing together Heidegger's phenomenology of technology and Andrew Feenberg's social constructivist theory. Together, they help to reveal the ontological, historical, and social dimensions of technology, especially reproductive technology.

I

In 'The Question Concerning Technology' (1954), Heidegger identifies the ontological characteristic (*Grundzug*) of the technological age as a 'mode of revealing' (*aletheuein, Entbergen*) (Heidegger, 1977, p. 14) that humans did not create or produce. He describes this revealing as a 'challenging-forth', a historically (*geschichtlich*) unique attitude that starts to emerge in the seventeenth century and increasingly discloses nature and things as a heap of orderable, fungible raw materials.[2] These resources or

---

2   According to Iain Thomson this captures the second definition of essence (or the positive sense of essence) in his three fold account of Heidegger's *Gestell*. I am indebted to Thomson's insightful account as presented at *The Disentangling Heidegger on Technology Retreat*, Buchnerhof, Italy, June 2024, organizers, Mark Wrathall and Jonathan Krude. For more on this differentiation see Thomson's forthcoming manuscript *Heidegger on the Danger and Promise of Technology, or What is Called Thinking in the Age of Artificial Intelligence?*, pp. 43-46, New York and Cambridge: Cambridge University Press, 2025.

'standing reserve no longer stand over against us as object (*Gegenstand*)' (Heidegger, 1977, p. 17). Seen together, challenging forth and standing reserve define the phenomenon of enframing (*Gestell*), the technological revealing. This revealing stamps modern technology with the character of flexible orderability. Heidegger describes this character as:

> a setting-upon, in the sense of a challenging-forth. Such challenging happens in that the energy concealed in nature is unlocked, what is unlocked is transformed, what is transformed is stored up, what is stored up is in turn distributed, and what is distributed is switched about ever anew. Unlocking, transforming, storing, distributing, and switching about are ways of revealing. But the revealing never simply comes to an end. Neither does it run off into the indeterminate. The revealing reveals to itself its own manifoldly interlocking paths, through regulating their course. This regulating itself is, for its part, everywhere secured. Regulating and securing even become the chief characteristics of the revealing that challenges. (Heidegger, 1977, p. 16)

Thus, when the modern scientific-technological outlook challenges nature forth, it sets it up as a resource by 'eliminating self-movement and intrinsic potentiality. Nature is then meaningless and utterly dependent on the subject for which it serves as raw material' (Feenberg, 2023, p. 151). In this view, nature is no longer an object, and neither is technology.

According to Heidegger, the commonplace view that technology is a means to an end, an object for a subject, is phenomenologically naïve—it is 'correct but not true' (Heidegger, 1977, p. 6) because the instrumental explanation cannot account for itself, for the provenance of instrumentality, and for the hegemony of utility. Instrumentality describes a relationship of use between a subject and an object that often includes the wrongful objectification of persons and nature, usually for the sake of power and profit. But as we will see with IVF and even more so with IVG, objectification and utility do not quite capture the phenomena. While Heidegger's phenomenological questioning of technology can be used to reveal women's reproductive bodies as resources rather than objects, it is too formal and abstract to fill in and to concretize the revealing. The enframed attitude is said to reduce nature and people to raw materials and energy, i.e., fungible media. However, empirical support for this reduction is so lacking that the theory cannot differentiate between, say, the medicalization of maternal labour, the standardization of education, the deskilling of work, mass deforestation, or the digitization of information. Thus, a concretization of enframing is needed so that it can make sense of the variety of our lived technological experiences. In earlier work I introduced the term *reproductive enframing* to refer to the challenging forth of women's bodies, their decontextualization and reduction to reproductive parts and potential (Belu, 2017).[3] *Reproductive enframing* sums up the manipulation of this potential by describing a fragmented approach to conception and gestation, one that frames the uterus as a collection of discrete and movable reproductive parts: ovaries, follicles, eggs, fallopian tubes, and hormones. These parts are managed as 'stock', potential reproductive energy challenged forth in the petri dish. There the 'energy' of the sperm and the egg is 'unlocked' to achieve fertilization and then frozen, 'stored-up' until the embryo is implanted in the uterus of the future mother or that of a 'carrier', a gestational surrogate.

By combining Heidegger's phenomenology of technology with aspects of the social constructivist theory of Feenberg, I concretize Heidegger's theory through a two-step instrumentalization process that, I show, sets up the woman's reproductive body as a resource. Thus, the woman as a feeling and rational subject is reduced to her malfunctioning reproduction which is then further reduced to a collection of parts to be assessed and optimized. Let us examine this reduction to a resource in more detail.

In his 1949 lecture 'Das Ge-Stell' Heidegger describes the resource or 'stock' as follows:

> What the [medical] machine produces, piece by piece, it places in the standing reserve of the orderable (*Bestellbaren*). The product is stock [...] The stock-piece (*Bestandstück*) is something different than the part. The part shares itself with other parts in the whole. It takes part in the whole, and belongs to it. (It completes the whole.) The piece, on the contrary, is separate and is as a piece closed off from other pieces. It never shares itself with these others in a whole. Nor does the resource piece share itself with others like it in standing reserve. On the contrary, the resource is made piece-meal for orderability. (Heidegger, 1994, p. 36, my translation)

---

3   This chapter contains revised material from chapter 3 in Belu (2017).

He highlights the fungible character of stock as follows:

> Stock pieces are piece by piece the same. Their stock character demands this uniformity. As the same, the pieces are in extreme competition with each other; in this way they raise and secure their stock character. The uniformity of the pieces guarantees (*verstattet*) that all pieces are interchangeable on the spot. A stock-piece is replaceable by another. The piece is, as a piece, put up for exchange. Stock-piece means that what is delimited as a piece is exchangeable in the ordering. (Heidegger, 1994, p. 36, my translation)

This fungible character of stock defines the treatment of women's reproductive bodies during IVF and, as we will see later, IVG. Because Heidegger's phenomenology of enframing is excessively formal and abstract, it cannot explain the details of this fungibility even though it is essential for framing the fungibility, making it visible. But reproductive enframing helps to bring out the resource status of women's reproductive bodies in IVF by coupling enframing with feminist and social constructivist analyses. I begin by applying key aspects of Feenberg's 'primary and secondary instrumentalization' to the use of ART.

In *Questioning Technology*, Feenberg develops a two-level instrumentalization theory that presents the 'functional constitution of technical objects and subjects' and describes their place in the lifeworld as the 'realization of the constituted objects and subjects in actual networks and devices' (Feenberg, 1999, p. 203). Applying elements of his theory to IVF helps to critically illuminate the 'functional reduction' and fungibility of the woman. Feenberg's theory criticizes the reductive understanding of technology that sees devices merely as *functional* things, tools that get things done. As a social constructivist, he insists that function depends on social context and thus is of contingent value only. For example, while Western industrialized countries value the function of technologies, other cultures place the emphasis elsewhere. He writes:

> What differentiates technology and tools in general from other types of objects is the fact that they appear always already split into 'primary' and 'secondary' qualities, i.e., functional qualities and all others. We do not have to make that distinction deliberately as we would in the case of a natural object since it belongs to the very form of the technical device.

> Thus, an *initial abstraction is built into our immediate perception of technologies.* That abstraction seems to set us on the path toward an understanding of the nature of technology as such. However, it is important to note that this is an assumption based on the form of objectivity of technology in our society. Function is not necessarily so privileged in other societies. The functional point of view may coexist peacefully with other points of view, religious, aesthetic, none of which are essentialized. (Feenberg, 1999, p. 211, my emphasis).

Feenberg's theory strives to avoid a poorly differentiated, reductive understanding of technology by foregrounding the connection between secondary instrumentalization (the cultural integration or world of new technologies) and primary instrumentalization (their function). His theory allows us to see how the socialization of IVF underscores the resource status of the woman and her eggs.

Feenberg analyzes primary instrumentalization into four component steps, which he calls 'reifying moments of technical practice' (Feenberg, 1999, p. 203). These are decontextualization, reductionism, autonomization, and positioning. I will focus on the first three. A phenomenological interpretation of conception through IVF shows that the lifeworld of the woman as a whole person and potential mother is concealed even *as* she is revealed (to the medical gaze and to herself) as a collection of malfunctioning reproductive parts that need to be fixed. Here is where Feenberg's decontextualization of the 'object' comes in. He writes: 'To reconstitute natural objects as technical objects, they must be "de-worlded", artificially separated from the context in which they are originally found so as to be integrated into a technical system. The isolation of the object exposes it to a utilitarian evaluation' (Feenberg, 1999, p. 203). The eggs are tested for their reproductive usefulness as well as the usefulness of the sperm. Their potential is technologically extracted so that it is more efficiently actualized. Once they are extracted from the uterus, the eggs 'reveal themselves as containing technical schemas, potentials in human action systems which are made available by decontextualization' (Feenberg, 1999, p. 203). This means that they are now made available for fertilization, freezing, or to be stored as embryos for future implantation or experimentation. Cryopreservation opens up possibilities for embryo research and experimentation often *unrelated* to reproduction and that may be unknown to the donor. Whether immediately fertilized and implanted or cryopreserved through vitrification, the decontextualization of the eggs reveals the woman and the eggs as stock, fragmented into a collection of *interchangeable* reproductive parts. This is a significant step in the control and ordering of human (re)production and a steppingstone toward more advanced IVF-derived technologies, such as IVG.

Decontextualization is coupled with a second step, *reductionism*, in which the natural object, the egg, is reduced to its primary qualities, such as 'size, weight and shape' or anything else about the 'object that offers an affordance' (Feenberg, 1999, pp. 203–204). In the case of the eggs, doctors seek high-quality (functional) eggs that contain the proper chromosomes, are young enough and resilient enough to combine with sperm, and are energetic enough to divide and multiply after fertilization.[4] The eggs are reduced to these primary qualities because those seem most conducive to technical production: that is, embryo fertilization, growth, and implantation. Whatever the secondary characteristics of the eggs, they remain undiscovered. Feenberg notes: 'Secondary qualities are what remains, including those dimensions of the object, that may have been most significant in the course of its pretechnical history. The secondary qualities of the object contain its potential for self-development' (Feenberg, 1999, p. 204). Since the potential for self-development is denied, this aspect of the egg becomes irrelevant. Feenberg provides the example of a tree whose secondary quality as 'habitat' no longer nourishes and shelters numerous species of flora and fauna once it is reduced to its primary quality—that is, a cylinder of wood. It is unclear what the secondary qualities of these extracted eggs may be, but they might relate to the uterine 'habitat' or 'umwelt' to which the eggs belong: an environment that is especially disturbed by superovulation.

Finally, the reproductive enframing in IVF can be seen to be underscored by what Feenberg calls the process of autonomization. Autonomization refers to the interruption of *reflexivity* in technical action, its impact on the user, so that the subject can affect the object of technical production without being significantly affected in return (Feenberg, 1999, pp. 207–208). The autonomization of IVF becomes visible when the medical industry treats the women in an administrative

---

4   These standard features are widely available and can also be found online on the popular and sentimental site https://www.sharedjourney.com/

manner, i.e., without caring for their feelings, their hopes and fears. It either abandons women with unsuccessful cycles of IVF by not providing care for their mental distress and/or collapsed life project and empty pockets, or simply encourages them to 'try again'. By dismissing the patient's experience and distress, the medical industry promotes an administrative or 'purely functional', indifferent attitude toward its patients when they are especially vulnerable. This affords it a kind of immunity from the consequences of its actions and casts the women as disposable resources.

In addition to primary instrumentalization, all technical production involves what Feenberg calls secondary instrumentalization. The steps of decontextualization, reduction, and autonomization loosely correspond to moments in secondary instrumentalization—a process that refers to the lifeworld or the social realization of the technology—to be distinguished from its primary counterpart only analytically, since the two cannot exist separately. Secondary instrumentalization involves systematization, mediation, and vocation (Feenberg, 1999, pp. 205–206). According to Feenberg: 'to function as an actual device, isolated, decontextualized technical objects must be combined with each other and reembedded in the natural environment. Systematization is the process of making these combinations and connections [...] of "enrolling" objects in a network' (Feenberg, 1999, p. 205). In IVF, systematization refers to IVF's commercial and social recontextualization. This means that the fertilized egg, which now appears as a technical object, must be reintroduced into the living womb of a woman and the woman must be successfully integrated into a network of doctor's visits and regular administrative and medical protocols. Since many women who undergo IVF are older, sometimes well into their forties, the social recontextualization of an older pregnant woman challenges traditional values, especially ageist prejudices about conception and motherhood. All of this involves ethical mediation. Feenberg writes: 'Ethical and aesthetic mediations supply the simplified technical object with new secondary qualities that seamlessly embed it in its new social context [...] Recently, medical advances and environmental crises have inspired new interest in the ethical limitations of technical power' (Feenberg, 1999, p. 206).

Some of the ethical limitations consist of legally deceiving women about their chances of having a baby by inflating the success of IVF and, as mentioned above, administratively dismissing their hurt after failed IVF cycles. For instance, clinics still misrepresent their success rates by reporting in vitro fertilization success rates as successful *in vivo* implantation and/or live births, though the number of live births are typically much lower than successful implantations. Moreover, the 'IVF pregnancy rate is usually based on the chance of getting pregnant *after* undergoing egg retrieval' (Sherr, Davis, & Stoess, 1995, p. 64) and successful egg retrieval is often not possible. This manipulation of success rates[5] entails a manipulation of the participants, those women who opt for IVF on the basis of misleading statistics. When the woman's disappointment is not taken into account, her subjectivity is ignored and this puts her on the path to being treated as disposable, an interchangeable resource for the technology that she now serves, rather than being served by it. In this case, attention to the ethical mediation reveals a *lack* of care for the well-being of the *whole* woman. This lack is a consequence of the overidentification of technology with function, with efficient conception. But neglect by itself does not yet frame the woman as a resource—it merely points to a kind of wrongful objectification. However, when it is coupled with the woman's voluntary acceptance of this objectification and thus her self-objectification in the interest of a functional outcome, her status as a resource is sealed. Both the ethical dismissal and the self-objectification are consequences of a reductive and one-dimensional conflation of technology with function, i.e., with efficient conception.

Finally, as mentioned in the discussion of primary instrumentalization above, the autonomization process refers to a lack of reflexivity on the part of the doctors and the medical staff. Autonomization corresponds to what Feenberg calls *vocation* in his secondary instrumentalization theory. He characterizes vocation as follows:

> The technical subject appears autonomous only insofar as its actions are considered in isolation from its life process. Taken as a whole, the succession of its acts adds up to a craft, a vocation, a way of life. The

---

5   According to the most recent numbers from the CDC, live births from IVF had a 22% success rate (Centers for Disease Control, 2023).

subject is just as deeply engaged as the object [...] The doer is transformed by its acts [...] The rifleman will become a hunter, the worker in wood becomes a carpenter. *Vocation* is the best term we have for this *reverse impact* of *tools on their users*. (Feenberg, 1999, p. 206, my emphasis)

So, from the point of view of the woman who uses IVF, vocation refers to the subjectification of this technology—its transformative power, whereby the technology is made her own through repeated use. That is, over time, this technological internalization shapes her identity as the user of the technology. But what is curious about the use of IVF is that recognition of this internalization is ultimately resisted. IVF continues to be widely solicited[6] and yet, when it is successful, its use and significance are downplayed. In other words, every effort appears to be made—by the media, the medical industry, and by the women themselves—to frame pregnancy by means of this invasive medical technology *as if* it had been achieved without the technology; as if the technology merely gave 'nature' a helping hand and had no lasting impact.[7] Downplaying the technology is a way of resisting identification with the technology, keeping it at a distance even as one relies on it. The popularity of 'mild IVF' is one evidence of this phenomenon. Women opt for a 'mild IVF cycle'—that is, a shorter cycle with fewer shots—because 'mild IVF' stays closer to 'mother nature' (Payne et al., 2012). This wild perception is interesting since even mild IVF relies on disembodied fertilization and acutely medicalizes conception, and so it is quite removed from whatever 'mother nature' might mean. Invoking 'mother nature' has the effect of undermining the role of the technology used for the precise purpose of suppressing 'mother nature'. When it is successful, parents and family members tend to avoid discussing their children's IVF origins—though, when it fails, women more openly discuss the 'ordeal' and debate with themselves whether to try again.

---

6   According to recent CDC statistics: in 2020, 2.3% of babies in the USA were born through IVF (Centers for Disease Control, 2023).

7   In Belu (2017, pp. 61–75), I discuss this common misperception of IVF merely giving nature a 'push' as being conceptually, however unwittingly, stuck between an Aristotelian understanding of *physis* as self-generation and a Heideggerian understanding of *physis* as being challenged forth into standing reserve.

II

According to Sarah Franklin's social constructivist analysis of ART in *Biological Relatives: IVF, Stem Cells and the Future of Kinship*, women still face enormous pressures to reproduce and this accounts for women trying IVF. Equally important is to 'be seen as trying IVF'. Both events provide women with a maternal identity and thus with a reprieve from societal pressures, at least for a while (Franklin, 2013, pp. 212–213). Because genetic parenthood is still considered a 'cultural gold standard' (Notini, Gyngell, & Savulescu, 2020, p. 132) for making a family, IVF is the most efficient route for women to meet the standard. Thus, even when they know that, with less than a 50% success rate, the procedure is likely to fail, women enrol in the process. Sometimes they enrol because they know that it will fail. 'Trying' masks their maternal ambivalence or disinterest.

Franklin mentions Heidegger briefly, mostly to use his phrase 'the question concerning technology' (Franklin, 2013, p. 196, p. 300) in order to point to her own thinking. Like Heidegger and Feenberg, Franklin does not see modern technologies as just value neutral tools but as mediations for our self-understandings and for pointing beyond themselves to the general culture they express. So, there is no such thing as IVF, although this view that appeals to the neutrality of IVF is still used in non-dialectical and non-phenomenological bioethical and social scientist commentaries on ART (e.g., Notini, Gyngell, & Savulescu, 2020; Suter, 2016). But this view is untenable because by situating the technology in a socio-scientific vacuum it also affirms, paradoxically, that it is useless.

But as Franklin's account of women's ambivalent IVF identity or their 'vocation' shows, the technology does not exist in a vacuum. Far from endorsing the view that technology is neutral, Franklin can be seen to echo Heidegger when she calls the age of IVF 'the age of biological control' (Franklin, 2013, p. 188). However, unlike Heidegger, she does not follow the question into its ontological ground—she does not look for the essence of (reproductive) technology. Rather, her analysis is dialectical as it emphasizes the mutual constitution of IVF and kinship, and various exchanges between biology and technology, technology and gender, and biology and values. She writes, 'IVF can be understood both as a technologization of substance and a substantialization of technology' (Franklin, 2013, p. 258). Or, more specifically, 'IVF is a new model of reproductivity in which the birth of viable offspring both depends upon and changes the social conditions that activate reproductive substance' (Franklin, 2013, p. 308). Fundamentally, for Franklin (and for Feenberg), production is the ultimate reality and it underlies the dialectical relationship between ART and gender. She writes, 'reproduction, like gender and kinship, must also be produced; it is not simply there to be presumed as a self-acting force' (Franklin, 2013, p. 182).[8]

IVF is not only a reproductive technology but also a technology of gender, a cultural technology (Franklin, 2013, p. 241). As such, it 'renaturalizes the maternal goal' even as it intensifies the desire for women to do everything they can to make conception happen. Their IVF related hardships and sacrifices recast maternity, once it is attained, as a 'heroic' triumph (Franklin, 2013, p. 241) or, if it fails, a heroic defeat. But even women who 'fail' succeed at having tried and so perpetuate the enduring notion that genetic parenthood is the 'cultural gold standard' for making a family.

However, contra Franklin's interesting work on describing IVF-women's identities as warriors and heroes, I have found that after successful IVF, women tend to ignore the impact the use of IVF has had on their lives. They minimize it or delete it altogether. There are many sociological reasons for this behaviour. As Franklin notes, they include the real or imagined satisfaction that their marriage, incomplete without a biological child, has now been fulfilled, as well as the successful display of 'devotion to a spouse or partner' and the achievement of 'a greater sense of belonging to friendship networks' (Franklin, 2013, p. 233). Not surprisingly, successful results are reported to ameliorate the pain and stress of IVF so much so that some women report that they 'forgot' all about the stress of IVF, and this seems to include glossing over the use of IVF itself (Verhaak et al., 2007). Whatever the reasons may be, it is extremely rare to meet women or parents who will boast

---

8   But this recurring emphasis on production as somehow ontologically primary is anthropocentric and phenomenologically naïve. Seen through Heidegger's phenomenology of technology, production—as a dialectical process of making and remaking—only appears fundamental in a world that is already historically enframed, i.e., defined by a reduction, a remaking of people and things into fungible raw materials.

about their 'miracle' IVF children even though these very same people initially rejoiced at a successful IVF pregnancy. Since, paradoxically, the successful result with IVF too often results in the individual user's denial of her social identity (or her subjectification) and vocation as an IVF user, the identity is then standardized. It is supplied by contemporary, advanced, industrial societies as the mere consumer of an expensive medical service. This underscores the suppression of the user's subjective, technological identity or vocation.

This denial is likely to be bound up with a woman's experience of shame at her inability to 'fulfil' her primary social role of bearing children and thus to conform to dominant social norms. Shame expresses feelings of deficiency, failure, and humiliation before an authority figure. In *The Obsolescence of Man*, Günther Anders aptly sums it up as a 'self reflexive act, a reference to self that fails [...] an interference in processes of identification, a condition of being confused or distraught' (Anders, 1956, p. 63). He coins the term Promethean shame to capture the pervasive feeling of inferiority that late moderns experience before the machines that they made (Anders, 1956, p. 31, p. 51). Moreover, it is a hopeless longing to emulate those machines, to escape the fragile and perishable 'natural' human condition. In short, it is a longing to become dehumanized. While shame seems like a good explanation for women's rejection of an IVF identity, it is not quite Promethean shame because IVF is devalued rather than admired, and every effort is made to absorb the technology into a narrative that exalts nature and natural reproduction. There is no desire to identify with the technology. Thus, minimizing or deleting the role of successful IVF has the perceived effect of restoring a woman's sense of self and lessening her humiliation. She did, after all, bear a child and is not willing to share the laurels with the technology that helped her to do it. She can now enjoy her freedom from the social pity reserved for women who cannot conceive biologically, and freedom from the silent contempt reserved for women who put their careers ahead of their maternal role, missing out on their fertile years.[9]

In sum, in both the social constructivist work of Feenberg and Franklin, the subjectification of the IVF user plays an important role. In my application of Feenberg's two-step instrumentalization theory, I

---

9   Women who are not interested in motherhood rarely show up or speak up and so are not part of this conversation.

analyzed the reduction of a woman's reproductive body and applied his account of technological subjectivity or vocation to show how users of IVF deny this vocation. This leaves them in the role of technological resources. We can see Franklin's account of women's conflicted use of IVF as supporting Feenberg's appeal to technological subjectivity as women use IVF in their strive for a gendered, maternal identity. While I agree that this technologized striving animates women during their use of IVF, it does not seem to stick around after the live birth of their children. Motivated by feelings of shame, the technologization of their bodies is forgotten as they become absorbed in naturalizing their offspring and minimizing discussions about their IVF experiences. This acceptance and naturalization of extreme reproductive reordering appears to be itself an act of self-objectification, i.e., treating oneself as an object. When this act and its consequences are dismissed, the subject accrues no memory, identity, or vocation, and the subject is then effectively recast as a resource.

The resource status of IVF users is even more visible when IVF is pursued by *fertile* women for the sake of testing the fertility of the woman's male partner or simply for experimental reasons whose end goal is open ended. As Françoise Laborie remarks: 'The increasing use of IVF to treat (and diagnose) male infertility means that healthy fertile women are exposed to the dangers of repeated doses of hormones and drugs and major surgeries [...] Experiments have been made with what is called "cross fertilization", i.e., sperm given by different men are tested for their capacity to fertilize the eggs of a single woman' (Laborie, 1987, p. 51). This example reveals a couple of things. It reveals the fungibility of women's reproductive bodies now enlisted to serve the interests of men and it also illustrates the resource status of eggs, their energy held on call for what Heidegger describes as a 'further ordering' (Heidegger, 1977, p. 17).

This further ordering is clearly seen in derivative IVF procedures such as cytoplasmic transfer (CT). CT

> revitalizes old eggs by combining the nucleus of an older woman's egg (that is, the egg of the woman trying to become pregnant) with the cytoplasm of a younger woman's egg (that is, the donor). The resulting embryo is thought to be healthier and more likely to implant in the uterus, but it may also contain genetic material from both eggs because

> the mitochondria in the younger egg's cytoplasm also contain genetic material. (Harwood, 2007, p. 12)

This procedure reveals the fungibility of the women participating in this process, since each is reduced to her egg-bearing function and her eggs are now recast as 'extractable resources'.[10] The combination of two eggs has the unintended consequences of multiplying genetic motherhood without addressing the social burdens of motherhood. Because it enables fertilization in older women, CT ends up *de facto* reproducing classist social structures. Instead of liberating women, CT distracts attention from feminist concerns with racial and economic gender inequities, such as the lack of support for working mothers, the working poor, and the high demands of career life—inequities that often compel women to postpone pregnancy until well into their forties when they require IVF and CT.

While IVF enables reproduction with two living genetic mothers, as in cytoplasmic transfer procedures, it also enables the production of offspring with no living genetic mothers. This process results in biologically motherless babies, babies whose mothers were never persons: 'unborn mothers'—mere genetic reproductive stock. In this procedure, 'viable eggs [are] collected from the ovarian tissue of aborted foetuses for use in fertility treatments such as IVF. Success has been limited; by stimulating the tissue with hormones, researchers are able to develop primary and secondary egg follicles about halfway to the point of maturity' (Guenther, 2006, p. 156). We see how the potential reproductive energy contained in this fungible stock—that is, in the ovarian tissue of the dead foetus—is extracted (stolen?) and challenged forth so that, as Heidegger presciently remarked, 'the energy concealed in [its] nature is unlocked, what is unlocked is transformed, what is transformed is stored up, what is stored up is, in turn, distributed, and what is distributed is switched about ever anew' (Heidegger, 1977, p. 16). The procedure dispenses with the woman as subject and with the egg as object so that both 'disappear into the

---

10 See Thomas Sheehan's *Making Sense of Heidegger* (2015). He writes: 'But the "positing" and "imposition" that Heidegger has in mind with *Gestell* is the particular dispensation that is imposed on us today and that compels us to posit and treat nature and people in terms of *extractable resources*' (p. 258).

objectlessness of standing reserve' (Heidegger, 1977, p. 19).

In such cases, the thorny issue of informed medical consent is bypassed altogether since the content of the abortion automatically becomes the property of the medical institution and there is no woman to consult. The process dispenses with the need for the female person as biological mother, woman, and subject because the so called 'unborn mother' is nothing but 'a body part without a body, an egg donor but not a person' (Guenther, 2006, p. 156). In fact, there is no 'donor' at all and no activity of gift-giving. Rather, the phenomenon is one of extraction, or what Heidegger calls a 'plundering' (*Geraff*) (Heidegger, 1949). The medical production of 'unborn mothers' redefines the meaning of human stock or resource in terms that even Heidegger could not foresee. It introduces a kind of fungibility predicated on fragmentation that was merely implicit in the earlier and more innocuous forms of low-tech reproductive interventions, such as artificial insemination, that still presupposed the presence and cooperation of the woman as person and subject. Here, the subject-object relationship is 'sucked up into standing reserve' (Heidegger, 1974, p. 173). The woman as subject is now a body part, an object—that is, viable ovarian tissue, merely an egg *in potentia*: a storehouse of reproductive energy on call for future use. And this egg now becomes the future 'unborn mother', reordered as the new subject that is really just a fungible resource through and through.

A feminist phenomenology of technology allows us to see how the living woman plays an increasingly smaller role and begins to fade from view in IVF and its subsequent developments, such as the one described above. Yet, most IVF-based forms of ART still require the living body of a woman or, at the very least, female ovarian tissue. The invention of IVG, however, dispenses with this need, since—as I noted earlier—it can develop eggs by reprogramming and differentiating somatic cells. This flexibility further entrenches control and predictability over human reproduction.[11] There is no limit to the number of eggs it can produce (Sutter, 2016, p. 95) and fertilize, and so no limit to the number of human embryos that can be stored.

---

11   IVG is developed for therapeutic purposes and not just reproductive purposes.

III

IVG is still in its experimental stages and there is no guarantee it will become available for human reproduction (Notini, Gynggell, & Savulescu, 2020, p. 124). However, if it becomes medically available, it will be historically unprecedented as it will dispense with the need for both men's and women's reproductive bodies. Since the availability of sperm for ART has always been plentiful compared with the scarce availability of eggs, IVF often struggled with getting 'eggs' and getting 'good eggs'. IVG ends that struggle and erases that limitation. Moreover, IVG allows us to see how the living woman is not merely fungible but, for the first time in reproductive history, superfluous for motherhood. Since somatic cells can be collected from anyone—young or old, male or female—and then reprogrammed, even the recently dead can 'donate' cells. Although current research shows that it is more complex and dangerous to produce babies from somatic cells than from induced pluripotent stem cells extracted from embryos, the somatic cell is the new frontier for easy human reproduction.

It is easy to see how this totally disembodied form of human reproduction makes parenthood increasingly flexible and fungible. This is reflected in the already debated IVG phenomena of 'multiplex parenting'—when more than two people contribute genetic material to one child—and also 'solo parenting'—when one parent contributes all of the genetic material to the child (Sutter, 2016, p. 106). But, despite facing considerable medical, social, and legal concerns with the consequences of multiplex and especially solo parenting,[12] the race to (re)produce babies from skin cells is on.

Viewed through the lens of reproductive enframing, these advanced forms of ART—especially IVG—can be seen not as a 'new technology' but rather as the culmination of a prevailing way of thinking that appears to resemble instrumentality but is, in fact, substantially different. In 'The Question Concerning Technology', Heidegger insists that the commonplace view that sees technology as an instrument, a means to an end, or an object for a subject is 'correct but not true' (Heidegger, 1977, p. 6) because it cannot account for itself, for the provenance of

---

12 Solo IVG is especially prone to producing children with severe birth defects. For more on the bioethics of IVG, see Notini, Gyngell, & Savulescu (2020).

instrumentality, and for the hegemony of utility. Instrumentality describes a relationship of use between a subject and an object that often includes the wrongful objectification of persons and nature, usually for the sake of power and profit. But as can be clearly seen with IVG, objectification and utility do not quite capture the phenomenon. The goal is to dispense with the subject but without turning it into an object, something that is relatively fixed and stable. Rather, IVG achieves what IVF could not—the dissolution of the subject/object boundary and the articulation of the resource as an entity that lacks a fixed and stable form or purpose—and is thus fungible through and through.

In acts of self-objectification performed by women in IVF, relatively stable medical and social boundaries still exist, though they have grown more porous and flexible. Even when IVF works, it does so by challenging the woman's body forth, and the process can be obtrusive and painful. On the other hand, IVG promises to be painless and more efficient, easily dispensing with the obtrusiveness of IVF. This can be seen to concretize Heidegger's claim in 'What are Poets For?' that enframing works best when it is invisible. By challenging the body forth, now almost entirely from the ground up, IVG can be seen to more thoroughly deny the cell's intrinsic 'potentiality'—i.e., to become skin—and thus it produces a 'free space of exploitation' (Feenberg, 2023, p. 159) and manipulation that feels easy, natural, and scientifically progressive. Humans have never experienced such freedom from the toils and uncertainties of reproduction.

Collecting somatic cells is indeed easy and science is working hard to make the use of skin cells for IVG happen. The difficulty of treating the IVF patient with dignity and respect is no longer an issue since the interpersonal part of the IVG procedure is just a brief collection of skin cells. The future parent, the user of the technology, is fungible and gone after donating the cell sample, and the sample itself is completely fungible since it can be taken from almost any part of the body. No medical follow up or doctor is necessary since the lived body of the patient is not part of this process and so does not require treatment. The collected sample is worked on by scientists in labs to derive eggs and sperm in order to then fertilize them through IVF, again in a lab. The finished product, in principle, would be the live baby taken home who would not be seen as a scientific product, if attitudes toward IVF-produced children are a good indicator, but as a piece of nature. Through IVG, eggs could in principle be produced *en masse* and stored for purposes that are yet to be determined, large supplies of human biotechnological stock standing reserve for medical experimentation and treatment. Products without a specific purpose.

In the conclusion to her book, Sarah Franklin asks, what comes after IVF? The question is not so much about subsequent IVF-based ART, such as pronuclear and maternal spindle transfer techniques (Franklin, 2013, p. 297) and now IVG, but more about identity as the continuous exchange flow between kinship and ART. She argues that new technologies have always been met with a strong dose of 'technological ambivalence' which she defines as 'the fear of degeneration in the wake of technological change, set against the more confident expectation of an improved, more fruitful, future' (Franklin, 2013, p. 300). This ambivalence can be seen to describe the long-standing tension between technophilia, a love and pursuit of technology, and technophilia, a fear of technology—a tension that has tended to resolve itself in favour of technophilia. Heidegger warns against subscribing to such binary, reactionary attitudes and instead urges us to question our relationship to technology, including our constant pursuit of more technology which he claims has run out of our control long ago and is now controlling us. Whether or not the pursuit of IVG[13] expresses this loss of control is perhaps the most urgent question concerning technology in our lifetime.

References

Anders, G. (1956). *The obsolescence of man*. C. H. Beck.

Belu, D.S. (2017). *Heidegger, reproductive technology and the motherless age*. Palgrave Macmillan.

Centers for Disease Control (2023, September 25). ART success rates. https://www.cdc.gov/art/artdata/index.html#:~:text=Based%20on%20CDC's%20

---

13 It is worth exploring whether IVG illustrates aspects of Anders' theory of Promethean Shame as elaborated in *The Obsolescence of Man* (1956). For instance, the promise of IVG to *produce* the human almost from the ground could be seen as a response to Promethean Shame—an experience of the inadequacy of the human as a natural, non-produced entity in need of technological remaking.

2021%20preliminary,and%2097%2C128%20live%20born%20infants

Feenberg, A. (1999). *Questioning technology*. Routledge.

Feenberg, A. (2023). *The ruthless critique of everything existing: Nature and revolution in Marcuse's philosophy of praxis*. Verso.

Franklin, S. (2013). *Biological relatives: IVF, stem cells and the future of kinship*. Duke University Press.

Guenther, L. (2006). *The gift of the other: Levinas and the politics of reproduction*. State University of New York Press.

Hart, R. J., & Wijs, L. A. (2022). The longer-term effects of IVF on offspring from childhood to adolescence. *Frontiers in Reproductive Health, 4*, 1046762, https://doi.org/10.3389/frph.2022.1045762

Harwood, K. (2007). *The infertility treadmill*. The University of North Carolina Press.

Heidegger, M. (1977). *The question concerning technology and other essays*. Garland Publishing.

Heidegger, M. (1994). Das Ge-stell. In *Gesamtausgabe. Band 79, Bremer und Freiburger vorträge*. Vittorio Klostermann.

Laborie, F. (1987). Looking for mothers you only find foetuses. In P. Spallone & D.L. Steinberg (Eds), *Made to order: The myth of reproductive and genetic progress* (pp. 48–57). Pergamon.

Notini, L., Gyngell, C., & Savulescu, J. (2020). Drawing the line on in vitro gametogenesis. *Bioethics, 34*(1), 123–134, https://doi.org/10.1111/bioe.12679

Payne, D., Goedeke, S., Balfour, S., & Gudex, G. (2012). Perspectives of mild cycle IVF: A qualitative study. *Human Reproduction, 27*(1), 167–172, https://doi.org/10.1093/humrep/der361

Sheehan, T. (2015). *Making sense of Heidegger: A paradigm shift*. Rowman & Littlefield.

Sherr, G., Davis, V. M., & Stoess, J. (1995). *In vitro fertilization: The A.R.T. of making babies*. Facts on File.

Stein, R. (2023, May 25). Scientists near a breakthrough that could revolutionize human reproduction. *NPR*, https://www.npr.org/2023/05/25/1178103188/scientists-near-a-breakthrough-that-could

Suter, S. M. (2016). *In vitro* gametogenesis: Just another way to have a baby? *Journal of Law and the Biosciences, 3*(1), 87–119, https://doi.org/10.1093/jjlb/lsv057

Verhaak, M., Smeenk, J. M. J., Evers, A. W. M., Fremer, J. A. M., Kraaimaat, F. W., & Braat, D. D. M. (2007). Women's emotional adjustment to IVF: A systematic review of 25 years of research. *Human Reproduction Update, 13*(1), 27–36, https://doi.org/10.1093/humupd/dml040

7. Artificial Intelligence and the Need to Redefine Human Traits

Galit Wellner

Introduction

The basic claim of postphenomenology is that technologies mediate the world for us and in doing so they transform our experience of the world (Ihde, 1979, 1990). This is what makes postphenomenology 'post' in comparison to classical phenomenology. In this chapter, my goal is to show how technologies in general, and Artificial Intelligence (AI) in particular, not only transform our experience of the world but also require us to rethink and redefine basic human capacities such as imagination (Wellner, 2018, 2021) or attention (Wellner, 2022). Instead of arguing that technologies have become so powerful that they can replace humans, as often claimed in the media, I suggest that we redefine our human capacities in light of the interactions we have with technologies such as AI. Postphenomenology has already done this with the notion of embodiment, which takes into account the technologies that surround us and reveals how we produce with them a new body schema (Ihde, 1990). The role of phenomenology in this theoretical development is crucial, as it offers a methodology and theory that focuses on the human lived experience. The postphenomenological challenge is to update the understanding of the lived experience in light of our new technologies.

This chapter will briefly explore the experiences of technology-mediated imagining and attending, as two examples of human capacities that are substantially impacted by digital technologies. The chapter will further show the ways in which technologies mediate even our understanding of imagination and attention. To begin with, a general overview of postphenomenology is provided, with a special emphasis on its origins in phenomenology. The next part deals with imagination as the first case study. It reviews imagination from the classical phenomenological viewpoint on the embodied experience as developed by Maurice Merleau-Ponty and adopted by Don Ihde. Then it proceeds to examine the impact of AI technologies on the classical understanding leading to the reformulation of imagination as 'post human imagination' (Wellner, 2018). The second case study focuses on attention and follows a similar path, from classical phenomenology to the challenges of AI resulting in the notion of 'multi attentions' (Wellner, 2022). In the conclusion, some commonalities between the two case studies will be discussed.

From Phenomenology to Postphenomenology

If phenomenology is the study of our experience in and of the world, *post*phenomenology examines the experience with an additional element—technology. Ihde (1979, 1990) represents this addition through an elegant formula built in several steps. First, classical phenomenology is illustrated as:

I—world

Next, technology is added, thereby producing the basic postphenomenological formula:

I—technology—world

This basic formula undergoes several permutations to depict the various ways in which technologies mediate the world for us. Ihde's original set of permutations is based on a playful addition of brackets and arrows. The brackets, in the spirit of Husserl, denote two alternative positions: (1) that something withdraws to the background, and (2) that two objects are united and operate as if they are one unit. The arrow signifies intentionality and thus in Ihde's formulation always points from the experiencing I towards the technology and the world.

Ihde (1979, 1990) suggests four postphenomenological relations. The first is embodiment relations, and it follows the logic of phenomenology that emphasizes the central role of the body in our experience of the world. Being the first in the set of relations, embodiment relations reflect the importance of the body in phenomenological analyses. In fact, Ihde embraces Merleau-Ponty's concept of embodiment and adds to the concept a technological element. He highlights Merleau-Ponty's examples of the blind man's stick (1962, p. 143) and the Parisian Lady's feather hat and explores the changes these artefacts-technologies introduce to the body schema of the blind man and the Parisian lady. The permutation for embodiment relations is:

(I—technology) → world

In this permutation, the I and the technology act as one unit in the world. The body schema changes with the presence of the 'technology' element, as for example in the case of a feathered hat. The Parisian Lady moves in the world as if she is taller.

Second is hermeneutic relations that refer to the ways in which meaning is generated through technology. Here the permutation 'reverse mirrors' embodiment relations so that now the brackets connect the technology and the world elements:

I → (technology—world)

The world is read and interpreted through the mediation of the technology element, and both are conceived as one entity. This process often involves some reading and interpretation, and hence the name 'hermeneutic'. When one watches the news, may it be on television or on social networking applications, the experience consists of the news item (reporting what happens in the 'world') and the media ('technology' in the form of an app, television, or a printed newspaper) operating as one entity.

Third there are alterity relations in which the technology is referred to as a quasi-other. This happens when children play vividly with dolls and when adults interact with an ATM or a cellphone. In these cases, a dialogue is maintained with the 'technology', even when it is clear that there is no one (physically) behind it. The permutation for alterity relations uses the brackets differently, indicating that the world withdraws to the background:

I → technology (—world)

Fourth are background relations, where the technology withdraws to the background and operates there unnoticed. These relations can be identified for technologies such as our clothes, eyeglasses, electricity, and Internet connection, all functioning in the background. As long as they operate as expected, we do not notice them. The postphenomenological formula is a kind of a reverse pattern to that of alterity relations, with the difference that here it is the technology that is bracketed:

I → (technology—) world

Since Ihde formulated these four postphenomenological relations, additional permutations have been developed to reflect contemporary situations. Peter-Paul Verbeek (2008) suggested three new relations involving technologies that have become an integral part of the body (e.g., pacemakers), or that extend reality into something that does not exist in the world and yet is accessible through the technology. In my own work, I have shown how Augmented Reality (AR) and Artificial Intelligence (AI) lead us into dramatically different permutations (Wellner, 2020a, 2021c, 2020b). These will be described in the sections describing posthuman imagination and multi-attentions.

Imagination, Perception, and Embodiment

A lesser-known part of Ihde's work is that which was written before he developed postphenomenology. Whereas his publications referred to many aspects of phenomenology, an almost neglected part is that which deals with imagination. In his 1973 book *Sense and Significance*, he develops some of the ideas that led him in *Technics and Praxis* (Ihde, 1979) to lay the foundations to postphenomenology. But as per 1973, he is still bound to classical phenomenology. He praises phenomenology as 'a revolution in man's understanding of himself and his world' (Ihde, 1973, p. 162).

In this early work, Ihde regards imagining as 'an "active synthesis" [that] *exceeds* perceptual modes of experience' (Ihde, 1973, p. 51). He warns that 'imaginative activity in general is more difficult to deal with because it has something to do with the very way in which we are present to ourselves' (p. 52). This presence poses a challenge to the identification of embodiment as bodily presence. The solution was to focus on perception (Langsdorf, 2020, p. 130). Merleau-Ponty pursues this path in *The Primacy of Perception* (1962) and Ihde follows him, terming it 'hermeneutic phenomenology' (1973, pp. 123–127). Such a phenomenology places key importance on the 'bodily present' perception (Ihde, 1973, p. 124). It is a 'version of perceptualism' (Ihde, 1973, p. 125).

In fact, Ihde adopts Merleau-Ponty's interpretation of the Husserlian late phenomenology, with a special emphasis on the notion of lifeworld. Regarding imagination as a form of bodily perception, Merleau-Ponty focuses on the 'real' world as perceived, that is 'rich in its contents' and not just 'bracketed world' (Ihde 1973, p. 125). In this landscape, the lived body becomes prominent, because through it the world is perceived (Ihde, 1973, p. 126). These understandings of Merleau-Ponty inspired Ihde's early hypotheses and led him to study the world as something populated by mostly biological and geological entities. Six years later, in *Technics and Praxis* (1979), technological entities were added to the mix. The shift to technology enabled him not to be bound to questions of language as he was in his 1973 book.

After 1979, technology dominated most of Ihde's work. Imagination was an exception and his analyses on this topic were not closely tied to technology. In *Experimental Phenomenology* (1986), for example, he demonstrates the role of bodily perception in imagination by examining how multiple perspectives on the Necker Cube (and its permutations) can form the basis of phenomenological variational theory. He shows that the same drawing can be imagined as various 'things'—a stage, a hallway, a gem, or a headless robot, to name a few. Some of these imagined possibilities 'appear' when the point of view (POV) is 'from above', others when it is 'in front'; some are extracted from a three three-dimensional perspective, others emerge from a flat two-dimensional view; and so on. All these variations are based on 'the subject as an active perceiver' (Ihde, 1986, p. 89). Being active means seeking new POVs. Ihde presents these examples to develop the notion of multistability, according to which there can be more than a single meaning to a phenomenon, especially when it comes to technologies. What is interesting to me in the context of imagination is the production of novel variations (such as the insect or the headless robot) that do not exist 'in the world' based on different POVs.

Later analyses of imagination were done in a more technological context. In 2015, Ihde introduces two technology-oriented concepts, one termed 'instrumentally enhanced perception' and the other 'instrumentally translational perception' (Ihde, 2015, p. x). The first represents an experience mediated by technologies that could not have been perceived without the technological mediation, such as 'seeing' radiation of remote stars with radio astronomy technologies and thereby exceeding the optical range of human sight. It involves the body and is related to the postphenomenological notion of embodiment relations. The other concept, the 'instrumentally translational perception', relates to the hermeneutic aspects of the experience. Ihde's example is the ability to sense the Earth's magnetic lines that can be found in animals. The equivalent human experience is mediated by the technology of the compass that requires reading, and hence the terms hermeneutic and translational. The two bodily perceptions described in Ihde's 2015 writings produce knowledge in imaginative ways. They operate in a different way than the seeing of the Necker Cube as described in 1986. They do not involve alternative POVs. Rather, they provide layers over reality through technological mediation (Wellner, 2021b). Ihde shows how bodily perceptions are technologically-saturated. However, there is no explicit reference to imagination.

Between the 1986 and 2015 studies, we can identify a certain decline in the primacy of perception. In *Bodies in Technology* (2002) Ihde returns to imagination as a phenomenological technic and explains what it's like to imagine that one is flying in the air. He distinguishes between 'a quasi-primacy to the here-body' and 'the quasi-otherness of the disembodied perspective' in which virtuality arises for the image-body (p. 5). In other words, 'this is the RL body in contrast to the more inactive and marginal VR bodies that make the shift to the quasi-disembodied perspectives possible' (p. 6).

This shift from perception to the 'VR body' has probably inspired Ingrid Richardson's focus on the body. She studies mobile media usage as a manifestation of embodiment relations (Richardson, 2020, p. 162), especially when experiencing tele-presence (p. 163). She identifies three bodily aspects: firstly, 'the physical macro-movement of the pedestrian body which can be traced geospatially through the gamer's GPS navigation' (Richardson, 2020, p. 166); secondly, 'the micro-movements and motor coordination required of the mobile player' (Richardson, 2020, p. 166) which are still visible to the phenomenologist-observer; and thirdly 'the virtual movement and exchange of objects and creatures "into" the gamers' mobile devices and their passage through the hybrid game-space' (Richardson, 2020, p. 166), visible only to the experiencing 'I' and requiring some form of imagination. When Richardson studies the experiencing body she is actually drifting away from the primacy of perception.

Today, I ask: should the phenomenological hypothesis regarding the primacy of perception be revisited in a world populated by virtual chatbots and augmented reality eyeglasses? What happens when we gain knowledge of the world less through our perceptions and more through the mediation of AI-based search engines and social networking apps? And what are the consequences for the phenomenological concepts of body and perception when our experiences of the world are heavily based on AI-generated texts and images?

Posthuman Imagination, Cryptocurrency, and AI

The concept of a point of view (POV) is founded on the primacy of bodily perception and is therefore paradigmatic for the modern imagination (Wellner, 2018). The transition from modern imagination to digital *postmodern* and posthuman imagination would entail a shift from the POV mode of operation to a layered mode of operation (Wellner, 2018). In this new paradigm, imagination operates by selecting different layers, changing the order of layers, or combining layers into new ones.

The notion of layers is typical to our thinking of contemporary technology. Developers and designers use it to conceptualize the underlying architecture of technologies like 3D printing and augmented reality (Wellner, 2020a, 2021a). Philosophers use it to conceptualize how a technology interacts with various users. The layer logic functions phenomenologically in a mode which I term 'plateaus' (Wellner, 2019) to designate parts in our subjectivity that can intersect and co-shape each other.

With the layer model, we can rethink the concept of imagination as formulated by Kant who provides us with a framework of productive and reproductive imaginations. These require some connection to reality, otherwise we are in the realm of 'phantasy'. Today, however, we realize that all three forms of imagination are encoded in AI systems through schematization performed on vast amounts of data (Wellner, 2018). Moreover, we need additional categories of imagination that would allow us to think, for example, about cryptocurrency. It is a form of digital money that is not represented by coins available to our bodily senses (reproductive imagination), albeit it is sometimes presented with the terminology of coins. It does not involve imagining representations of monetary value as in the case of bank notes or plastic cards (productive imagination), nor is digital currency a simulation or 'radically new visualizations' as offered for computer-aided design (CAD) software (Ihde, 2009, p. 465; see also Wellner, 2021b). Cryptocurrency is not a phantasy but rather a reality that exists in the digital sphere. We can analyze it in terms of embodiment and hermeneutic relations, but they are of secondary importance. It makes little difference whether we read how many digital coins are stored in a digital wallet on a computer screen or on a cell phone. Their value remains the same, regardless of the embodied perception with which we experience them. Assigning meaning to currency, whether fiat, crypto, or otherwise, requires imagination: what can I buy with this money? How can its amount affect my social status? How can I obtain more 'coins'? All of these questions refer to the future, leaving the body and perception aspects as of secondary importance. Likewise, hermeneutic relations provide a limited understanding of cryptocurrency if they don't take into account the value (or content). It is similar to the situation with digital media which requires us to refer not only to the mediating technologies but also to the content they carry (Wiltse, 2014; Liberati & Nagataki, 2015; Wellner, 2020a).

Similarly, embodiment and hermeneutic relations will provide limited understanding of generative AI that 'imagines' images, texts, etc. DALL-E is one of the currently common examples, but an older software program has been more transparent as per its operation and hence can better reveal how such systems work. My example is Google's 'Deep Dream Generator' that alters an uploaded picture through multiple rounds, each producing a layer in which the picture is slightly altered and becomes more 'dreamy'. The result is a picture that looks like an hallucination (Wellner, 2018). The developers state that 'when you reach level 6, the dream will become a rare one'.[1] The more layers are added, the more digital imagination operates. This digital imagination operates not in accordance with the intentionality of the experiencing 'I'. Moreover, it shapes perceptions in unexpected ways. Therefore, I suggested reversing the intentionality arrow:

I ← technology—world

I termed this new type of relations 'relegation' to denote a downgrade of the human intentionality while hinting at Latour's notion of 'delegation', according to which technologies take over and operate instead of the human actor. The reversal of the intentionality arrow can redefine hermeneutic relations in the age of AI in which meaning is not freely produced by the 'I' but rather is imposed by the technological system. As in the case of fake news, for example. Instead of humans imagining their world, fake news that repeats in different forms, sometimes produced by AI bots, imposes on the 'I' a certain world view and a certain way to imagine the world.

AI and cryptocurrency demonstrate how changes in the technologies that mediate our imagination will necessarily alter not only the operation of our imagination but also its definition and meaning (Wellner, 2021a). The experiencing subject imagines differently in the presence of software technologies which mediate the world. Examining our bodily perceptions will not provide a major understanding of crypto-currencies or AI systems or our imagination. Just like examining the embodiment aspects of a watch will result in an analysis similar to that of a bracelet and will fail to recognize the hermeneutic aspects of time reading.

If the focus on embodiment led us to think of imagination in terms of producing new POVs, where should the 'relegation' lead us? In other words, how can we resist the intentionality of AI and reverse the arrow? Inspired by Gilles Deleuze and Félix Guattari, I propose to conceive imagination as plateaus where some are governed by the technology and some by the experiencing 'I' (Wellner, 2021a, 2019). This model should remind us of our role as those who provide the resources for the system to function, and as those who produce meaning from the results. We can

---

1 https://web.archive.org/web/20160108021107/http://deepdreamgenerator.com/rare-deep-dreams

also play a more active role in recombining different layers-plateaus and adding new ones, thereby redirecting the technological imagination in new pathways. Whereas POV requires the body and hence the extensive discussion on embodiment in the context of imagination, a layered approach to imagination shifts towards a combination of hermeneutic relations and relegation. The intentionality is distributed among the 'I' and the 'technology' and the perception is not as primary as it was for the embodiment-POV understanding of imagination. Embodiment does not disappear altogether, but rather loses its primacy.

Attention and Embodied Perception

Since the late nineteenth century, one of the common understandings of a properly functioning attention has been as a selection process of an object or thought out of a certain collection of potentialities. This type of attention is served by the searchlight metaphor that usually represents the fast switching of a highlight from one object to another. Such an attention consists of a mental selection of a specific object instead of others. This approach is imputed to Husserl (Kelly, 2004, p. 89), who describes attention as a ray of light. It is a 'bodily metaphor', as it is relatively easy to 'feel' how attention leads the body towards the object of attention and thereby puts it under the light of the attentive mind.

Merleau-Ponty criticized the searchlight approach for being too rigid and fixed. First, the reference to a searchlight that 'shows up objects preexisting in the darkness' (Merleau-Ponty, 1962, p. 26) assumes the priority of the objects over the attention paid to them. For Merleau-Ponty, the searchlight approach postulates that the objective world already exists and thus is fixed and unchangeable. Second, not only is the world fixed but the searchlight effect is fixed as well. He writes, 'The searchlight beam is the same whatever landscape be illuminated' (p. 26), thereby assuming that the formulation of attention is a uniform revealing force that only scans the surface of the world. As a result, a second 'visit' of attention-as-searchlight should yield the same impression. However, in practice, a second visit does provide a different impression and therefore this model of attention, according to Merleau-Ponty, is flawed.

While the searchlight metaphor may be limited by presupposing a fixed light and a pre-given object of attention, it may still be useful for conceptualizing how attention can be fast switched from one object to another. As Jonathan Crary notes, 'part of the cultural logic of capitalism demands that we accept as *natural* switching our attention rapidly from one thing to another' (1999, pp. 29–30). Additionally, the superficial illumination of the surface is implicit in the searchlight image and serves well the paradigm of shallow and flat involvement. This logic has been implemented for the Internet, echoing the searchlight metaphor to describe Internet activity in terms of 'skimming' and 'scanning' (cf. Carr, 2010).

Merleau-Ponty provides an alternative explanation as per how attention works: the first operation of attention is, then, to create for itself a field, either perceptual or mental, which can be 'surveyed', in which movements of the exploratory organ or elaborations of thought are possible (1962, p. 29). He asserts that attention 'bring[s] to light the object of attention itself' (p. 29). For him, the relation between the experiencing 'I' and the object of attention is yet another manifestation of the indispensable role of the body.

No technology mediates this process in Merleau-Ponty's description. This absence can be spotted even in more recent works on attention, like Bernard Waldenfels' 'Thresholds of attention' as part of his *Phenomenology of the Alien* (2011), Sean Dorrance Kelly's 'Seeing Things in Merleau-Ponty' (2004), and Maren Wehrle's 'Horizontal Extensions of Attention' (2016). This lack of reference to technology stands in stark contrast to the discussion on the attention economy and how the Internet and mobile apps distract the users' attention. Although attention has been managed by media technologies as such, and to an even larger extent since the introduction of electronic media (e.g., cinema and radio), these technologies hardly appear in the phenomenological discussions on attention.

Another lack in the classical phenomenology of attention is with regards to multi-tasking. The implicit underlying assumption is that since we have one single body, then our attention functions on the singular. This assumption leads to attempts to measure attention by the eyes' movement and to examine the gaze through a device called an eye tracker. It is assumed that wherever the eyes look, this is where the 'ray of attention' is directed. Hence, there can be only one object of attention. But we can look at one object and listen to another and even think in parallel of a third object. Even if our sight is limited to one object of attention (and it's not, as captured by terms like 'peripheral vision'), our body as a multiple-sense system can be attentive to several targets.

A much-discussed example is driving a car while talking on the cell phone (also known as 'celling') or navigating with the help of a GPS-based app (Besmer, 2014; Irwin, 2014; Michelfelder, 2014; Wellner, 2014). These usage modes can be easily classified as multi-tasking. Once we think of the concept of multi-tasking in the context of new technologies, we realize that multi-tasking as such is not a new phenomenon. It has been present before the Internet and the cell phone in mundane acts like talking to someone while reading the newspaper or washing the dishes (Tun & Wingfield, 1995); playing football, which requires paying attention to the ball, the player's group members, the other group members, and the referee (Tripathy & Howard, 2012); or driving while talking to the other passengers (Irwin, 2014). In these everyday situations, attention must be paid to more than a single object simultaneously.

Attempting to understand the multi-tasking experience of driving with classical phenomenology requires identifying a field of awareness and examining how the exploratory organs operate within that framework to produce bodily perceptions (Rosenberger, 2014). It fails to describe the experience of driving properly with children 'fighting' in the back of the car (Irwin, 2014), a dog sitting on the driver's lap (Michelfelder, 2014), talking on the cell phone (Wellner, 2014), or all of the above at the same time.

Multi-Attentions

To address attention in the context of technology (especially digital technology) and multi-tasking, I have introduced the term multi-attentions. The term draws inspiration from Donna Haraway's (1998) conceptualization of 'knowledges', wherein the addition of the 's' may be read by the spell-checking software as an error. However, this plurality aims to challenge the conventional view towards the plurality of tasks and attention. The concept of multi-attentions means that our attention is not necessarily directed at a single object. It can do that, and in that situation, we are focusing, but this is just one mode-of-attention among others. Multi-attentions involve various levels of attention directed at different objects. It is not limited to the structure of foreground-background that implies 'one focus' (foreground) and 'one awareness' (background), but can encompass three, four, or more attentions.

The term 'multi-attentions' describes various experiences. Think of the attentions involved in crossing a busy street: attentions are paid to the act of walking; to noticing holes in the road due to endless roadworks; to noticing cars and attempting to create eye contact with the driver to ensure they stop their car; to the other pedestrians and more importantly to e-scooters that ride on the sidewalks; and possibly to thinking—on family matters, on the political situation, or plans of where to go and what to do in an hour, tomorrow, or next week. All these happen simultaneously and non-hierarchically.

My first work on attention was focused on the role of cell phones. In the debate between those who assert that cell phones are distracting and therefore dangerous while driving, and those who use them regardless, I unfashionably supported the latter. The distraction claim presupposes single attention as the only possibility, whereas the pragmatic approach regards multi-attentions as an always-already part of our lives. The two positions were presented in a special issue of *Techné Research in Philosophy and Technology* (Volume 18, issue 1/2) that examined the multiple aspects of driving while celling and related topics. On the single-attention side, Robert Rosenberger (Rosenberger, 2014) claimed that celling while driving is dangerous based on a phenomenological analysis and cognitive research. On the multi-attentions side, I presented (Wellner, 2014) a contestant view based on a genealogy of the notion of attention that uncovered how attention had attracted negative vocabulary in the nineteenth century (Crary, 1999) and how this negativity is duplicated into the discussion of driving while celling. The concept of multi-attentions conceptualizes how seeing (e.g., the road) and hearing (e.g., the cell phone) can be accompanied by calculating the route to one's destination and recalling the day one had in the office. Driving while celling means one can drive and see the road while talking on the cell phone and navigating towards the destination.

This multiplicity of senses is in sharp contrast with the single-attention view which implicitly assumes that seeing means being attentive, so that the operation of any other sense—such as hearing—is likely to impair driving. From a technological perspective, multi-attentions turned into a viable mode-of-attention when the cell phone, and especially the smartphone, became part of our everyday life. Philosophically, the cell phone enabled us to recognize that we always already practice multi-attentions, be it because of our multiple senses (e.g., seeing one thing and listening to another, like driving through busy traffic while listening to the radio), or because of the technologies that we have around us, such as the radio and cell phone that accompany us in everyday life. The various senses and technologies can each be regarded as a layer, and together they compose a whole experience. Here, the observation of Merleau-Ponty regarding a 'second visit' that yields new experiences is relevant and productive. The layers explain the mechanism that generates such new experiences through endless combinations.

The concept of multi-attentions does not mean that attention is necessarily spread equally. Each object of attention can enjoy a various degree of attention (Watzl, 2017). For example, while listening to jazz music, 'you might focus your attention on either piano or saxophone, but remain conscious of both in either case' (Watzl, 2011, p. 723). If, while commuting, reading the headlines on the news app (or my friends' statuses on a social networking app, or any other activity involving the cell phone's screen) attracts most of my attention, I am still attentive to the happenings around me and the stations. I can notice who among the other passengers stood up, and can realize (almost always) when the train or the bus is nearing the station where I disembark. Hence, multi-attentions are a set of attentions given to several objects to various degrees and extents. This represents a complex real-life experience.

A Genealogy of Attention: Attention in AI

In my work on attention and technology, I discovered that the notion of attention changes over time and cannot be considered ahistorical. It has a genealogy. Crary (1999) mapped this genealogy up to the early twentieth century. He marked the last quarter of the nineteenth century as the moment in which attention became a problem, known as distraction. The negative discourse on attention unfolded once workers in factories were obliged to remain attentive to the monotonous work near machines for long hours. This 'problem' migrated from the factories to schools and other social institutions. It is not a coincidence that the cinema was invented during that era and shaped so that spectatorship was sedentary in a dark hall and leading the viewers to concentrate on the movie. The cinema can be regarded as an attention machine that operates within the logic of the searchlight and ensures the viewers' attention is equal to focusing on a single object, which is presented on the illuminated screen.

Crary's genealogy ends at the beginning of the twentieth century and portrays the 'modernity moment' of the notion of attention. My genealogy continues from that moment and carries into the next step in the mid-twentieth century, with the introduction of electronic mass media, i.e., radio and then television. Here the prevalent mode of attention transforms into a scanning, from one broadcasting station to another. Like the cinema, mid-century mass media was mostly consumed while sitting and preferably being attentive to the broadcast content. The difference is the fast switching of attention between several objects. The third step was with regards to the cell phone and how it participated in the multi-tasking experience of driving as described above.

Now it is time to move forward and refer to AI. AI developers have embraced the common understanding of attention that equates it to focusing. It was a kind of 'delegation', to use Latour's terminology, that attempts to transfer a human action or capability to a technological artefact. The adoption of attention into AI systems was done in two parallel paths, one regarding text and the other regarding images.

In 2010, the notion of attention was integrated into AI systems that deal with texts in order to solve a problem in which the system ignored early inputs and referred mostly to those that came later (Larochelle & Hinton, 2010). Thus, the concept of attention originates as a variation of memory in the context of multiple inputs over time,[2] and later evolved into a mechanism for choosing a direction to go ('hard direction', in the words of the AI Summer). Thus, attention becomes a way for an AI system to encode only part of the information in the source input.

In image recognition systems, the integration of attention can be spotted already in the late 1980s as a selection mechanism and target

---

[2] See N. Adaloglou (2020, November 19). How attention works in Deep Learning: Understanding the attention mechanism in sequence models. *AI Summer,* https://theaisummer.com/attention/

detection, but '2015 [was] the golden year of attention mechanisms' (Soydaner, 2022, p. 13373). Interestingly, Derya Soydaner opens her review of attention mechanisms in AI with an explanation of the visual attention as developed in neuroscience that follows the logic of focusing on a single target. As a result, attention serves as an algorithmic mechanism that leads a model to focus on what it considers to be the important part of the picture, like a human body. Consequently, one definition of attention in AI frames it as: 'the ability to dynamically highlight and use the salient parts of the information at hand'.[3] This approach of attention in visual processing is similar to that of traditional attention that equates it with focusing. It uncritically adopts the searchlight metaphor. Technology specialists explain that, in practice, attention allows neural networks to approximate the visual attention mechanism humans use. Like people processing a new scene, the model studies a certain point of an image with intense, 'high resolution' focus, while perceiving the surrounding areas in 'low resolution', then adjusts the focal point as the network begins to understand the scene.[4]

From the textual and visual processing technics, algorithmic attention further developed and became a way to solve a 'big problem': attention models, or attention mechanisms, are input processing techniques for neural networks that allow the network to focus on specific aspects of a complex input, one at a time, until the entire dataset is categorized. The goal is to break down complicated tasks into smaller areas of attention that are processed sequentially, similar to how the human mind solves a new problem by dividing it into simpler tasks and solving them one by one.[5]

The result is a model that can handle a 'big problem' like translation from one language to another not linearly word by word but rather on a higher level of overall meaning. The limitations of human sight and the reliance only on the sense of sight have led the development of AI systems towards an attention that is focused on a single subject. A wider conceptualization would have enabled the development of more complex systems where attention is given to more than one object, what

---

[3] S. Cristina (2023, January 6). What is attention? *Machine Learning Mastery*, https://machinelearningmastery.com/what-is-attention/.
[4] Attention models. *DeepAI*, https://deepai.org/machine-learning-glossary-and-terms/attention-models
[5] Ibid.

I termed here as multi-attentions. It is an attention that is not limited to the embodiment aspects (i.e., the eye gaze), but can include also a stream of thoughts that runs in parallel to the sight, or to hearing.

Summary and Conclusions

This chapter is structured as a two-dimensional matrix. One axis delineates phenomenology, stretching from classical phenomenology to postphenomenology and its subsequent developments; the other axis expounds two basic human traits, namely imagination and attention, and the challenges that digital technologies pose to our understanding of them.

In imagination, bodily perception has been the prevalent perspective in phenomenology since Merleau-Ponty's *The Primacy of Perception*. Digital technologies have led to a kind of return to the body itself, but this return serves as a springboard to discuss the virtual body, that which exists in the mind, as in the case of computer games and virtual reality apps.

In attention, a significant discussion assumes—in most cases implicitly—that attention can be directed to a single object, using the metaphor of a searchlight. Much of the phenomenological literature does not refer to technologies as participants in attentive processes, and outside this field the reference is mostly negative, as a source of distraction that hampers attention. Also lacking from the phenomenological discussions is the possibility of multi-tasking, and again, outside the field it is considered in a negative manner.

The challenges to the phenomenological approach are described through the lens of technology. In the case of imagination, the examples of cryptocurrency and generative AI apps like DALL-E and Deep Dream Generator exemplify the need for new postphenomenological relations, and even draw some guidelines to its operation as layers.

In attention, the notion of multi-attentions was introduced along with the examples of driving while celling and crossing the street. These examples show how multi-attention works and how it fits to our contemporary everyday experiences. The more recent examples from the field of AI demonstrate how the nineteenth century understanding of attention is duplicated into technological systems to identify images, translate texts, etc. Now the challenge is to move in the development of AI systems from a searchlight, single-target attention to multi-attentions that take into account multiple inputs from various kinds and sources.

Imagination and attention in the age of AI demonstrate the applicability of the concept of co-shaping, which conceptualizes how the development of new technologies leads to new possibilities of imagination and attention, which leads to the development of new technologies, and so on in an endless loop. This process ties imagination and attention on the one hand and technology on the other, so that they can hardly be separated. Co-shaping also assists in answering difficult questions such as the embodied aspects of imagination for AI algorithms. How can algorithms imagine if they do not have a body? A co-shaping analysis would regard embodiment as one element in the imaginative process that is contributed by the human actor: there is a difference between listening to jazz in a lab versus listening in a club with a live audience. An AI algorithm like Shimon the robot that improvises jazz would play differently in these two settings. Co-shaping models how the various layers interact and how they produce vibrant experiences.

Another insight refers to the primacy of perception. For classical phenomenology, understanding of imagination and attention is tightly related to the body and the perceptions. In the case of imagination, perception seems to lose some of its primacy and there is now some room for the virtual body, especially in the presence of digital technologies like cell phones and VR. In the case of attention, the body has been orienting the analysis to focus on a single attention while overlooking the possibility of multi-attentions. Technologies like the cell phone accentuate such possibility. AI technologies are accelerating these processes. While they have important bodily aspects, their focus is on intelligence, mind, and other non-bodily-oriented concepts. The non-bodily orientation can be examined with the relatively new concept of embrainment. Rosi Braidotti (2013) coined the term but did not elaborate on it. Is it possible to use this term as a complementary aspect of embodiment by focusing on mind-related aspects of imagination and attention? It can be regarded as a response to the embodied cognition paradigm shift that aimed to show how cognition is embodied.

Phenomenology places a strong emphasis on bodily aspects, and now it is time to bring the mind into focus. When considering the mind, the term embrainment might need to be reconsidered in order to reflect the shift away from the body-brain connection and instead emphasize the mind. In any case, for postphenomenology, this could involve moving beyond embodiment and hermeneutic relations to incorporate embrainment relations. These could be useful for analyzing many digital technologies that have minimal or even negligible bodily aspects.

References

Braidotti, R. (2013). *The posthuman*. Polity Press.

Carr, N. (2010). *The shallows: What the internet is doing to our brain*. W. W. Norton & Company.

Crary, J. (1999). *Suspensions of perception: Attention, spectacle, and modern culture*. MIT Press.

Ihde, D. (1973). *Sense and significance*. Duquesne University Press.

Ihde, D. (1979). *Technics and Praxis*. D. Reidel Publishing Company.

Ihde, D. (1986). *Experimental phenomenology: An introduction*. State University of New York Press.

Ihde, D. (1990). *Technology and the lifeworld: From garden to earth*. Indiana University Press.

Ihde, D. (2002). *Bodies in technology*. University of Minnesota Press.

Ihde, D. (2009). From Da Vinci to CAD and beyond. *Synthese, 168*(3), 453–67, https://doi.org/10.1007/s11229-008-9445-0

Irwin, S.O. (2014). Technological reciprocity with a cell phone. *Techné: Research in Philosophy and Technology*, 18(1–2), 10–19, https://doi.org/10.5840/TECHNE201461613

Jansen, J. (2016). Husserl. In A. Kind (Ed.), *The Routledge handbook of the philosophy of imagination* (pp. 69–81). Routledge.

Kelly, S. D. (2004). Seeing things in Meraleau-Ponty. In T. Carman (Ed.), *Cambridge Companion to Merleau-Ponty* (pp. 74–110). Cambridge University Press.

Langsdorf, L. (2020). Relational ethics: The primacy of experience. In G. Miller & A. Shew (Eds), *Reimagining philosophy and technology, reinventing Ihde* (pp. 123–140). Springer.

Liberati, N., & Nagataki, S. (2015). The AR glasses' 'non-neutrality': Their knock-on effects on the subject and on the giveness of the object. *Ethics and Information Technology, 17*(2), 125–37, https://doi.org/10.1007/s10676-015-9370-0

Merleau-Ponty, M. (1962). *Phenomenology of perception* (C. Smith, Trans.). Routledge & Kegan Paul.

Michelfelder, D. P. (2014). Driving while beagleated. *Techné: Research in Philosophy and Technology, 18*(1–2), 117–132, https://doi.org/10.5840/techne201461818

Rosenberger, R. (2014). The phenomenological case for stricter regulation of cell phones and driving. *Techné: Research in Philosophy and Technology, 18*(1–2), 20–47, https://doi.org/10.5840/TECHNE201461717

Soydaner, D. (2022). Attention mechanism in neural networks: Where it comes and where it goes. *Neural Computing and Applications, 34*(16), 13371–13385, https://doi.org/10.1007/s00521-022-07366-3

Verbeek, P.-P. (2008). Cyborg intentionality: Rethinking the phenomenology of human-technology relations. *Phenomenology and the Cognitive Sciences, 7*(3), 387–395, https://doi.org/10.1007/s11097-008-9099--x.

Watzl, S. (2011). The philosophical significance of attention. *Philosophy Compass, 6*(10), 722–733, https://doi.org/10.1111/j.1747-9991.2011.00432.x

Watzl, S. (2017). *Structuring mind: The nature of attention and how it shapes consciousness*. Oxford University Press.

Wehrle, M., & Breyer, T. (2016). Horizontal extensions of attention: A phenomenological study of the contextuality and habituality of experience. *Journal of Phenomenological Psychology, 47*(1), 41–61, https://doi.org/10.1163/15691624-12341304

Wellner, G. (2014). Multi-attention and the horcrux logic: Justifications for talking on the cell phone while driving. *Techné: Research in Philosophy and Technology, 18*(1–2), 48–73, https://doi.org/10.5840/techne201432712

Wellner, G. (2018). Posthuman imagination: From modernity to augmented reality. *Journal of Posthuman Studies, 2*(1), 45, https://doi.org/10.5325/jpoststud.2.1.0045

Wellner, G. (2019). Digital subjectivity: From a network metaphor to a layer-plateau model. *Azimuth: Philosophical Coordinates in Modern and Contemporary Age, 14*, 55–66.

Wellner, G. (2020a). Postphenomenology of augmented reality. In H. Wiltse (Ed.), *Relating to things: Design, technology and the artificial* (pp. 173–187). Bloomsbury Visual Arts.

Wellner, G. (2020b). When AI is gender-biased: The effects of biased AI on the everyday experiences of women. *Humana.Mente, 13*(37), 127–50.

Wellner, G. (2021a). Digital imagination, fantasy, AI art. *Foundations of Science*. https://doi.org/https://doi.org/10.1007/s10699-020-09747-0

Wellner, G. (2021b). Digital imagination: Ihde's and Stiegler's concepts of imagination. *Foundations of Science*, https://doi.org/10.1007/s10699-020-09737-2

Wellner, G. (2021c). I-algorithm-dataset: Mapping the solutions to gender bias in AI. In J. Büssers, A. Faulhaber, M. Raboldy, & R. Wiesner (Eds), *Gendered configurations of humans and machines: Interdisciplinary contributions* (pp. 79–97). Verlag Barbara Budrih.

Wellner, G. (2022). Attention and technology: From focusing to multiple attentions. In M. Wehrle, D. D'Angelo, & E. Solomonova (Eds), *Access and mediation* (pp. 239–258). De Gruyter Saur.

Wiltse, H. (2014). Unpacking digital material mediation. *Techné: Research in Philosophy and Technology, 18*(3), 154–182, https://doi.org/10.5840/techne201411322

PART III

PHENOMENOLOGY AND TECHNOLOGICAL PRACTICES

8. Nothing in Practice: Entanglements of Sartre's Nothingness and Social Media Practice

Annie Kurz

Introduction

Artists and designers could be considered the most likely to profit from image-based social media such as Instagram.[1] An attempt towards a phenomenology of the artist-social media relationship, however, reveals that the way in which 'we within the creative industries' relate to this technology is at best deeply ambiguous. Web 2.0 offers new opportunities for self-expression, interaction, and thus for potentially far-reaching self-promotion. Yet, artists rarely describe this medium as a straightforward helpful tool but rather as a Janus-faced technology—often referred to as a 'necessary evil' (e.g., Cheong, 2023). As creative professionals become financially more successful, they might be able to outsource the 'necessary evil'—online marketing and certain parts of the social media practice. However, even those highest in ranking ideally must regularly produce *content* showing insights into their personal lives with claims of presenting their true, 'authentic' selves, or at least well-curated personas that appear that way (consider the paradoxicalphenomenon of the plandid).[2] So how

---

1 With the general term 'social media' or 'social network sites', I refer to the medium generally. However, this chapter only considers image-based and image sharing social media—mostly used within the creative industries—excluding, e.g., text-based social media or search engines such as Google, often also considered to be a variation of the social media technology.

2 The term *plandid* denotes a 'planned candid' photo—an image that appears to be

do artists and designers experience social media in practice and how can philosophers (of technology) deal with the aforementioned 'evils' without falling into dystopian one-dimensionality?

The main problem addressed in this chapter is how to describe specific phenomena observable in social media practice, that I consider overlooked within the school of thought known as *postphenomenology* and the related field of *mediation theory*. These underdiscussed phenomena that I call 'absence phenomena', however, can be made explicit through the work of French philosopher Jean-Paul Sartre and his concept of *nothingness* (1993). *Absence phenomena* are not exclusive to the experience of artists and designers; yet they are frequently expressed within artistic works that I can rely on for my arguments. In this exploration, I draw from two well-known artistic examples within popular culture; Cindy Sherman's 'Instagram selfies' (Russeth, 2017) and comedian and singer Bo Burnham's account of the 'human-content relation' in his song titled 'Content' (2021). Designers and artists use and experience social media in many versatile ways. Therefore, when using postphenomenology and the concept of multistability,[3] it is necessary to clarify that the use of the collective pronoun 'we' to describe a hypothetical coherent group of creative professionals is a strategic choice. This choice is intended to highlight the relevance of Sartre's nothingness and related absence phenomena as collectively significant, while acknowledging that these phenomena are not experienced uniformly by everyone. Such a multistable reading of nothingness and social media brings forth new questions on the human-social media relationship. In this chapter, I seek to build on existing postphenomenological work (e.g., Wiltse, 2017) towards a more holistic view of social media as a technology tinkering with existential issues and core human principles, as expounded by Sartre. I discuss a modestly small part of the practice—the experience of setting up a new profile and sharing content on two platforms typically used within creative communities: Instagram and TikTok. As mentioned, contrary to a simple instrumentalist view, most artists acknowledge social media's ambiguity and fear that their work would not be able to

---
spontaneous but is planned down to the smallest detail.
3   Postphenomenologists describe variations of possible use cases (actual or hypothetical) as multistability. Technology is always multistable (can be used in many ways).

stand a chance without the 'aggressive' self-expression and promotion that social media offers to facilitate. What many creatives experience can already be identified as one of the most obvious 'evils'—the lack of choice that creative professionals seem to have. Phenomenologically, social media non-use (absence) equals non-existence - not a choice or at least not a good one if an artist aims to take her work and thus herself seriously. Aware of contemporary digital power relations, many within the creative industries thus stoically embrace or at least accept the fact that social media must be wrestled with in one way or another. Many put aside nostalgia towards 'authentic choice', accepting that a profile breeding social media has become the dominant contemporary way to produce identity (cf. Moeller & D'Ambrosio, 2021).

In the following, I seek to show why the existential potency of social media and in some cases the 'necessarily evil' stabilities can be better understood within American Philosopher Don Ihde's postphenomenology, in dialogue with Sartre's concept of nothingness Consequently, I argue that social media practice cannot be conceptualized only as an *actuality* within an *in-use paradigm*, which is central to postphenomenology (e.g., Ihde, 1990; 2002; 2009; 2012; Rosenberger & Verbeek, 2015; Wellner, 2016; Kudina, 2021). The versatile corpus of postphenomenology offers insightful details on how specific technologies transform experience, how they shape human reality and perception of the *lifeworld* and the *self* within (co-constitution). However, postphenomenology does not seriously consider technological practice entangled with Sartre's nothingness—as *perceived absences* come into consciousness even before the evaluations of hypothetical usefulness. A careful phenomenology shows that the artist-social media relationship already begins before moments of evaluation, before and after use-cases occur.[4] In other words, to understand social media more holistically, postphenomenology should consider the dialectic between *use* and *nonuse*, between actuality and *potentiality* of the technology (Kiran, 2012). Sartre's existential phenomenology offers useful vocabulary to better describe such tensions of being *present* on a social media platform OR

---

4 (Post)phenomenologist recall concepts such as technological 'affordances' (compare De Boer, 2021) to deal with questions of evaluating general usefulness (versus use), yet the problem of absence (and nothingness) is not adequately addressed within postphenomenology.

being *absent*—what and when to share and when not to, when to be or not to be online. This digital version of Sartrean dialectic, per my hypothesis, weighs heavily on how people interpret the world as well as their and other's personal identities (I call this sense-making). To fill this analytical gap, I propose to (re)integrate the concept of nothingness into postphenomenology through reminding readers of Sartre's vocabulary and Ihde's early work (e.g., Ihde, 1973; 1986; 1990). The subproblem that follows is how Sartre's main concept of nothingness can be framed conceptually within Ihde's relational ontology and related mediation theory (Verbeek, 2016; Kudina, 2020; 2021). On these grounds, I suggest determined negations (see section 4) within Ihde's threefold formula, *human—technology—world*, to represent the experience of absence and nothingness that Sartre's existential phenomenology famously lays bare. This chapter argues that the convergence of Sartre's existential project with postphenomenology offers analytical tools to better understand the experience of social media practice as typically done by artists and designers. While I consider postphenomenology as best suited for my task at hand—to be able to discuss fragments of social media practice—I push the boundaries of postphenomenology with an attempt to coin the term *absence relations* based on Ihde's analytical method expanding his *background relations*. With the forestallment of the notion of 'perceived absence'—the nuance of Sartre's nothingness I consider most useful and programmatic for this exploration—I discuss the phenomenology of artist-social media relations in some of their existential meanings. Absence relations then are in entanglement[5] with Sartre's nothingness as well as with Ihde's technological practice that is *self-making* through technologies. I therefore propose Sartre's project as potentially contributing to philosophy of technology (Siegler, 2022) beyond the connection to social media I make here.[6] I argue that Sartre's nothingness

---

5   I use the word 'entanglement' to describe co-dependence.
6   Sartre never developed a philosophy targeted specifically towards technology, but he builds on Heidegger and uses numerous examples especially in his later works. Marcel Siegler (2022) points out that only through reading Sartre's early as well as later works such as *Critique of Dialectical Reason* does this insight unfold. Siegler, however, does not understand postphenomenology as compatible with Sartre's views on technologies. Sartre, in his understanding, frames human consciousness as the trigger for technological developments which Ihde, in his understanding, does not: 'Sartre escapes the technomorphic conception of subjectivity that can be found in postphenomenology/ANT. By considering human existence as a

finds amplifications online, while social media in return offers a banal caricature and reductive answer to existential circumstances of the artist (human) condition. Thus, in my interpretation of Ihde and Sartre, social media reveals some of its necessarily evils as not far from the trivial or the banal (Arendt, 1964).

1. Bracketing the Shock

When relying on words such as 'evil' to describe certain human-technology relations, and, more specifically, artist-social media relations, it is unavoidable to recognize that while the number and variations of social media sites rapidly grow, increasingly accurate research has been able to unfold the ambiguous, in some cases problematic, impacts of these technologies (trade-offs). In postphenomenological language, social media networks are not neutral—they inevitably change perception, the human, and thus the world. The so-called 'toxic' impacts of this technology, however, might have recently come as a 'shock' to some.[7] Over the past decade, sociologists, psychologists, Silicon Valley insiders, educators, and others have begun investigating empirically the causal nexus, identifying types of technological 'shocks' that are linked, for instance, to mental health decline amongst teenagers (e.g., Heidt, 2019; Turkle, 2011; Lanier, 2018; Zuboff, 2019; Haugen, 2023). Linked problematic behaviours or habits are often blamed on some form of digital addiction. Some empirical correlations have been found with social media use but cannot be clearly identified as causations. At this stage, civil society, researchers, and philosophers only can hold suspicions towards these connections. Growing movements known, for example, as digital detoxing[8] are taking these suspicions seriously, trying to find ways to individually and collectively keep people away from digital 'evils'. These

---

primarily instrumentalizing endeavor, it is human subjectivity and intentionality that constitutes what is technology, not the other way around' (Siegler, 2022, p. 23).

7   Compare the discussion on 'the shock of technology'—technologies 'shock' when disrupting our routines, exposing our entanglements with them (Lemmens et al., 2022).

8   Digital detoxing movements are on the rise (Halpert, 2022), as well as so-called neo-Luddite communities (Vadukul, 2022) trying to keep their peers away from the smartphone and specifically from social media.

phenomena have provoked new research fields (Altmaier et al., 2024) and new postphenomenological questions (Kurz, forthcoming).[9]

One important puzzle Ihde poses is how to find the adequate analytical nuance between a doomsday dystopian verdict[10] and an overoptimistic hype of a technology. One pressing question to answer then for postphenomenologists is how not to fall into reactionary moves yet adequately acknowledge the philosophical steps necessary to more holistically describe social media and what people (and, increasingly, artists and designers) are experiencing.

Having mentioned what is bracketed, I shall not discuss straightforward social media trade-offs, nor will I represent counter positions of likewise versatile advantages and concrete gains that social media platforms provide (specifically for artists and designers). Beyond the research mentioned, both positions are well observable through everyday experiences, in schools, in private lives, or in professional contexts. Postphenomenological inquiries are usually more agnostic, not preoccupied with the 'either or'—these technologies good for humankind *or* harmful in essence. This exploration is rather interested in working towards details of the 'how?'—how is social media both? Why is this technology so effective in tinkering with and manipulating core human principles? With postphenomenology in dialogue with Sartre, the question becomes: how does *mediation of nothingness* occur?

2. Sartre's Nothingness

French philosopher Sartre's concept of nothingness—in French: *le néant*, as theorized in *Being and Nothingness* (1993)—most importantly must be defined as his umbrella term holding many nuances. Sartre's overall aim in his treatise is to phenomenologically show that the human experience of the self and others emerges in consciousness entangled with nothingness. This nothingness reveals itself in different forms—both as a source of vulnerability and as the freedom to 'make' the self. Sartre recognizes pre-reflective ways that we ascribe meaning to the world and to (self-)identity - I call this *sense-making*. Most reductively put,

---

9   Compare the so-called new research field of 'disconnection studies' (Altmaier et al., 2024).
10 Ihde finds this within the work of classical phenomenologists such as Heidegger.

consciousness for Sartre is entangled with the experience of *negations*[11] or potential *nihilations* within human interpretations of the lifeworld as well as the self. This is to show that perception of nothingness is most urgent to the human condition (that perhaps eastern philosophers have understood better than the continental kind). The human then most fundamentally experiences herself as 'lacking', inevitably linked to the awareness of nothingness as perceived negations within. Sartre's consciousness is haunted by the possibility of its very nihilation.[12] These vulnerabilities are neither concrete nor imaginary, they are flickering in-between and are the sources of core human judgments and motivations, as well as desires and emotions. Nothingness is inseparably entangled with Sartre's other subordinate concepts composing his existential phenomenology. The question explored in this chapter is how to acknowledge Sartre's flickering nothingness within Ihde's analytical methods and within the context of social media use as typically practiced by artists. All variations and nuances of Sartre's nothingness connect to the ways in which an individual directs herself towards the world and others. Thus, Sartre's consciousness is not only aware of the positive and that which is *present* but is co-shaped by what is *absent*. For my line of arguments, it will be relevant to keep this in mind to differentiate between nothingness as an overarching concept and subordinate nuances of negations such as 'perceived absences' that I further use within Ihde's formula (section 4) to make explicit the ways in which nothingness can be concretely experienced on social media.

The human condition according to Sartre is a dynamic interplay between being (the positive) and nothingness (the nihilation). Sense-making of the world is, for Sartre, the perception of nothingness—a dialogue between what 'is' and what 'is not' and is thus entangled with what 'could be' (potentiality). Sartre is very clear in pointing out that the awareness of one's identity is the experience of the lack of such a thing. Contrary to an object, like a chair—which in-itself is perceived as holding intrinsic meaning—Sartre's human does not stand *in-itself*. The human is always directed towards the future and

---

11   Sartre relies on Hegelian negations to address his nuances and variations of nothingness.
12   Nihilation can mean non-being or death, but also the impossibility to make the authentic self. It can also mean negation more generally.

thus acts *for-itself*. Humans are motivated by nothingness to try to fill the void or the lack they find within self-identity. Sartre calls this the *condemnation to be free*. This freedom and its void orient the individual in the world, indicating what actions (including technological and societal) can and must be taken. Thus, the concept of nothingness is tied closely to human freedom as a responsibility towards the self and the world. Sartre famously declares that humans are not born with predetermined meanings or 'essences'. Instead, individuals create their own essence through their choices and actions. This freedom of having to choose and make the self is accompanied by anxiety over the responsibility of creating meaning in a seemingly absurd world. Because human consciousness is always transcending itself, it is reaching towards potentialities (experienced as endless on social media). The awareness of nothingness is crucial in sense-making, pointing to bodily needs as well as emotional desires. Perception of nothingness likewise motivates technological action for-itself. Sartre's nothingness most famously culminates into absolute responsibility towards the making of the self—that is, thriving for an *authentic self*. For the purposes of this text, I need not further discuss Sartre's notion of *authenticity*, but it is important to keep in mind that the concept is one of his most central lifelong projects that he considers tied to the perception of self-identity that is worth striving toward.

A growing body of literature proposes that Sartre's existential philosophy can shed light on core principles of the human condition immersed in contingency and uncertainty amplified by social media technologies (e.g., Lopato, 2015; Qi et al., 2018; Jose, 2019; Cheong, 2023). Marc Cheong, for example, argues in this context 'that harm to existential well-being is a persistent, but often under-discussed threat, where existentialist concepts are pivotal in unpacking our relationship with social media' (Cheong, 2023, p. 2).

Once the concept of nothingness is established as useful to explicate the dialectics of human sense-making and the forming of self-identity, it becomes clear that it is independent of or prior to any concrete human-technology relation. The role of nothingness on social media, then, leads to the next question of how it tinkers with existential well-being and self-identity.

3. Identity and Social Media: The Relevance of Nothingness for Postphenomenology

The brisk expansion of Web 2.0 social media platforms increasingly enables artist-generated content to be shared and interacted with online instantly. Over time, this content potentially (if cared for well enough) becomes an online artist's identity. Intricately connected to and embedded within another complex technology of the smartphone, these platforms such as Instagram (frequently used within the art world) record and archive user's photographs, video clips, and short texts, composing a toolkit of what I refer to as identity- or profile-technologies.[13] Currently, most popular platforms use networks (based on friendships or followers) to build connections and allow for interactions.[14] Curated and visually 'embellished', searchable self-archives build new forms of online communities. These advancements have profoundly changed existential circumstances and how people today understand human connection and self-identity and how artists understand themselves and the world. It is safe to say that today, the quest for identity and related performances and *presentations of the self* (Goffman, 1959) are deeply involved with the virtual world and online profile productions. Identity already in its analogue forms could not be reduced to simple solvable steps nor fully understood from one totalizing perspective, as Sartre illustrates in his versatile attempts to demonstrate the existential conundrum and the complexities of his pursuit of identity (being toward authenticity). Sartre's phenomenology thus stands valuable without any need for acknowledgment of the role of technologies to better understand human sense-making as the quest for identity and the meaningful. Yet the connection between identity and social media is self-evident and becomes explicit as soon as artists and designers begin building their online profiles; the link to Sartre's nothingness follows.

---

13 Cf. Moeller and D'Ambrosio (2021). They coin the term 'profilicity' to emphasize the role of profile technologies in identity production.

14 Lopato (2015) differentiates between *static* and *dynamic* features of social media. According to him, *static social media* does not allow for person-to-person communication that face-to-face communication or communication via messaging services, such as email, would allow. Dynamic social media, on the other hand, has a symmetrical structure allowing person to person communication.

Contemporary debates around identity can be protracted. The term is used in many ways. It can be put in political contexts to express rivalries of recognition, rights, or inclusion of certain people or groups. The concept of identity more fundamentally references a personal understanding of the self or selfhood (Ricœur, 1992). Identity then implies sameness as well as difference and the felt connections between the individual person and some wider collective or group (Taylor, 2015). For Sartre, self-identity is a quest toward the authentic self that must make its own essence. Sartre's missing human essence (or the lack within identity) shows that identity must be framed as a 'wicked problem', impossible to be solved and difficult to define or break down into solvable steps. In naming three prominent thinkers, who come to a similarly intricate conclusion, it becomes clear that tinkering with identity inevitably means tinkering with violence. In my interpretation, this shows that the quest for identity reaches into the most fundamental human principles and perhaps into those of the most primitive kind. Francis Fukuyama (2019), for instance, regards the quest for identity as an intersubjective, highly political, and therefore sensitive struggle because it is human dignity, the recognition of self-worth, and meaning that people are searching for. Amartya Sen (2020) stands not far from Fukuyama. He rejects a static interpretation of identity, arguing against reducing identity to a single fixed or locked dimension. He advocates for 'complicating' identity instead of viewing it as a caricatured one-way strategy. According to Sen, identity must go beyond simplistic, singular categorizations to allow for societal well-being. He promotes an inclusive and pluralistic approach. Sen emphasizes the multifaceted nature of human identity, which includes various affiliations and attributes, such as social, political, and economic dimensions. Sen encourages a nuanced understanding that is necessary to avoid violence tied up in rigid, fixed, or blown-up, out-of-proportion identities. A few decades earlier, Marshall McLuhan (1977) put it more bluntly—according to him, the lack of identity always leads to violence.[15]

To return to my specific case of the artist and social media practice

---

15   McLuhan understands violence in a broad sense—for him, even a sports game can be considered violent.

within creative communities, the second 'evil' of social media (after the apparent lack of choice mentioned in the introduction) can be identified as another lack of choice and the simplistic rigidity in which profile building can happen, namely, *only* through posting content. This seems like a paradox, as on the other hand social media allows for unprecedented possibilities to express the self. Posting' as the only method to build online identities reveals itself as fixed and rigid or at least one-dimensional, which Sen rejects.

It is relevant to point out that social media for artists is not just another marketing tool for their businesses but is often inevitably tied to their personal identities. This connection can be understood through Sartre's exploration of authenticity, which is often associated with an artistic life. Claims of authenticity make profiles (that is, social media content infused with personal/insider information on one's life) more interesting and useful for self-promotion than previously used brands: 'Profiles reflect a much livelier and more interactive type of identity than traditional brands' (Moeller & D'Ambrosio, 2021, p. 29).

It would go beyond the scope of this text to further discuss Sartre's authenticity in relation to the artist, but perhaps I can establish that social media disrupts or 'shocks' (Lemmens et al., 2022) identity as the quest for authenticity (the original/honest self).[16] With the rise of social media as *the* 'identity technology' for artists, the discussion on authenticity is back on the table. Historically, it can be argued that people have developed different ways of aiming to 'solve' the wicked problem of identity—the trendy one being (digital) profile building. While the 'profile phenomenon' is not new, it has found major amplification through new media such that other forms of identity concepts like 'sincerity' or—as already mentioned—'authenticity' are weakened, perhaps to the point of irrelevance (cf. Moeller & D'Ambrosio, 2021). This view that technologies amplify or weaken certain ways in which people perceive reality is not only compatible with postphenomenology but one of its central points. Social media is therefore not a neutral tool—it changes (co-shapes) the artist and how they make sense of the world.

---

16   We explicitly see this, for instance, with apps such as 'BeReal' claiming that 'regular' social media do not allow for authenticity.

To circle back to my guiding question of why postphenomenology should care about Sartre's nothingness, I make the case that any account of social media that does not acknowledge Sartrean dialectic will fail to describe our relationship with this technology's role in identity building. Central, namely, are moments when assessment of the technology happens before and after the social media use-case, when usefulness (potentiality) of the technology is evaluated—whether to post content or not to post on social media. Whether to be online or not to be, and which platforms to use in the first place?

To think with Sartre and Ihde simultaneously, it becomes useful to keep in mind Sartre's *action for-itself* alongside Ihde's *leaving of the nurturing garden* to conceptualize technologies as human action facing nothingness. Later in Sartre's work, the preoccupation with nothingness turns towards *scarcity* of material and social forces[17]—in Sartre's understanding, scarcity is the very motivation for (personal, technological, and societal) action and making (Siegler, 2022). Similarly, for Ihde, making, and therefore the making of technologies, pushes back to counter 'harsh conditions' of the natural environment when leaving the garden (Ihde, 1990, pp. 11–20).

The bridge from the existential- to the postphenomenological thus is not a difficult one, as Don Ihde himself experienced existentialism as a philosophical as well as a popular movement, and he comments on and critiques existentialism on different occasions (e.g., Ihde, 1967). Ihde in his essay titled *Existentialism Today* acknowledges with Sartre that '[…] man is a negation; he is NOT identical with himself'—'MAN IS A PROBLEM TO HIMSELF' (Ihde, 1967, pp. 25–26).

As an artist, I dare to take on the risks of discussing empirical traces of negations and nothingness as a phenomenologically detectable experience, arriving at something like an *empirical transcendental* case study of social media practice. The challenge is to not drift into the 'trivial', nor the 'hardcore metaphysical' (Priest, 2017).[18] Thus, I admit to the limitations or perhaps the problems of the methodology.

---

17 Culminating in his interest in and closeness to Marxism.
18 The analytic philosopher Priest (2017) refers to the inquiry into the question of nothingness as 'hardcore metaphysics'—this is his conclusion after a mereological analysis.

4. Nothingness as Absence: Introducing Absence Relations

Human desires and needs and what 'a good life' means are increasingly mediated by social media. But why does this technology have such a nauseating and potent effect on human fragility, core human emotions, and sense-making? To better understand the artist-social media relationship, postphenomenologists need to be able to deal with both concrete use (stabilities) as well as social media phenomena that I identify as linked to the experience of absence (perhaps well described as instabilities)—such unintended or purposeful non-use of certain available social networks—during which the hypothetical evaluation (assessment) of the usefulness of the technology happens in the first place. Another form of absence appears when, for instance, individuals are 'socially absent' from the dinner table while scrolling social media or other online sites.

Visual or image-based social media platforms are preferred by those within the creative industries for obvious reasons. With this specific situatedness, I express that social media can be used in many versatile ways. Even though this analysis will remain close to basic use habits such as setting up a profile, it is important to acknowledge *multistability*, i.e., different possible use variations across different cultures, industries, and, most likely, generations and even individuals.

With Sartre, however, the question of multistability and possible use-cases expands into the problem of how to conceptualize not only use but also technological non-use of social media. Thinking along my own experiences using two concrete platforms—Instagram and TikTok—and two well-known artistic examples exploring these apps reveals the manifold nuances of how artists deal with nothingness, and how non-use is just another form of potentiality or perhaps even another form of technology that needs to be dealt with.

After clarifying the necessary vocabulary, I can now propose to think with Sartre's nothingness and the concept of identity in dialogue with Ihde's postphenomenology through introducing the concept of *absence relation*. My wording has already forestalled the 'variation' of Sartre's nothingness (discussed in section 2) which I consider the most useful and programmatic for the next step. One way or one nuance of how to experience nothingness, according to Sartre, is what he describes as absence—that is, an 'absence perceived' (Sorensen, 2022, pp. 289–308). This is the sub-concept I borrow for an entry into Ihde's relational ontology and material hermeneutics. To be able to illustrate the entanglements of Sartre's absence, his related ideas as well as the umbrella term nothingness must be kept in mind.

Phenomenology as proposed by Husserl is the study of structures of consciousness. Sartre sets out to study the problem of consciousness as the pre-reflective consciousness of consciousness. Sartre names the most obvious form of experiencing this nothingness as experiencing absence. Roy Sorensen in his recent book *Nothing. A Philosophical History* briefly discusses Sartre's concept. He notes that 'absences are always particular absences whereas presences can be general' (Sorensen, 2022, pp. 289–308). In this sense, absence always appears in relation to presence and thus within the limits of human *expectations*.

With Sartre in mind, I now can turn to Don Ihde's basic threefold formula (e.g., 2009):

human—technology—world

This phenomenological skeleton, according to Ihde, allows for an entry into descriptive attempts to deal with the relationships people can have to specific technologies and the mediated world. But how to acknowledge nothingness in this equation? The reasons for my next move to propose *determined negations* have perhaps become obvious. These negations are staged as follows:

a) (~~Human~~ → Technology)—World
b) Human → (~~Technology~~)—World
c) Human → (Technology—~~World~~)

This conceptual step can be backed up by Ihde's early work and his own dealings with nothingness. Ihde provides, especially in his early, pre-postphenomenology, insights into his views on nothingness as a concept that, in the human mind, becomes a significant force driving intentionality and action. Consequently, I conclude, an agent within technological practice. For example, in his early book *Sense and Significance* (1973), Ihde discusses the experience of sound and silence: he calls it the 'Heideggerian Model':

> The horizon of sound is silence, but at the same time it is the 'absence' which is never attained. Silence is the unspoken background for sound. (Ihde, 1973, p. 67)

> Silence is nothingness, but nothingness is sheer possibility. (Ihde, 1973, p. 68)

I propose an analytical tool to deal with phenomena that Ihde acknowledges here and I connect to social media practice. I consider my *absence relation* a variation or sub-concept of Ihde's *background relation*. This version of Ihde's human-technology relation needs to be conceptualized holistically in the context of his other relations. Ihde (1990, chapter 5) proposes analytic tools to phenomenologically describe what he calls human-technology relations. He identifies four types of relationships people might have to their technologies: *embodiment* (e.g., wearing glasses), *hermeneutic* (e.g., interpreting the world through an instrument, such as a thermostat), *alterity* (e.g., interacting with an ATM machine), and *background relation*.[19] Background relation is perhaps the one that the least attention has been paid to. One reason for this might be that this type of relation is not a straightforward use case. A technology in the background is one that is not used actively but might be running unnoticed—like an AC system or a refrigerator. Background technologies are usually only noticed when something is wrong, for instance when there is a breakdown or malfunction.

With Sartre, I hope to deepen the understanding of this background context, in which technologies 'do' something even when they are not actively in use, not yet in use, or no longer in use. What I call absence relations thus seeks to expand the vocabulary and perhaps the possible research program of postphenomenology.

The concrete example of encountering a new, potentially helpful social media app for the first time (the discovery) initially strikes the artist with her own very absence. 'I am not (yet) on this platform'. The first encounter is an in-the-face visualization of the absence of one's own face (human). This type of absence that I call the *absence-avatar*, has a distinct and well-known icon—most platforms such as Instagram or Facebook provide an 'empty' profile image with a simplistic illustration of a generic head

---

19 Ihde's four relations have been added to by other philosophers—e.g., 'cyborg relations' added by Peter-Paul Verbeek.

in shades of grey or light blue that might be stylistically male or female, depending on the name and gender assigned in the first instance. This generic head is increasingly becoming a more playful illustration (e.g., on TikTok or Reddit). The absence-avatar is a placeholder until the profile is considered complete. A second step human absence phenomenon would be the discovery of an expected person to not be on the platform. 'Pierre' might not be on TikTok ~~(human)~~.[20]

> So that what is offered to intuition is a flickering of nothingness; it is nothingness of the ground, the nihilation of which summons and demands the appearance of the figure—the nothingness which slips as a nothing to the surface of the ground. It serves as a foundation for judgment; 'Pierre is not there'. (Sorensen, 2022, p. 293; Sartre, 1992, p. 41)

Likewise, the absence of any connections in general appears. Social media companies, consciously or not, immediately play into this void by making suggestions on how to fill this nothingness. Admittedly it is a rather simple move to represent nothingness and absence through a determined negation in Ihde's formula. Yet, in my interpretation, it can achieve more than we might think at first. It allows for a discussion of Sartrean nothingness and Kiran's potentialities (2012), and allows me to go beyond the in-use paradigm unfolding a framework to describe non-use as a relation. While staying loyal to Ihde's main analytic system and materialism, the dialectic laid bare then helps to show the evaluation of usefulness (versus use) of a technology more holistically describing how co-constitution occurs. Thus, I argue that this move towards the a), b), and c) of absence relations (as mentioned, a subset of the background relation) helps to decode what *non-use* is.[21]

Ihde's relations entangled with Sartre's nothingness help to describe important fragments of the social media experience and how the mediation of nothingness can occur in our relationships to technologies. In a), as already discussed, the 'I' or the human is crossed out within Ihde's model: a) (~~Human~~ → Technology)—World. This aims to illustrate the hermeneutic digital landscape in which artists are trying

---

20 Compare Sartre's description of his friend Pierre not showing up at a café in Paris (1992, p. 41).

21 Elsewhere, I have argued that the absence relation is likewise helpful to describe the aforementioned *digital detoxing* phenomena when a technology is purposefully put aside—related apps are designed to achieve non-use—e.g., 'Digitox' (2018), 'Digital Detox' (2019), 'Freedom' (2019), 'AppBlock' (2020), 'Forest' (2021).

to make sense of the situated self that is nowhere to be found on TikTok. Yet, it is more complicated than just one negation. What appears next is what I call *co-absence*.[22] If I decided not to be on this platform, all the others are excluded from my possible *lifeworld*. Another form of absence relation appears when not the human, but the technology is absent—for instance when a phone is *lost*: b) Human → (T̶e̶c̶h̶n̶o̶l̶o̶g̶y̶)—World. The third variation based on Ihde's model is the absence of world: c) Human → (Technology—W̶o̶r̶l̶d̶). My prime example for c), a *world-absence* phenomenon, would be noise-cancelling headphones.[23]

Staying close to Ihde and his pragmatism allows for this concreteness of absence to more holistically illustrate the experience of social media practice likewise explored within my two examples from contemporary art (see next sections). This concreteness of absence on the other hand contains the risk of displaying the *self-evident* and the *trivial*. Which eventually becomes the concluding point of my exercise—to expose *triviality and* the *banal* (Arendt, 1964) within the way that social media 'makes' identity. This brings up a possible discussion—if we consider Sen's call for a more complex view of identity, social media, when analyzed using Sartre and Ihde, turns out to be a simplistic and *caricatured* answer to the search for meaning (of the self). Social media then are quite obviously playing into human vulnerability and existential anguish faced with nothingness (consider the seemingly innocent triviality of the absence-avatar).

5. Nothingness in Action: Staring at Nothing

'Why does everyone stare at their phones?' My three-year-old daughter asked while travelling on the F train from Queens to Manhattan in New York a few years back.For Sartre, nothingness culminates in absolute responsibility towards the making of the authentic self. Nothingness is the manifold experience of freedom and potentiality in practice. Sartre's nothingness finds digital amplifications through new media culminating into new ways of dealing with the responsibility and the *condemnation to be*

---

22 The term *co-absence* was suggested by Marc Ries in a personal discussion in 2020.
23 Further postphenomenological questions follow. For instance: can nothingness or absence be embodied? Can nothingness also 'appear' within alterity or hermeneutic relations?

free. Freedom online on social media is experienced as a growing *multi(in)stability* (Redström & Wiltse, 2015) of the technology and the self—the technology, as well as the artist, are always in flux. The artist on Instagram is someone who is never 'enough', always directed towards sharing into a 'higher' version (high profile) of the self that is potentially located in the future or perhaps on other platforms. But how is this different from life in general? The short answer is that it is not, yet with Ihde we can argue that nothingness and the experience of the 'never enough' artist, are amplified (through the ubiquity of the technology always allowing the potential to be 'higher profile' and to share more).

In this section, I turn to the social media practice of the so-called 'selfie'. The social media *self-portrait*[24] becomes an unavoidable, often enjoyable playground for artists exploring the *potentiality of being* and *freedom*. An example of such an exploration on Instagram is the work of the artist and photographer Cindy Sherman. Sherman is one of the best-known contemporary artists experimenting with social media and identity performance. Her technologically mediated variations of possible concepts of the self embrace existential inquiries into interchangeable virtual forms of identity. Sherman questions society and technology as accomplices in producing her *identity-obscuring* variations. Her photographs and numerous experimental self-portraits (she would herself not refer to them as such) were well known before Instagram, *selfies*, or *plandids* (candid photographs that were planned) were a thing.[25]

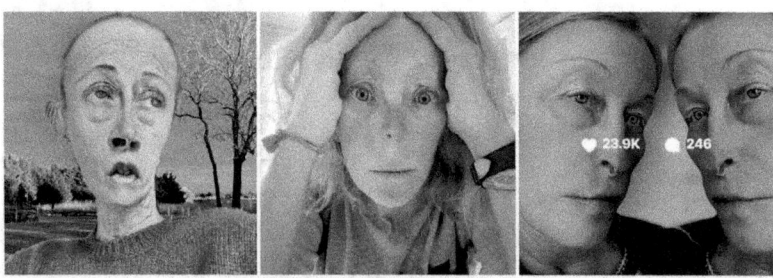

Fig. 8.1 Instagram post by Cindy Sherman. Photo by Cindy Sherman (2020), public Instagram account, https://www.instagram.com/cindysherman/

---

24 By 'social media self-portrait', I refer not only to the famous 'selfie' but to the representation of the self more broadly, which might entail images or texts beyond the image of one's face and body.

25 See A. Russeth (2017, November 6). Facetime with Cindy Sherman: The artist on her 'Selfie' project for W, and what's behind her celebrated Instagram. *W Magazine*,

Sherman criticizes social media practices of the masses and questions Instagram aesthetics. In a New York Times article, Blake Gopnik (2016) discusses Sherman's process:

> Ms. Sherman expresses contempt for the superficialities of social media. 'It seems so vulgar to me'- her new images of old-time film stars also hint at our digitized present.[26]

Sherman, in her contemporary work, embraces heavy layers of digital filters to place herself (or the characters she develops from her own image) into different backgrounds and imaginary social environments. She uses apps such as 'Facetune', 'Perfect365', and 'YouCam Makeup' to heavily manipulate her portraits. As she illustrates through her photographs behind the screen, her multiplied presence is a default in cyberspace unfolding of the status-quo of radical freedom to *become* whatever and whoever one might be. Sherman's exaggeration of herself asks existential questions concerned with the potentialities of human existence being *for-itself*. For Sherman, existence is a contingent state. Existence *precedes* her *essence,* always in the process of becoming an object, always *for-itself*, showing us the dialectics of the *for-itself* and *in-itself* that is *being-for-others*. Sherman does not accept *existential nothingness*, she embraces it.

Reimagining Sartre's existential dilemma shaped by social media and through the lens of postphenomenology comes with the risk of discovering 'the trivial' or, with Sherman, 'the vulgar' within this seemingly innocent, fun, and easy technology, finally offering a solution on how to fill the *existential void* of *non-being*.

---

https://www.wmagazine.com/culture/cindy-sherman-instagram-selfie

26 Sherman's description of Facebook's and Instagram's 'vulgarity' perhaps provides an accurate analysis, considering the origins of Facebook's beta site FaceMash, developed to compare the pictures of different Harvard students' faces to allow users to rate them according to attractiveness. See, e.g., A. Horton (2018, April 11). Channeling "The Social Network", lawmaker grills Zuckerberg on his notorious beginnings. *The Washington Post,* https://www.washingtonpost.com/news/the-switch/wp/2018/04/11/channeling-the-social-network-lawmaker-grills-zuckerberg-on-his-notorious-beginnings/. Also consider Sean Parker in 2017 admitting to knowing what social media would do to the human psyche: Sean Parker (2017, November 11). Facebook exploits human vulnerability [Video]. YouTube, https://www.youtube.com/watch?v=R7jar4KgKxs

> But non-being is not the opposite of being; it is its contradiction. This implies that logically nothingness is subsequent to being since it is being, first posited, then denied. (Sartre, 1992, p. 47)

As my daughter well observed at a young age, social media and related identity play, embedded into the technology of the smartphone, is an embodied technology. The smartphone is always close to the body, like shoes, glasses, or a hat. People on the F train stared at their phones, motivated by their suspicions of nothingness being close to their bodies, lurking somewhere.

6. Artist-Content Relations

Once a social media profile is set up, Sartre's possible nihilations appear as a void to be filled with possibilities—sharing content can begin. Once artists commit to a social media profile, they are condemned to continue to be 'free'. They must sustain that very profile over time (preferably in consistent aesthetic language), sharing content repeatedly, ideally, and as—some recommend—several times a day, with no long breaks in-between. Now locked into the duty to not miss posting, they can turn to apps to help schedule content, to calculate the 'best' times for posting. Artists also may set up several accounts they have to 'care' for or, better, 'share' for, to avoid confusing aesthetics in case their different projects compete visually or conceptually. A coherent (to the online mass, understandable) identity is the goal. Many feel guilty, formulating apology notes when they happen to miss posting for a while—with several active profiles, this easily can happen. Comedian, musician, and insightful phenomenologist Bo Burnham explores this experience in his song 'Content', from the 2021 Netflix special titled *Inside*.[27] He provides an accurate and humorous phenomenology of the 'human—content—world' relationship. In his lyrics 'I'm sorry I was gone, but look I made you some content!', Burnham apologizes for his online *absence* and makes it up with offering freshly produced content. His absence demands an apology and the 'filling in' of the void with

---

27 See 'Content'—Bo Burnham song video, from 'Inside', new special on Netflix. YouTube, June 16, 2021, https://www.youtube.com/watch?v=pQvrap19Eng

'sparkling' content. The content of the content is only secondary.[28] When not sharing for a longer period, such notes of apologies are not unusual. Additionally, sometimes an explanation might be offered to justify the absence, always presented next to new visual content.[29] Burnham shows how *mediation of nothingness* can play out—how being absent/offline for too long leads to emotions of *neglect* and *guilt* and the need to apologize or at least explain the absence to the online crowd.

A colleague and friend who owns a concept store in Germany describes a similar relationship to content. She never feels she has done enough sharing, never enough 'social media content work'. There is always more that potentially could be done to care for her online project closely entangled with her private life. Content, potentially, could always and everywhere be produced. Like a fragile child, her online store profile is always in need of attention, with lots of potential if only 'shared for' well enough. Her conclusion: self-care means self-share with fragility lurking in every act of *missing content*.

> And what is fragility if not a certain probability of non-being for a given being under determined circumstances. A being is fragile if it carries in its being a definite possibility of non-being. (Sartre, 1992, p. 40)

The logical conclusion of this type of absence relation—people who experience guilt when 'not sharing enough' or 'not producing enough content', coupled with ubiquitous digital technologies allowing one to always share—is self-evident: a whole generation has been accused of 'oversharing' and 'narcissism' (Chokshi, 2019).

Concluding Note

In this paper, I reflected on French philosopher Jean-Paul Sartre's notion of nothingness in his treatise *Being and Nothingness*, and his sub-concept *absence*—that is *perceived absence*—in dialogue with

---

28 German Philosopher Markus Gabriel (2022) in a lecture at the IWP (Institut für Schweizer Wirtschaftspolitik, 4 August 2022, defines social media as nothing but 'post-modernism' without content (my translation from the German) (https://www.youtube.com/watch?v=3CRzqkpePaY).

29 Burnham in a different song also explores *boredom*, another variation of nothingness and the second self-evident motivation for content production and consumption.

American philosopher Don Ihde's relational ontology. The aim was to phenomenologically describe fragments of social media practice (using Instagram and TikTok), as typically done and experienced by artists and designers, that I found overlooked within the school of thought known as postphenomenology and related mediation theory. To better dialectically map out the workings of image-based social media as a 'necessary evil' for those within the creative industries, I suggested considering the notion of *mediation of nothingness* within the artist-social media relationship. With Sartre, I made the case for determined negations within Ihde's threefold model of human—technology—world, to integrate what I have described as *absence phenomena*. I used the example of the *absence-avatar* to show the banal or trivial workings of how social media plays into Sartre's nothingness. With the convergence of Sartre's nothingness and Ihde's early work I could expand on Ihde's *background relation* adding three variations, a), b), c), of *absence relations*. Widening the analytical repertoire of postphenomenology allows for a better understanding of identity as a wicked problem entangled with Sartre's nothingness that I see amplified through image-based social media. Absence relations open up a framework to discuss under-examined existential issues within postphenomenology, such as *actuality* in relation to *potentiality*, questions on *use* versus *non-use*. Sartre's project and vocabulary became helpful for developing a more holistic understanding of social media practice (within the creative industries). What there is to be gained from the convergence of Sartre's dialectics and Ihde's pragmatism is a philosophical space to discuss human-technology relations beyond the in-use paradigm that postphenomenology has famously excelled in.

Finally, I put my absence relations to work, showing two well-known artistic examples—artist and photographer Cindy Sherman's Instagram selfies and comedian Bo Burnham's human-content phenomenology performed in his song 'Content'. The artist-social media relationship illustrates that artists are skilled in exploring and coping with the *multi(in)stability of nothingness* through identity play, humour, and irony. Artists thus often skilfully embrace nothingness questioning the depth of the fragility of 'human wholeness' (sanity). Yet a careful phenomenology of the social media-artist relation that has not given up on the human subject will also recognize that this also shows that humanity has embraced a rigid or one-dimensional method of *making* the artist through content. I conclude that to stay relevant in addressing pressing contemporary technological issues around, human (digital) well-being tied to social media, postphenomenology must reintegrate existential questions into its corpus. In this first step of analyzing absence relations, I remain agnostic in evaluating social media normatively in relation to the artist; however; I observe and conclude that artists and designers often consciously embrace a technology preoccupied with answering to a caricatured version of Sartre's existential 'conundrum'. The idea of *condemnation* and the *absolute freedom* to make the self is no longer met with a nostalgia for higher states of authenticity (that historically tends to be attributed to the artist) but rather with working toward a *higher profile*. Nostalgia for Sartre's authentic self is replaced by sharing content to literally 'face' nothingness.

References

Altmaier, N., Kratel, V. A. E., Borchers, N. S., & Zurstiege, G. (2024). Studying digital disconnection: A mapping review of empirical contributions to disconnection studies. *First Monday, 29(1)*, https://doi.org/10.5210/fm.v29i1.13269

Arendt, H. (1964). *Eichmann in Jerusalem: A report on the banality of evil*. Penguin.

Cheong, M. (2023). Existentialism on social media. *Journal of Human-Technology Relations, 1*, https://doi.org/10.59490/jhtr.2023.1.7022

Chokshi, N. (2019, May 15). Attention young people: This narcissism study is all about you. *The New York Times*, https://www.nytimes.com/2019/05/15/science/narcissism-teenagers.html

De Boer, B. (2021). Explaining multistability: Postphenomenology and affordances of technologies. *AI & Society*, https://doi.org/10.1007/s00146-021-01272-3

Fukuyama, F. (2019). *Identity: Contemporary identity politics and the struggle for recognition*. Profile Books.

Goffman, E. (1959). *The presentation of self in everyday life*. Anchor Books.

Gopnik, B. (2016, April 21). Cindy Sherman takes on aging (her own). *The New York Times*, https://www.nytimes.com/2016/04/24/arts/design/cindy-sherman-takes-on-aging-her-own.html

Haidt, J., & Rose-Stockwell, T. (2019, December). The dark psychology of social networks. *The Atlantic*.

Halpert, J. (2022, June 14). A new student movement wants you to log off. *New York Times*, https://www.nytimes.com/2022/06/14/style/log-off-movement-emma-lembke.html

Haugen, F. (2023). *The power of one: Blowing the whistle on Facebook*. Hachette UK.

Ihde, D. (1967). Existentialism today. *Journal of Thought, 2*(4), 19–27.

Ihde, D. (1973). *Sense and significance*. Duquesne University Press.

Ihde, D. (1986). *Consequences of phenomenology*. State University of New York Press.

Ihde, D. (1990). *Technology and the lifeworld: From garden to earth*. Indiana University Press.

Ihde, D. (2002). *Bodies in technology*. University of Minnesota Press.

Ihde, D. (2009). *Postphenomenology and technoscience: The Peking University lectures*. State University of New York Press.

Ihde, D. (2012). *Experimental phenomenology: Multistabilities*. State University of New York Press.

Jose, J. M. M. (2019). Sartre misconstrued: A reply to Michael Lopato's 'Social media, love, and Sartre's look of the other'. *Philosophia-International Journal of Philosophy, 20*, 60–79, https://doi.org/10.46992/pijp.20.1.a.4

Kiran, A. H. (2012). Technological presence: Actuality and potentiality in subject constitution. *Human Studies, 35*(1), 77–93, https://doi.org/10.1007/s10746-011-9208-7

Kudina, O. (2020). *Technological mediation of morality* [Video]. TED Conferences. https://www.youtube.com/watch?v=vwqi8C04Gsk

Kudina, O. (2021). 'Alexa, who am I?': Voice assistants and hermeneutic lemniscate as the technologically mediated sense-making. *Human Studies, 44*(2), 233–53, https://doi.org/10.1007/s10746-021-09572-9

Kurz, A. (forthcoming). *Offline, unplugged, disconnected: A postphenomenological inquiry into absence relations to technologies*. [PhD dissertation, Hessen State University of Art and Design].

Lanier, J. (2018). *Ten arguments for deleting your social media accounts right now*. Random House.

Lemmens, P., Sharon, T., Swierstra, T., & Vermaas, P. (2022). *The technical condition: The entanglement of technology, culture, and society*. Uitgeverij Boom.

Lopato, M. S. (2015). Social media, love, and Sartre's look of the other: Why online communication is not fulfilling. *Philosophy & Technology, 29*(3), 195–210, https://doi.org/10.1007/s13347-015-0207-x

McLuhan, M. (1977). *Violence as a quest for identity TV Ontario 1977*. The Mike McManus Show, https://www.marshallmcluhanspeaks.com/media/mcluhan_pdf_11_fNfqnAl.pdf

Moeller, H. G-., & D'Ambrosio, P. J. (2021). *You and your profile. Identity after authenticity*. Columbia University Press.

Priest, G. (2017). *'Everything and nothing' (Robert Curtius Lecture of Excellence)* [*Video*]. Internationales Zentrum für Philosophie NRW, https://www.youtube.com/watch?v=66enDcUQUK0

Qi, J., Monod, E., Fang, B., & Deng, S. (2018). Theories of social media: Philosophical foundations. *Engineering*, 4(1), 94–102, https://doi.org/10.1016/j.eng.2018.02.009

Redström, J., & Wiltse, H. (2015). *On the multi-instabilities of assembled things* [Conference Paper]. 4S 2015, Denver, Colorado, USA, https://www.researchgate.net/publication/289533292_On_the_Multi-Instabilities_of_Assembled_Things

Ricœur, P. (1992). *Oneself as another*. University of Chicago Press.

Rosenberger, R., & Verbeek, P.-P. (Eds). (2015). *Postphenomenological investigations: Essays on human–technology relations*. Lexington Books.

Russeth, A. (2017, November 6). Facetime with Cindy Sherman: The artist on her 'selfie' project for W, and what's behind her celebrated instagram. *W Magazine*, https://www.wmagazine.com/culture/cindy-sherman-instagram-selfie

Sartre, J. P-. (1993). *Being and nothingness. The principal text of modern existentialism*. Washington Square Press.

Sen, A. (2020). *Identität Und Gewalt*. C.H. Beck.

Siegler, M. (2022). The dialectics of action and technology in the philosophy of Jean-Paul Sartre. *Philosophy & Technology, 35*(2), https://doi.org/10.1007/s13347-022-00536-0

Sorensen, R. (2022). *Nothing: A philosophical history*. Oxford University Press.

Taylor, S. (2015). Identity construction. In K. Tracy, T. Sandel, & C. Ilie (Eds), *The International Encyclopedia of Language and Social Interaction*, https://doi.org/10.1002/9781118611463.wbielsi099

Turkle, S. (2011). Alone together: Why we expect more from technology and less from each other. *Choice Reviews Online, 48*(12), 48–7239, https://doi.org/10.5860/choice.48-7239

Vadukul, A. (2022, December 15). 'Luddite' teens don't want your likes when the only thing better than a flip phone is no phone at all. *New York Times*, https://www.nytimes.com/2022/12/15/style/teens-social-media.html

Verbeek, P.-P. (2016). Toward a theory of technological mediation: A program for postphenomenological research. In J. K. B. O. Friis & R.P. Crease (Eds), *Technoscience and postphenomenology: The Manhattan papers* (pp. 189–204). Lexington Books.

Wellner, G. (2016). *A postphenomenological inquiry of cell phones: Genealogies, meanings, and becoming.* Lexington Books.

Wiltse, H. (2017). Mediating (infra)structures: Technology, media, environment. In Y. Van Den Eede, S. O. Irwin, & G. Wellner (Eds), *Postphenomenology and Media* (pp. 3–25). Lexington Books.

Zuboff, S. (2019). *The age of surveillance capitalism: The fight for a human future at the new frontier of power.* Profile Books.

9. Attending to the Online Other: A Phenomenology of Attention on Social Media Platforms[1]

Lavinia Marin

Introduction: Attention Scattering on Social Media Platforms

In scholarly discussions on the ethics of social media,[2] a recurring point of concern around the heavy usage of such platforms is their detrimental effects on the well-being of their users (Dennis, 2021; Hoffner & Bond, 2022), with one of the most visible effects being the scattering of users' attention (Roholt, 2023). With the constant usage of smartphones, users are always connected to their social media platforms (SMPs) of choice, constantly updated but with a scattered focus as users find themselves compulsively checking their social media updates whenever they have a free moment and even when they are doing something else, multi-tasking (Koralus, 2014). In these discussions, attention is usually seen as a resource depleted by SMP usage,[3] with long-term effects on

---

1   This work is part of the research programme Ethics of Socially Disruptive Technologies, funded through the Gravitation programme of the Dutch Ministry of Education, Culture, and Science and the Netherlands Organization for Scientific Research (NWO grant number 024.004.031).
2   The platforms discussed here are mainstream social media platforms (SMPs) such as Facebook, Twitter ('X'), Instagram, YouTube, TikTok, and Threads.
3   There are exceptions to this mainstream view—most remarkably, Galit Wellner's work (2014), which has pointed out that our notion of attention as an undistractible capacity to focus on one thing is problematic and culturally constructed (Wellner, 2014, p. 49) and that multi-tasking is not only possible and

diminishing users' attention and capacity to focus on one thing at a time (Fisher, 2022). The framing of scattered attention as detrimental is seen as one of the main ways in which online social media platforms are disruptive of the day-to-day lives of their users as a standard example of how a socially disruptive technology acts (van de Poel et al., 2023). In this chapter, I turn to a less-discussed dimension of the attention disruption of SMPs—namely, how the capacity for attention enables us to relate to others as moral agents. By focusing on this relational aspect of human attention, I will argue that SMPs are disruptive for our moral and social lives in specific ways previously ignored in most scholarship on social media ethics.

In this chapter, I use a phenomenological approach to disentangle the features of the relational mode of attention and use this analysis to argue that SMPs' constant bid for users' attention has detrimental consequences for how users attend to other users, and for recognizing their moral agency. I claim that SMPs do not merely distract us from our surroundings but also hinder us from perceiving distant others as moral agents and worthy of our attention. I first analyse how the other-oriented attention is distinctive from other modes of attention that objects demand. I will draw from conceptualizations of attention in the phenomenological tradition to flesh out a phenomenology of attending to the other or other-oriented attention. Then, I will use these phenomenological insights to investigate the ways in which SMPs affect the other-oriented attention detrimentally, in ways that short-circuit our moral perception of others.

1. Attention and Moral Agency

The shaping of human attention through technological artefacts is an ethical issue that has been widely discussed, with online social spaces such as SMPs playing a significant role in this shaping. Thus far, the ethically focused discussions on attention in online social spaces have followed two broad directions: the first one concerns the deceitful

---

assumed by specific jobs (piloting an aircraft, parenting), but also that specific technological designed experiences make multi-tasking feasible and rewarding, becoming an experience which is 'greater than the sum of its parts' (Wellner, 2014, p. 69).

practices enacted by design, where attention is seen as a scarce resource that is consumed by online platforms without the users' awareness, leading to problematic issues such as accountability in design choices and user consent (Brady et al., 2020; Fogg et al., 2007; Timms & Spurrett, 2023, p. 24), or user manipulation (Klenk, 2022) when users do not notice how certain choices are already made for them by the platform. When design choices affect a user's capacity for focused attention without the users' noticing or consent, we are in the realm of the ethics of (interaction) design. The second direction of ethical analysis concerns what attention as a mental capacity enables for our moral lives: it has been discussed that we are autonomous and self-directed agents precisely because we can choose what we pay attention to (Williams, 2018), hence attention is a resource that we need for enacting moral agency (Watzl, 2023; Bombaerts et al., 2023). My concern in this chapter aligns with the second direction of ethical analysis, namely how attention is fundamental for moral agency, to which I add the distinctive concern of recognizing the moral agency of others. Thus, while it has been argued that we need to be able to freely focus our attention on the matters of concern to us—as a precondition of our own moral agency, acting in the realm of moral ends—I will argue here that we need to pay attention to others in particular ways such that we recognize their moral agency. Attention has a particular relational aspect, which I will explore in this chapter while also highlighting the distinct ways in which online attention can hinder this mode of attention.

Before we dive into the phenomenology of attention to others, we need to establish what makes attention a distinct experience. An example will help us discern the fundamental dimensions of attention. Imagine you are walking in a park with the purpose of finding a spot to have a picnic. You scrutinize the grass and the trees, looking for the perfect spot, not too shady, sunny, or wet. Then, a toddler runs at you and throws a ball at you, so you notice the toddler and wonder where the ball will go next. As you scrutinize the grass, you also wonder if this spot would also be good for playing a football game, so you move your gaze to the trees surrounding it and wonder if their branches are too low for this purpose. Then you hear a bus passing by on the street next to the park and think you could take the bus back home instead of walking. In a few minutes, you switched what you noticed seamlessly—

the grass, the toddler, the ball, the grass again—but looked at different aspects of the field, the trees, the sound of the bus. At the same time, you were thinking and imagining things while also paying attention to these thoughts and the surroundings. Attention is this capacity for dynamic rearrangement of what you focus on while also holding all the other things in the periphery of perception. As you moved your focus to the football game, the toddler did not disappear, but it only became less central and slowly faded away from your perception.

Attention is the individual capacity to rank things subjectively in a dynamic manner: some things become the centre of our focus, and some are pushed to the background (Watzl, 2017). We cannot pay equal attention to everything in our surroundings; thus, we need to dynamically shift what we notice and involuntarily ignore. The capacity to rearrange spontaneously what we focus on, shifting between what becomes central and what fades at the periphery, ranking and selecting subjectively the things we attend to (Panizza, 2022, p. 157), is what attention is all about phenomenologically. Sebastian Watzl has described this implicit hierarchy-setting in the experience of paying attention as the arranging of saliences: 'attending to something creates a structured field, in which the object of our attention plays a special role' (Watzl, 2017, p. 209). Attention is a mode of consciousness that arranges everything into ordered sets based on the perceived importance of the elements of the set (salience), whereby this arrangement is subjective and idiosyncratic to the one paying attention, heavily dependent on their particular ways of experiencing the world. For example, a field covered with grass will be perceived differently based on who is paying attention to it and given their interests. A sports player will perceive the features of a field, looking for what game actions it affords (D'Angelo, 2020, p. 964), while others may look at the same field, noticing good places for having a picnic. What we perceive as salient is already shaped by what we want to do but also, at the same time, by the unfamiliar. Some things capture our attention, with attention hijacked from us when we cannot help but pay attention to the unfamiliar (Fredriksson, 2022, p. 31).

Attention is experienced by humans on a continuum from voluntary to involuntary. There is an effortful way of paying attention (presupposing voluntary intention from our side) and a general attentiveness or perception,[4] both are part and parcel of the faculty of attention (Panizza & Hopwood, 2022, p. 162). Both modes of attention have ethical implications but in different ways. While voluntary attention is something we direct at others, we cannot say the same thing about our perception (attention as awareness), which can be hijacked and is seemingly out of our voluntary control. It seems that one cannot be held responsible for what one perceives. Still, there is room for responsibility, even in passive attention. Previous experiences of voluntary attention shape our passive attention or perceptual awareness; that is, we train ourselves to know what to pay attention to through habitual interactions. What strikes us as attention-worthy is shaped by our past experiences of attention, our relations with others, and our embodied history of being alive in the world. If we want to pay attention to other things, we need to train ourselves by paying voluntary attention to some aspects of the world until, given enough interactions, we become experts at passively noticing these aspects after a while. In the ethics of attention, we are autonomous about what we pay voluntary attention to—based on our interests and preferences—and agentic about our involuntary attention, as we are responsible for our habits that shape what we notice and what strikes us as interesting. To sum up, attention is a capacity to arrange saliences which is both voluntary and involuntary, shaped by our particular history of interactions with the world, by our interests, and by our way of being-in-the-world as embodied agents.

2. Relational or Other-Oriented Attention

Attention is the currency of social media exchanges, while posts, notifications and images are the attention attractors. Mainstream social media platforms are primarily seen as places for socialising but, at the same time, places where we bid for other users' attention and offer it to others through the informational snippets that we publish, share, or consume. It has been argued that every share on social media is a gesture of pointing at the interestingness of the original post. The speech act entailed in sharing would be pointing at something interesting to draw

---

[4] See the work of Sebastian Watzl (2017) for more fine-grained distinctions between the kinds and modes of attention.

other's attention (Arielli, 2018). But if every post, image, or comment is an attention bid, then the overall environment becomes overwhelming for users who are constantly asked to pay attention to this or that. This is already recognized as an issue for psychological well-being but also an ethical concern. This constant bid for attention from everyone makes SMPs feel like exhausting places. When you decide to share someone's post, you cannot only look at what is said in the post (informational and epistemic content) but also who said it, and you also need to think carefully about what kind of attention you want to disclose about that person. You may agree with a post by Trump, factually, but you may withhold from sharing it if you disagree with him politically. Every gesture of sharing, linking, or commenting is primarily a gesture of signalling attention. In deciding whom to share and whom to like, I also decide whom to ignore. This renders a quality of premeditation to any act of attention online, which also becomes a morally loaded choice.

The angle of my approach to moral agency is relational. Relational approaches in ethics highlight the role that other moral agents play in our own shaping as moral agents, seeing as we all inhabit the same social environment and our moral actions are connected. Moral agency is 'the property of humans and other animals in their capacity as actors who more or less intentionally bring about results in the world' (Alfano, 2016, p. 219). Moral agency presupposes agents with responsibility and autonomy (Watson, 2013, p. 1): we are responsible for the things we bring about in the world through our actions. If these actions rely on autonomous decisions, how we act in the world is the result of our choices and preferences. Moral agency concerns what someone can do, and it relies on their being autonomous and deciding for themselves what they want to do. Moral agency is already relational to some extent, given that, to act in the moral realm, it is assumed that we are responsible for our actions in front of others: our actions are not morally relevant unless we accept accountability for them. Furthermore, we never act in a social vacuum: our actions encounter the resistance and reaction of others. Sometimes, our moral actions presuppose that others receive these actions, and then they are the patients of our agency. As Mark Alfano (2016) has put it, our moral agency is intertwined with the moral patiency of others, and vice-versa: 'people can be simple patients, to whom things just happen; they can be simple agents, who just do things; but they can also be complex agents and patients: they can do things to each other. In such cases, agency and patiency are inextricably intertwined' (Alfano, 2016, p. 20). One's actions can diminish another's moral agency and enhance it, for example, by promoting another's autonomy in decision-making (Raskoff, 2022). To sum up, the relational dimensions of moral agency are visible in the following ways: agency is not possible without responsibility and autonomy, and sometimes it entails the patiency of others (when we do things to others, e.g., we decide for them). Responsibility is already a relational concept, while autonomy has already been discussed as a relational concept (MacKenzie, 2019)—albeit some Kantian philosophers will not agree that autonomy is fundamentally relational.

If moral agency is a relational concept, then what we can do in the moral domain is constrained or enhanced by others' actions and responses to our own actions. Hence, our moral agency is constrained by the attention we pay to others and the attention they pay to us.

In exploring the part played by attention in exercising our moral agency, the phenomenology of attention can help us to understand what exactly is relational in our attention. While we use the same term of 'attention' for the capacity to notice other humans as we do for objects or environments, there is a qualitative difference between the attention we give to other humans versus everything else. When we perceive others, usually, we cannot see them merely as objects—we also see them as subjects at the same time. There are, of course, exceptions to this rule. When we are running through a crowd—to catch a train, for example— we do not see the others as subjects, just obstacles we must avoid as we navigate the public spaces. But in most cases, when people surround us, we pay attention to them as subjects as well, meaning that they can also pay attention to us. There is always a possibility for reciprocity in the attention we give to others, even if this possibility does not always become actualized. We are able—partially due to technological artefacts—to create our social bubbles into which nobody can enter without our consent; for example, we may walk on a street and completely ignore the people around us as we scroll social media feeds on our phone and listen to music with noise-cancelling phones. In this walk, we notice those around us only as bodies and potential obstacles, things not to bump into, but still, we do not perceive them in the same way as we would the stop signs or buildings around us. Any of these persons around us can emerge at any time as a moral agent, demanding a different kind of attention from us, for example, by asking us for directions, for our help with something, or to start a conversation. Even when we create a social bubble around us, we are not immune from others soliciting our attention, and then we feel obliged to respond. In granting attention to others, reciprocity is always possible: they can also notice us in their subjective field of attention. This reciprocity embedded in the other-oriented attention affects how we relate to others as moral agents.

Is there something distinctive in the attention we pay to others, from the attention to inanimate objects? Yes, and this distinctiveness has to do with moral agency, both our moral agency and that of the others we pay attention to. We notice that others are moral agents when we feel responsible for our actions in front of them and demand accountability for their actions—at least in principle. To dive deeper into this object-person difference within the phenomenology of attention, I will draw on the concepts of the classical concepts of the gaze and empathy. Others can return our gaze and we can feel empathy towards others, even without wanting to.

2.1 The Gaze

The moral phenomenology of the gaze has been analysed on a continuum stretching between the opposing views of Sartre and Levinas (Gallagher, 2020, p. 101). For Sartre, the encounter with another's gaze discloses the experience of being objects of that gaze. We are objectified when we are looked at:

> The shock of the encounter with the Other is for me a revelation in emptiness of the existence of my body outside as an in-itself for the Other. Thus my body is not given merely as that which is purely and simply lived [...] [it becomes] extended outside in a dimension of flight which escapes me. (Sartre 1956, p. 352, cited in Gallagher, 2020, p. 102)

For Levinas, on the other hand, the other's gaze and the encounter of gazes is 'imperative' (Gallagher, 2020, p. 102) as it addresses us as subjects and makes a moral demand from us. The gaze can subjectify and objectify someone at the same time. When another person watches me, I can feel that I am the object of their scrutiny but also, if our eyes meet, a moral subject who is asked something. Both ways of reading the gaze are plausible and can happen at the same time or alternate.

Shaun Gallagher proposes an affective and interactive reading of the gaze: the gaze 'is neither a passive observation nor a disorganised glance; it appears, at the very least, as an active, interested questioning—and we experience it as something to which we need to respond' (Gallagher, 2020, p. 103). The gaze of the other carries an affective dimension and a demand for relating, which Gallagher calls an 'elementary responsiveness' (Gallagher, 2020, p. 103). When another looks at me, their gaze carries this implicit demand for affective relating. This is why, for example, staring for too long at someone else is experienced as uncomfortable because there is an implicit demand for relating in that gaze. However, without additional information, what is asked of us is unclear. When a moral request comes through words, asking for help is easily understood. However, a gaze signals the entering into a relation of attention awarding while also demanding attention from the other. The purpose of this bid for attention is unclear in the beginning. The gaze signals an initiating reciprocal attention exchange, which may or may not have moral significance.

There is a continuum between two modes of attention to others: the 'scientific' gaze and the affective one (Harney, 2020, p. 101), with various modes in between. We can see the other as an object of our scrutiny, and we see the other as a subject capable of returning our attention by returning our gaze or answering us. Many ethical issues arise when we are stuck only in the scientific gaze, looking at others as if they are merely objects of scrutiny (for example, a doctor looking at patients only as clusters of symptoms). Even in professional contexts, staying in the scientific mode of attention to others should be avoided since it is a dehumanizing gaze. Meanwhile, the affective mode of attention is about relating to others as subjects capable of affective responses, yet this mode of attention is difficult to maintain all the time.

Imagine you are travelling by public transport. While all other passengers are capable of being subjects of your attention and hence of being recipients of your affective gaze,[5] not all of them should be

---

5   Visually impaired people are also capable of full attention to another and being attended to. In these cases, the voice replaces the gaze as a marker of the lived body. Being spoken to and answering back, in real time, is what replaces the

because then your attention would be indiscriminate: when everyone is important, nobody is. As a fictional example, in Dostoevsky's novel *The Idiot* (1869), Prince Myshkin, the main character, is a very peculiar man who awards everyone affective attention in a way that makes them feel really seen. Initially, this feature of Myshkin is endearing, and he gains a lot of fans among the other characters of the novel. However, as the action progresses, Myshkin disappoints everyone as he cannot sustain this genuine interest in everyone else equally. While attending to others as moral agents entails having this capacity to see them as subjects and extending this affective attention to them, this is only a requirement in principle. In a Levinasian reading, we owe others our affective attention insofar as they ask, but we cannot always relate to others as subjects. In practice, both modes of attending to others are alternating—the scientific and the affective—since attention is a dynamic rearrangement of saliences, so this affective dimension also gets rearranged. Sometimes we see others clinically and sometimes we perceive them affectively, alternating modes for the same person depending on the context.

2.2 Empathy

As mentioned previously, a distinctive dimension of other-oriented attention consists in its affective modality, usually cashed out in terms of empathy. What makes the attention we pay to others as opposed to objects distinctive is the ever-present possibility of empathy. This does not mean we always need to experience empathy when we look at others—this would be too high a requirement for ethically relating to others as subjects—even when we see others as moral agents. A judge in a courtroom sees the accused as a moral agent, but empathy is not needed for this kind of attention to be awarded.

The link between attention to the other and ethical life passes through empathy. Attention to others is fixed by empathy, making it hard to dismiss the other as a moral agent or treat them as a non-person.

---

reciprocity of the gaze. If we are in the dark and someone speaks to us directly then this counts as establishing reciprocity between subjects, and is a grounds for recognition. We do not speak to inanimate objects in the same way as we do not look at the objects expecting a response. The response needs to be embodied to establish the common ground between the two subjects: the lived body.

Empathy is a mode of perceiving the other as embodied, similar beings to ourselves. We experience others as 'embodied minds' (Zahavi, 2014, p. 151) capable of feeling the same sensations as us (that is, the same type of experiences, not the same tokens). This ground of common sensations and ways of being-in-the-world is very hard to dismiss: 'the most fundamental form of empathy is the one that allows us to apprehend the perceptually given body as a lived body, that is, most fundamentally as a sensing body' (Zahavi, 2014, p. 138).

Other-oriented attention emerges in the tension of distance and interconnectedness: the other is similar to me (embodied being), and another that I cannot assimilate. 'Both polarities are required for ethical attention: a propensity to distinguish the other as that which is not governed by my self-interest, and the propensity to acknowledge our' (Fredriksson, 2022, pp. 168–169). I recognize their embodied reactions (Maurice Merleau-Ponty brings the example of the person who twitches when the sun hits their face) and a common ground of perceiving the world and, simultaneously, we are different, irreducible to another. To whom we choose to (not) give our attention divides the world into people like us and the other: strangers, aliens, and invisible: 'wilful non-perception, making a person socially invisible, is to deny recognition to that person' (Zahavi, 2014, p. 224).

Empathy is important for the ethical domain since it grounds recognizing others as moral agents in a way that short-circuits the deliberation or conscious decisions. I may not want to see another human as a moral agent, but empathy bypasses this tendency and forces me to see their moral personhood. Some historical instances of seeing other humans as sub-human are a counterexample to this claim (Smith, 2020, p. 63). However, I see this more as a boundary condition for recognition: awarding others our full attention does not mean that we will see them as moral agents, even when they return our gaze and even when we cannot help but feel empathy, due to recognizing our embodiment. Still, we cannot recognize others as moral agents without focusing some of our attention on them, thus making them important in our subjective ranking of attention.

Attention to others always has a moral dimension: ignoring others or paying the wrong kind of attention to them has consequences for the kind of relations we enter into and their moral weight. Choosing to pay attention to this person rather than that one is a moral choice, especially if the situation as such has moral implications (requesting help or care, for example). By contrast, what we pay attention to in the realm of inanimate artefacts or environments is not necessarily charged with ethical significance. We are drawn to the unfamiliar, the strange situations, as our attention is magnetically focused on such situations (Fredriksson, 2022).

The attention we pay to others is the basis for recognition and for effectively being-in-the-world as a moral agent. Moral agency, as previously highlighted, is not only about the actions I can perform and the relations I enter into but also about how others become moral patients for my actions and how others react and respond to my actions with a moral significance, for example, by demanding accountability. I may think I am an autonomous moral agent, making decisions for myself. However, if others do not recognize my agency and dismiss all my decisions, I am not effectively a moral agent. A similar case could be when I am a moral agent; I say and do things unimpeded, but nobody pays attention to me. Am I still a moral agent when I am ignored, given that my actions are not visible in the moral realm? Some would argue that being invisible does not remove one's agency, and at some point, I could be held accountable for my actions. But, outside the legal realm of being held accountable, we need constant recognition from others of our actions and their consequences, and this recognition routinely entails being paid attention to.

3. The Ethics of Paying Attention to Others

The moral features of attention to others can be briefly conceptualized within the following dimensions.

A. First, there is **an embodied ground** for attending to others. This means that when we attend to others, we cannot help but notice that we share an embodied common nature (the Husserlian 'animal nature'—see Gallagher, 2022) and that the other is capable of feeling and suffering. The experience of paying attention to another (be it voluntary or involuntary) is about the spontaneous recognition that we, like them, are embodied beings.⁶ The sources of this mode of attention are usually the gaze, as described previously, but also the voice. Hearing the voice of another reminds us of the embodied nature we share with them. We cannot 'hear away' as we can 'look away'. recognizing this embodied commonality with others, of having a lived body, is also the ground for empathy.

The attention we pay to others is grounded in our embodied being-in-the-world, as bodies recognize other bodies as having similar experiences. While all other-oriented attention is embodied in a basic way, our attending to others also seems to rely on us having some awareness of their bodies. However, this becomes problematic when we relate to others through digital intermediaries, such as social media platforms (messaging apps, emails, etc.). The affective or subject-oriented perception (Harney, 2020, p. 101) gives rise to moral obligations and recognition. Without the return of the gaze of the other, we would be hard-pressed to recognize them spontaneously as moral agents. We could still see their moral agency, inferred from their words and signs, but this requires a lot more effort in inference and induction, similar to the effort we put into consciously overcoming our biases.

B. Another moral feature of attention to others concerns **recognizing them as individuals**, not as class representatives. We notice a person, and almost immediately, we classify them into some categories, some broad generalizations of who they could be (these can be anything from culture, personality types, race, socio-economic status, and character traits). Iris Murdoch (2014) has conceptualized this kind of attention to another as an individual as the backbone of moral choices. We do not see the others until we pay continuous attention to them to notice how they evade the categories we fit into, prima facie. In Murdoch's famous example (2014), a mother-in-law is at first prejudiced against her daughter-in-law, actively disliking her, and then slowly changing her mind after paying attention to her more. Murdoch argues that this act of focusing attention and readjusting one's judgments could be happening

---

6   This embodied dimension works for any animate other, not only humans, but other animals. For example, many people eat meat but refuse to see video documentaries of how cattle are sacrificed in industrial settings. Most people prefer not to see where the meat for their consumption comes from. In deliberately ignoring this source of information, they are curating their attention to prevent this raw and embodied identification with the suffering of another living being.

entirely inside the mother-in-law's head (for example, by rearranging and reinterpreting past impressions of the other). Still, the contact with the daughter-in-law needs something to reinterpret, so the gaze or the voice needs to provide some input for this attention. It is possible that even after we decide to refocus our attention on a person and be open to who they could be, we still dislike them and judge them. But what matters here is that we judge them as individuals, going out of the broad categories we ascribed to them on the first impression. In this dimension of attention, we pay attention to the particulars of the other, and their manner of being, and we need to take the time to pay this attention.

The recognition of the other as a moral agent means we see the other who can do things to us (or others), which can be morally evaluated and thus held responsible for these actions (Watson, 2013). The moral significance of attention to others concerns the attention that makes this recognition of the other as a moral agent possible. When we pay enough attention to others and the right kind of attention, we recognize their agency: we see them as responsible agents capable of making decisions on their own. This point is somewhat different from the idea that we need to pay attention to our actions to be responsible for them—see Jennings (2020, p. 162), who argues that we are still responsible for our automatic actions even though we may not pay attention to them at the moment. To attribute moral agency to others, one needs to pay attention to them; particularly, we need to pay attention to their embodied being and individuality. It is difficult to spontaneously recognize others as moral agents, equal to oneself, without noticing their embodied nature and unique individuality. It does not follow from this that attention to their embodied nature and attention to their uniqueness necessarily lead to recognition of their moral agency. Many parents notice their toddlers, their uniqueness, and their individual manner of being but do not attribute to them full moral agency, at least not for a while. Both the embodied dimension and the recognition of individuality are necessary, albeit insufficient, attentional dimensions for recognizing another's moral agency.

Thus far, I have discussed other-oriented attention as a spontaneous capacity to notice others (or some of their features) and to arrange what we notice into degrees of importance or saliences (Watzl, 2022), focusing on some aspects while backgrounding the others (Fredriksson, 2022;

Jacobs, 2021). I tried to argue that attention to others has an ethical significance as the ground on which we establish moral recognition (Anderson, 2021). I did not discuss how attention is a socially learned capacity based on multiple previous interactions. Attention to others allows us to pick up on social affordances (behaviours, cultural markers) and act on these. Presumably, the more attention we pay to others, the more skilled we become at picking up on social affordances, the more occasions we have to interact with others in community-endorsed ways, and the better we get at being moral agents and recognizing other's moral agency. Thus, we do not always consciously choose to award others our attention (albeit sometimes we choose to withdraw it, as the example of homeless people being invisible demonstrates)—rather, attention is also something we practice (Bombaerts et al., 2023) to develop as social actors. Without attention to others—involuntary or voluntary—our social realms of rules and tacit knowledge would look completely different. Attention is the invisible glue holding together the social, the ethical, and the legal, making a life together bearable and, to some extent, predictable. It follows that how attention is expressed and experienced online will play an important role in how we perceive others as social and moral agents.

4. Other-Oriented Attention in Online Environments

In the offline realm ('IRL', or 'in real life'), we pay attention to whomever we choose, but, at the same time, much of our attention is hijacked by the awareness that spontaneously orients us to those who seem important for us to notice (again, this is a trained capacity shaped by the history of interactions we underwent, but it is still spontaneous). The gift of attention to someone else is simple and unmediated; a mere gaze suffices to acknowledge or ignore the others, or a spoken word lets others know that they are being noticed or ignored. What happens with this other-oriented attention when we engage in online interactions that are, by definition, always mediated by interfaces? There are two distinctive features of other-oriented attention online that deserve elaboration, as these features make the experience of paying attention to another distinctive: attention as a deliberate signal and the rigid saliences of online social platforms.

4.1 Rigid Salience Hierarchies

In 2015, an American dentist shot a lion during a hunting trip in Zimbabwe. The lion, called Cecil, happened to be famous. A wave of outrage ensues after the killing as the hunter is identified and later admits to the deed. Hatred waves follow on social media, with people sharing Tweets about the hunter's identity; the dental practice receives bad reviews on Yelp, while the dentist gets death threats.[7] Even today, if one were to search for the dentist's name, the lion incident would surface again in all search engines, affording a repeated cancellation of the hunter. New generations can feel outrage repeatedly since they say the Internet never forgets. In 2023, a philosopher posts a picture of herself on Twitter, next to a picture of Hume, with the caption 'what we actually look like',[8] intended to show in a funny way how the classic image of philosophers has changed and, presumably, how their public image should also change. After this tweet, she experienced a wave of hate and threats from what has been called the Twitter 'manosphere', with people outraged mostly that such a young and beautiful woman would dare to consider herself as a philosopher. Needless to say, the hate reactions did not come from academics, who happen to have seen young female philosophers, but from outside the profession. The female philosopher had stepped on an old taboo of who gets to do philosophy and suffered backlash consequently. What do the lion hunter and the young woman philosopher have in common? Twitter awarded them with too much attention from people who felt offended and wanted to express it. The hunter-dentist was not on Twitter; his identity and deed were made famous by a celebrity's Tweet. Meanwhile, the woman philosopher was active on Twitter. The hunter-dentist was cancelled as a dentist due to a wave of moral outrage, as people felt rightful about the cause and encouraged each other to pile on the online hate on this person. The

---

7   BBC Trending (2015, July 29). How the internet descended on the man who killed Cecil the lion. *BBC*. https://www.bbc.com/news/blogs-trending-33694075. See also (Pichford, 2020) for an academic discussion of the waves of outrage around this incident.

8   D. Dixon (2023, May 11). Women philosophers in the Twitter 'Manosphere' (or, that light-hearted Hume tweet that ended in r*pe threats). *The Philosopher's Cocoon*. https://philosopherscocoon.typepad.com/blog/2023/05/women-philosophers-in-the-twitter-manosphere-or-that-light-hearted-hume-tweet-that-ended-in-rpe-thre.html

female philosopher met a different kind of hate, not moral outrage, but outrage nonetheless, as she dared to be visible and assume the identity of a philosopher. She experienced being the target of a digital swarm or 'online shitstorm', as Byung Chul Han has described the phenomenon (2017)—a coagulation of anonymous hatred that has no political force, intended to change nothing, but to 'strike individual persons, whom they unmask or make an item of scandal' (2017, p. 12). The two cases discussed became the recipients of too much online attention, with the collective waves of hatred and threats that followed. Something about their identity became salient and sticky such that nobody who found their names online could forget this or focus on something else. This is a particular feature of online social platforms: they make certain features of one's identity salient with no possibility to appeal or change.

In a paper on saliences and the ethics of attention, Ella Whiteley (2023) argues that minorities usually are subjected to unwanted attentional patterns from others, which make some features of their identity salient while disregarding other aspects. For example, women philosophers usually want their work to be discussed as philosophers, not as a token of a 'woman philosopher' work. In introducing one's work to others as a 'woman philosopher' or 'woman coder', one makes a person's feature extremely salient to the audience. Sometimes this salience is wanted by the person if she wants to be an example for others that women can be philosophers or coders. However, Whiteley argues that when others present and acknowledge someone as a 'woman philosopher', the gender gets more attention than the context requires. Whiteley argues that this can be a form of 'morally problematic attention' (Whiteley, 2023, p. 527) because one dimension (the gender, in this case) distracts the audience from other more important or relevant dimensions of the message (the philosophical content in this case).

Online attention poses a problem of rigid saliences that has ultimately moral consequences for how we recognize others. Inspired by Whiteley's approach, SMPs are attentional environments that favour such morally problematic attention patterns. The main mechanism here is that of placing certain features as highly salient to the detriment of other features. Attention is dynamic, and one of its main features is that it can rearrange saliences instantly: something important fades to the background, and something else gets to be in the centre of our focus.

But, since what we perceive about others online is signalled by them, either deliberately or involuntarily, we rely on the other's signals (posts, reactions, content) to form our impressions of them and to revise such impressions. But revising saliences becomes difficult when nothing is forgotten and people keep reminding each other of one person's traits. A man shoots a lion in Africa and posts a proud picture on Twitter with the trophy. A storm of outraged reactions follows. He takes down the picture and apologises, but it is too late. Those who reacted to the post will remember him as the lion killer. In Murdoch's example of the mother-in-law, saliences are subtly rearranged across time. As the mother-in-law notices more things about the daughter-in-law and as she reinterprets them, a new relationship emerges between the two. The daughter-in-law is rediscovered, and the mother-in-law overcomes her prejudices by forcing herself to pay attention. With the lion hunter, there is very little extra information online to pay attention to so that we can paint a more complex picture of the person. Even if he apologises publicly, this is not enough to change what we find salient about him: his murder of the lion. To change our mind about the hunter, we would need to continuously observe the lion hunter's actions until he discloses more about himself than what we knew, gathering clues and reinterpreting. The reinterpretation would require that we make the effort to overcome our prejudices and that the lion-hunter gives enough information about his character to paint a complex picture of the human behind the hunter-persona. Without this effort coming from both sides, the class-like features of a person (where class means here any broad category to which we can attribute them: gender, race, social class, political inclinations, etc.) will always be more salient online than their individuality. This rigid salience arrangement makes it very difficult to dynamically and spontaneously focus on other traits of an individual user that we know only through social media, thus bypassing the individuality feature of relational attention.

The main point here is not that we cannot pay attention to someone online as an individual, but rather that the kind of attention that grounds our relating to others as moral agents—by seeing more than they aim to disclose and by potentially reevaluating them, considering new information—is difficult to achieve in online social spaces. As online users of SMPs, we are all reduced to a handful of salient features attributed to us by others or that we perform ourselves in front of others (the lifestyle influencer, the health guru, the conspiracy theorist, etc.) because it is these features that get picked up by the algorithms that make our posts visible to others. Our online profiles turn us into simplified sketches of who we are, almost caricatures. As Lucy Osler argued (2021), online empathy is possible in principle if enough effort is granted, and this should be the case with online attention awarded to others. Hyper-visible users like Donald Trump or Elon Musk are almost identical to their public persona. We know almost nothing about the real people behind those users. We could try to piece the puzzle by paying attention to every digital trace they leave, puzzling all the information about them, and looking for things they disclose unwittingly. But how much effort and time would this need? Meanwhile, having the real Donald Trump or Elon Musk in front of us would allow us to pay attention to them spontaneously while seeing more than they intended to signal about who they are. The issue is not that the online world is world-poor, but rather that there is too much signal-rich information going on in the online space, and we cannot help but pay attention to this information. We are all 'inforgs' (Floridi, 2009), meaning we are highly skilled at harvesting and interpreting information surrounding us. In the online realm of SMPs, all information coming at us is curated to be interesting and relevant to us hence we cannot ignore it. Adapting a phrase from the title of a book by Jonathan Safran Foer, the online information we get about others is 'extremely loud and incredibly close'. In such a strong stream of signals we get about others, the more subtle cues that would have picked up our attention—the embodied cues of tone of voice, gaze, and gestures—are lost and fade to invisibility.[9]

---

9   One could object that only the platforms relying on written messages and static images have this problem with asymmetrical and rigid attention to the other. Video streaming platforms such as YouTube or TikTok promise a more genuine access to the other's self, albeit this is always performed to some extent, as influencers curate their videos as much as they do their posts and images. A fundamental problem with video recordings of others remains the lack of reciprocity. The YouTubers seem to look at their audience, but there is no exchange of gazes. One large part of the ethics of attention to others is the potential for reciprocity: the other can gaze back, speak back, and suddenly we are the objects of their attention. With SMPs this is unlikely, albeit not impossible. The moral relations into which we need to enter with others are devoid of reciprocity, spontaneity, and recognition, which threatens to reduce us all to some rigidly salient features.

4.2 Online Attention as a Mediated Signal

All our online interactions are mediated by the platform's affordances (buttons, links, and fields to fill in), so that the attention to other users is expressed in a mediated way. To give an example: I may pay attention to all of my friend's updates on Facebook, keeping up with her life and worrying about her, but if I do not engage with these updates (by liking or commenting on them), my friend will have no idea about my attention awarded to her online. I need to deliberately signal my attention by interacting with the platform in a publicly visible way. Otherwise, my attention is not relational, and my friend will have no idea about my online gaze fixated on her. Without signalling my attention and thus affording reciprocity from the one gazing at me, my attention awarded to another looks more like stalking or watching from a panopticon tower. In stalking, I fixate my attention on someone who cannot answer my gaze because they have no idea they are being watched in the first place. I could, of course, let my friend know in real life that I am following her posts and I am concerned about her. This would be a form of reparatory attention after the actual attention has been awarded. This is possible when our relations with others happen both online and offline, but when relations happen only online, this cannot happen.

Attention awarded to another online user is voluntary and deliberate. Many interactions with content also count as awarding someone our attention: reacting to their posts (usually with an emoji reaction such as a like or heart, but any other emoji counts as attention), commenting on their posts (with words but also with a gif or a meme), mentioning them in one's public posts, linking to their posts, sharing their posts (citing them or retweeting, depending on the platform), making a video essay about someone else, or making a parody of their content. All these forms of paying attention range from a simple reaction to more sophisticated creations of content, but all involve deliberate launching of signals in the digital environment. Online attention to another is carried by various signals such as messages, reactions, and posts. Hence, we need to invest some deliberate effort in awarding this attention, and this removes some of the spontaneity involved in acts of effortless attention. To turn my gaze to someone in an offline environment, I do not need to think about it; I just do it, and then maybe I realise that it was impolite to stare at them like this if they also react with a gesture or a gaze directed at me. But to react with a like to someone's post, I have to click on a button. Even if liking or commenting does not involve much deliberation, as I can do it very fast, it is still more under my control than the spontaneous turning of one's gaze. This means that my attention to another is a deliberate choice I make each time I engage with another user's content. Meanwhile, ignoring another is the default option when we are online. We cannot be expected to signal attention to everyone we come across online through their digital content. The default action is to not like, comment, or click on their posts. This does not mean that we are ignoring others, as we are still aware of their online presence, but that this non-reaction is the default mode we engage with others online. Imagine if non-engaging was the default mode in how we related to others offline.

Online attention to one another is effortful, as each signal for attention must be carried through various actions. The effort we put into signalling our attention to others may vary and depend on our willingness to engage. We can pay attention to their content as well as to some embodied ways in which they act online—for example, how fast someone types, their hesitant messaging as they type and delete, as discussed in Osler (2021)—but this comes with a cost in energy that offline spontaneous attention does not seem to demand. There are also effortful ways of paying attention in the offline realm. When someone is speaking in a crowded bar, I hear their words, and I strain for them, but the noise is also competing. In the end, my attention will be exhausted. In online social spaces, the main question for our attention is: for whom are we willing to make the effort to signal our attention? While we will try to pay attention to our friends, we are not inclined to do so for strangers we find online. It is possible to pay attention to all the users we are subscribed to on SMPs, but it needs to be voluntary and expressed so that the other sees it. In addition to the costs in the effort for awarding voluntary attention, SMPs are environments where others constantly bid for everyone's attention. For many people, posting on an SMP is to get as much attention as possible and eventually become an influencer.

Influencers and celebrities are constantly harvesting attention from everyone without even trying because their posts become visible due to the algorithms that promote certain posts to many users. Whatever

Donald Trump or Elon Musk may post gets shared regularly and liked even when it may be meaningless. Another category is temporary attention attractors: someone who becomes the target of collective outrage or of being cancelled. These people do not want the attention they get from others, but after the online swarms of outrage are formed, it becomes very hard to immerse back into anonymity (Han, 2017). Both these kinds of unwanted and wanted attention to the attractors have no clear moral relevance. Attention awarded to influencers is not a recognition of their moral agency, only their social status, with no moral weight tied to this. When Trump or Musk receive thousands of likes to their posts, it does not mean that they are exemplary figures in any way, nor that people endorse their utterances. A like granted to a post usually means that we find it interesting enough that others should see it (Arielli, 2018), so we raise its visibility in our network.

Online attention as a mediated signal gives rise to a paradox: we need to deliberately and effortfully signal our attention to those we follow online, such that they can reciprocate our attention, thus allowing for relational attention to form; however, there is a threshold of online visibility from which no reciprocity can be reasonably expected. If we like or comment on a tweet of Elon Musk's, we cannot realistically expect any recognition from Musk due to the sheer number of likes he gets for each tweet. Once an influencer strains from their public image and tries to say something dissonant, they will receive backlash from their followers. We recognize the influencer's visibility, but not necessarily their moral agency since none of our usual signals of online attention create any reciprocity. This is problematic because, in the long run, we may be tempted to treat them as performers, as non-human entities that are there for our entertainment alone.

Social media platforms mediate other-oriented attention and the experiences that trigger it. I have tried to argue that this mediation is problematic insofar as other-oriented attention is needed for ethically relating with others as moral agents. In the two cases of Cecil's shooter and the woman harassed on Twitter, there is no denial of their moral agency; on the contrary, their moral agency is over-emphasized as their whole identity is reduced to a single act that cannot be forgotten. For Cecil's shooter, there is no reparation possible in front of the online crowd, no matter how much he apologised later. His identity cannot be reconfigured in a Murdochian way based on further moral perception and new signals that he gives; he will remain frozen in this identity of Cecil's shooter.

Conclusions

The attention we pay to others online is a systematic misreading of who they are, in which we either over-identify with them (as is the case with influencers, giving rise to parasocial relations for their audience) or we reify them. The distance between us and others, which is required to enable tension for ethical relating, is undermined. What ensues between users is not dynamic tension. We polarize our gaze: either the other is an alien, or they are just like us but in an overly identifying way. Too much distance from another or too close. Granted, this kind of misreading does not occur when we know the other users from offline life since offline settings give us more information about the other and allow the other to interact with us. For the woman harassed on Twitter for being a philosopher, there was no moral outrage since what she did was not immoral in any way; it was just hatred expressed in violent ways. Something about her manner of appearing in the online space was moralized as if it was an infringement of something unspoken, and then she was judged and condemned by the online crowds. Things about their identities become all too salient to the crowds' attention, and no further signals are effective in changing the focus of attention. Once you become viral, you are condemned to be remembered in a certain way, which directs the online crowds' attention to most future interactions. Thus, the kind of dynamic and spontaneous attention that allows one to reevaluate another's moral character and deeds—as described by Murdoch in the interaction with the mother-in-law and the daughter-in-law (2014)—is refused to those with the unfortunate fate of becoming viral. This threatens their moral agency differently than being ignored in real life—namely, their subsequent actions become invisible, as does their identity change. Attention online is remarkably sticky, rigid, and one-directional as it gets carried by deliberate signals to which we must constantly try to give rise. Every interaction with online others is like playing an attention lottery: how the others interpret our attention remains a mystery beyond our control since we are missing the embodied cues that would allow us to spontaneously recognize the other as an equal we can empathize with. Establishing an embodied empathy and a gaze exchange are not sufficient on their own to ensure that we get the right kind of attention that grounds moral recognition, but rather these act as fail-safes to ensure that something or our moral agency gets across to the others. In the absence of our embodied presence, the online audiences get to choose which aspects or our identity get reified beyond our intention or control.

References

Alfano, M. (2016). *Moral psychology: An introduction*. Polity Press.

Arielli, E. (2018). *Sharing as speech act. Versus*.

Bombaerts, G., Anderson, J., Dennis, M., Gerola, A., Frank, L., Hannes, T., Hopster, J., Marin, L., & Spahn, A. (2023). Attention as practice: Buddhist ethics responses to persuasive technologies. *Global Philosophy, 33*(2), 25, https://doi.org/10.1007/s10516-023-09680-4

Brady, W. J., Gantman, A. P., & Van Bavel, J. J. (2020). Attentional capture helps explain why moral and emotional content go viral. *Journal of Experimental Psychology: General, 149*(4), 746–756, https://doi.org/10.1037/xge0000673

D'Angelo, D. (2020). The phenomenology of embodied attention. *Phenomenology and the Cognitive Sciences, 19*(5), 961–978. https://doi.org/10.1007/s11097-019-09637-2

Dennis, M. J. (2021). Towards a theory of digital well-being: Reimagining online life after lockdown. *Science and Engineering Ethics, 27*(3), 32, https://doi.org/10.1007/s11948-021-00307-8

Fisher, M. (2022). *The chaos machine: The inside story of how social media rewired our minds and our world*. Little Brown and Company.

Floridi, L. (2009). Web 2.0 vs. the semantic web: A philosophical assessment. *Episteme, 6*(1), 25–37, https://doi.org/10.3366/E174236000800052X

Fogg, B. J., Cueller, G., & Danielson, D. (2007). Motivating, influencing, and persuading users: An introduction To captology. In A. Sears & J. A. Jacko (Eds), *The human-computer interaction handbook* (2nd edition, pp. 133–147). CRC Press.

Fredriksson, A. (2022). *A phenomenology of attention and the unfamiliar: Encounters with the unknown*. Springer, https://doi.org/10.1007/978-3-031-14117-1

Gallagher, S. (2020). *Action and interaction*. Oxford University Press.

Gallagher, S. (2022). *Phenomenology*. Springer, https://doi.org/10.1007/978-3-031-11586-8

Greenfield, S. A. (2015). *Mind change: How digital technologies are leaving their mark on our brains* (1st edition). Random House.

Han, B.-C. (2017). *In the swarm: Digital prospects*. MIT Press.

Harney, M. (2020). Perception and its objects. In A. Daly, F. Cummins, J. Jardine, & D. Moran (Eds), *Perception and the inhuman gaze: Perspectives from philosophy, phenomenology, and the sciences* (pp. 109–127). Routledge.

Hoffner, C. A., & Bond, B. J. (2022). Parasocial relationships, social media, & well-being. *Current Opinion in Psychology, 45*, 101306, https://doi.org/10.1016/j.copsyc.2022.101306

Klenk, M. (2022). (Online) manipulation: Sometimes hidden, always careless. *Review of Social Economy, 80*(1), 85–105, https://doi.org/10.1080/00346764.2021.1894350

Jacobs, H. (2021). Husserl, the active self, and commitment. *Phenomenology and the Cognitive Sciences, 20*(2), 281–298, https://doi.org/10.1007/s11097-020-09706-x

Jennings, C. D. (2020). *The attending mind* (1st edition). Cambridge University Press, https://doi.org/10.1017/9781108164238

Koralus, P. (2014). The erotetic theory of attention: Questions, focus and distraction: The erotetic theory of attention. *Mind & Language, 29*(1), 26–50, https://doi.org/10.1111/mila.12040

Mackenzie, C. (2019). Feminist innovation in philosophy: Relational autonomy and social justice. *Women's Studies International Forum, 72*, 144–151, https://doi.org/10.1016/j.wsif.2018.05.003

Murdoch, I. (2014). *The sovereignty of good*. Routledge.

Osler, L. (2021). Taking empathy online. *Inquiry*, 1–28, https://doi.org/10.1080/0020174X.2021.1899045

Panizza, S. C. (2022). *The ethics of attention: Engaging the real with Iris Murdoch and Simone Weil* (1st edition). Routledge, https://doi.org/10.4324/9781003164852

Panizza, S. C., & Hopwood, M. (2022). *The Murdochian mind* (1st edition). Routledge, https://doi.org/10.4324/9781003031222

Pitchford, M. C. (2020). The empire of outrage: Topical systems at the death of Cecil the lion. *Quarterly Journal of Speech, 106*(2), 156–178, https://doi.org/10.1080/00335630.2020.1744033

Raskoff, S. Z. (2022). Nudges and hard choices. *Bioethics, 36*(9), 948–956. https://doi.org/10.1111/bioe.13091

Roholt, T. C. (2023). *Distracted from meaning: A philosophy of smartphones*. Bloomsbury Academic, https://doi.org/10.5040/9781350172685

Smith, D. L. (2020). *On inhumanity: Dehumanization and how to resist it*. Oxford University Press.

Timms, R., & Spurrett, D. (2023). Hostile scaffolding. *Philosophical Papers*, 1–30. https://doi.org/10.1080/05568641.2023.2231652

Van De Poel, I., Frank, L. E., Hermann, J., Hopster, J., Lenzi, D., Nyholm, S., Taebi, B., & Ziliotti, E. (Eds). (2023). *Ethics of socially disruptive technologies: An introduction* (1st edition). Open Book Publishers, https://doi.org/10.11647/OBP.0366

Watson, G. (2013). Moral agency. In H. LaFollette (Ed.), *The international encyclopedia of ethics* (1st edition). Wiley, https://doi.org/10.1002/9781444367072.wbiee294

Watzl, S. (2017). *Structuring mind: The nature of attention and how it shapes consciousness* (1st edition). Oxford University Press.

Watzl, S. (2022). The ethics of attention: An argument and a framework. In S. Archer (Ed.), *Salience* (1st edition, pp. 89–112). Routledge, https://doi.org/10.4324/9781351202114-6

Watzl, S. (2023). What attention is. The priority structure account. *WIREs Cognitive Science, 14*(1), e1632, https://doi.org/10.1002/wcs.1632

Wellner, G. (2014). Multi-attention and the horcrux logic: Justifications for talking on the cell phone while driving. *Techné: Research in Philosophy and Technology, 18*(1), 48–73, https://doi.org/10.5840/techne201432712

Whiteley, E. K. (2023). 'A woman first and a philosopher second': Relative attentional surplus on the wrong property. *Ethics, 133*(4), 497–528, https://doi.org/10.1086/724538

Williams, J. (2018). *Stand out of our light*. Cambridge University Press.

Wu, T. (2017). *The attention merchants: The epic scramble to get inside our heads* (1st Vintage Books edition). Vintage Books.

Zahavi, D. (2014). *Self and other: Exploring subjectivity, empathy, and shame* (1st edition). Oxford University Press.

10. Three Embodied Dimensions of Communication: Phenomenological Lessons *for and from* the Field of Augmented and Alternative Communication Technology

Janna van Grunsven, Bouke van Balen, and Caroline Bollen

Introduction

Phenomenologists understand human beings as 'always already' intertwined with a meaningful world that is intersubjectively constituted and shaped by the affordances of tools and technological systems.[1] To take this intertwinement seriously is to recognize that there is an ineluctable link between how human beings experience other people and the sociomaterial world at large, and how they relate to themselves. People are, to speak with Maurice Merleau-Ponty, 'destined to the world' where it is 'in the world that [they] know [themselves]' (2012, lxxiv). As Merleau-Ponty has compellingly argued, *human embodiment* plays a vital role in the constitution of this experiential interconnectedness of

---

1   To be sure, we can adopt a scientific perspective onto the world, maximally stripped of any traces of subjectivity, for legitimate explanatory purposes. But the world that we experience in our everyday lives is a world shot through with significance; a world that we perceive in terms of the countless possibilities for action, interaction, and engagement afforded by the things and people around us.

self, other, and world. To capture this, he moves us away from a picture of the body as a 'mere physical object among objects', towards a view of the body as 'our general means of having a world' (2012, 147). From a phenomenological Merleau-Pontyan perspective, the body is a site of lived experience and expressive intentional agency. The body, thus understood, is connected to the world through countless 'intentional threads' that are enriched, extended, and maintained via interactions with other people as well as through embodied sensorimotor processes of habituation that enable the incorporation of tools and technologies into the body's 'schema' (Merleau-Ponty's familiar example is that of the blind person's cane, which, during active embodied manipulation, extends a person's experience of the perceived environment and of itself as an agent within that environment).

In the flow of everyday experience, we are typically not thematically aware of the constitutive role played by our embodiment in how we relate to the world and, by the same token, to ourselves. Hence, to make the implicit explicit, Merleau-Ponty and many contemporary phenomenologists with him turn to limit cases in which the dynamical embodied interplay between self and world is in some sense compromised. By pushing the limits of human experience, cases such as illness (Carel, 2016), depression (Ratcliffe, 2014), solitary confinement (Guenther, 2013), or a global pandemic (Van Grunsven, 2021) can reveal structures of ordinary experience that are usually taken for granted but that, when brought into view, can be appreciated for their profound existential significance. Limit cases, in other words, help 'loose[n] the intentional threads that connect us to the world in order to make them appear' (Merleau-Ponty, 2012, p. xxvii).

In this chapter, we too focus on a limit case. Specifically, we turn to the lived embodied experiences of people who are unable to use (some of) their bodily expressive resources due to congenital or acquired disability. People who find themselves navigating these communicative challenges often use some form of *augmentative or alternative communication technology* also called AAC tech. Think of picture boards, communication-supporting apps, eye-tracking technology, or, more recently (and still in the early stages of development and validation),

Brain-Computer Interfaces (BCIs) used for communication.[2] By incorporating AAC tech into their sensorimotor body schema, AAC tech-users can access new ways of relating to the world and to themselves as expressive communicative agents, thus enriching and diversifying their communicative lives.

That said, AAC tech usage can also be experienced as limiting, constricting, and narrowing a communicator's self and world relation. This depends in part on the design of a given AAC tech and its ability to appropriately reflect a user's communication needs. Currently, much AAC tech is designed to restore or augment people's communicative resources by facilitating information-transmissive speech acts that convey propositional content through words or images. Think of the computer-generated utterance 'I am thirsty' being produced by selecting an image of a cup of water or by spelling out a series of letters selected from a screen. Being able to convey such propositional information is undeniably important for AAC tech-users, supporting them in many daily practical activities and increasing their physical safety (cf. Beukelman & Mirenda, 2013). However, if phenomenologists like Merleau-Ponty are right, then interpersonal communication reaches far beyond the transmission of propositional content and is deeply embodied. To highlight the embodied dimension of interpersonal communication, Merleau-Ponty introduces the term *intercorporeality*. Intercorporeality refers to the 'pre-reflective intertwining of lived and living bodies, in which my own is affected by the other's body as much as his by mine, leading to an embodied communication' (Fuchs, 2017, p. 200). In this chapter, we articulate three dimensions within the phenomenon of intercorporeality or 'embodied communication', to put it more colloquially. These dimensions become perspicuous by combining insights from phenomenology with testimonial insights gleaned from the lived experiences of AAC tech-users. We will refer to these dimensions as *embodied mutual address, embodied enrichment*, and *embodied diversity*.

---

[2] In the United States alone, 2 million people make use of AAC tech 'to gain access to their human and civil right to communicate'. *National Institute on Deafness and Other Communication Disorders* (2022, July 20), https://www.nidcd.nih.gov/directory/united-states-society-augmentative-and-alternative-communication-ussaac

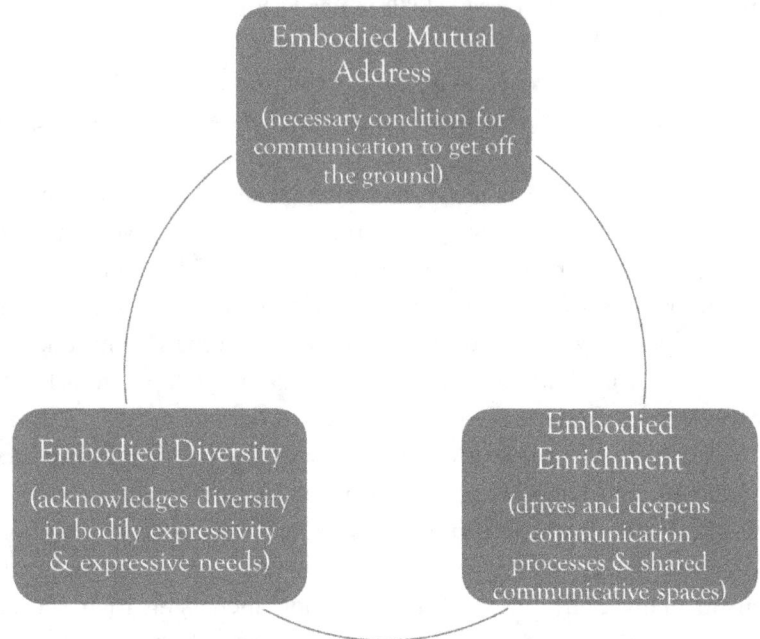

Fig. 10.1 Diagram illustrating the three interrelated dimensions of embodied communication. Figure created by authors (2024).

We propose that these three dimensions are vital for a robust understanding of the notion of embodied interpersonal communication and the existential significance it holds in human life. These embodied dimensions, which are overlooked when we understand communication primarily as the transmission of propositional content through speech, can have significant implications for the experience, design, policy, and socio-ethical decision-making surrounding AAC tech. As such, our chapter is in part a call for those working in the field of AAC tech to learn from phenomenological insights regarding the rich concept of embodied communication. These phenomenological insights are in part borrowed from Merleau-Ponty, but we also incorporate insights from Edmund Husserl as well as contemporary phenomenological thinkers. While we turn to phenomenological insights regarding embodied communication in order to reflect on the potential and limits of AAC tech, we simultaneously deepen the concept of intercorporeality (or embodied communication), within which we distinguish the above-mentioned three dimensions, in light of testimonial evidence provided by AAC tech users. As such, our chapter also calls on phenomenologists to attend to the lived experiences of people whose embodied and technologically-mediated lives are situated differently from those whose embodiment is more in line with what is typically considered as 'normal'.[3] In doing so, our chapter also takes a critical look at the methodological use of disabled embodied communication as a 'limit case'. More specifically, we problematize the use of disabled embodied communication as a limit case *understood primarily in terms of experiential deficiency or lack* and how it falls short of the 'normal'.[4] Instead, via the notion of embodied diversity, we propose an engagement with disabled embodied communication that takes seriously the rich lived experiential perspectives of those whose expressive bodily lives are lived on the margins of what is typically considered 'normal' and the diversity of ways in which technologies can be incorporated into the lived communicative body. Although our discussion is focused on a niche subfield of communication technology, we believe that our insights—much like other insights that have been gleaned from phenomenological discussions of limit cases—can be applied more broadly, offering a fine-grained embodied perspective on a range of mainstream and emerging communication technologies.

Smiles and Blinks: The Significance of Embodied Mutual Address

As mentioned, we will introduce *embodied mutual address, embodied enrichment,* and *embodied diversity* as three vital dimensions of embodied communication, which can inform how people experience, design, evaluate, and implement technologies that purport to mediate between people in communication. We begin, in this section, with the notion of embodied mutual address.

---

3   In that sense our chapter aligns with the project of critical phenomenology (cf. Guenther, 2021; Young, 1980).
4   The status of limit cases in Merleau-Ponty is complicated. While we can find reductive gestures in his work, he equally insists on the importance of understanding the lived experience of illness on its own terms, i.e., in its full existential significance, and not just in terms of what it is lacking in contrast with 'the normal'.

1. The Phenomenon of Embodied Mutual Address

Mutual address is constitutive of communication. That is, in order for your communicative acts to contribute to a communicative exchange, these acts need to be 'taken up' by a social other who sees you and who is seen by you as a minded subject whose communicative acts in turn warrant a response. Husserl articulates this point when he states, 'in an act in which one I addresses the other [...] I see the other as seeing and understanding me, and it is further in this that I "know" that the other in turn also knows himself as seen by me' (Husserl, 1973, p. 211). Husserl highlights that such mutual address requires 'engaged listening', where the addresser's expressive acts in turn 'motivate' a responsiveness in the addressee to genuinely engage 'with the aim of what is communicated' (Husserl, cited in Meindl & Zahavi, 2023). This makes acts of mutual address beholden to normative standards, where we can, in the midst of a communicative exchange, succeed or fail to properly attend to the other's communicative efforts. As our discussion below will indicate, such successes and failures can occur within multiple strata of embodied communication.

One's orientation towards the other, attending to her (listening to her, seeing her) as someone who aims to communicate something to us worth attending to, requires a particular stance towards the embodiment of the other.[5] The communicative other's body must be seen as more than a 'mere physical object among objects' (a *Körper*); it has to be seen as the expressive locus of an inner life (a *Leib*), as 'the place of a certain elaboration and somehow a certain "view" of the world' (Merleau-Ponty, 2012, p. 369). That is, the 'bodily comportment' of the addresser must be able to express a desire to communicate, which must be visible, and the bodily comportment of the addressee must be able to convey to the addresser that their act of address has been taken up—that they are heard or seen as an expressive communicator (Meindl & Zahavi, 2023). In the flow of everyday interaction, many of us can take for granted that our body is indeed seen by others in this way. It is predominantly in limit cases, discussed below, that the human body's primordial visibility

---

5   This is especially the case when communication unfolds in-person, but, as Lucy Osler convincingly discusses (2021), it is even the case in digitally-mediated 'offline' forms of communication.

as lived is replaced with a stance towards the body as first and foremost a 'mere' physical object. Typically, *when things go as they should*, we are directed at the body of another (and the other is directed at us) as the locus of personhood, where the other's bodily behaviour and expressive gestures are directly seen and felt as imbued with psychological meaning. In Merleau-Ponty's words:

> the communication [...] of gestures comes about through the reciprocity of my intentions and the gestures of others, of my gestures and the intentions discernible in the conduct of other people. It is as if the other person's intentions inhabited my body and mine his. (Merleau-Ponty, 1962, p. 215)

In the course of everyday communication, people are typically attuned to and invested in the embodied expressive other as an addressable interlocutor, who, in turn, shapes the addressee, 'co-determin[ing] me in his gaze, touch, attitude, etc' (Fuchs & De Jaegher, 2009, p. 477). To flag, the phenomenon of *embodied diversity* (section 4, below) complicates the picture of effortless embodied communication sketched here.

As Merleau-Ponty already argued, and as many developmental psychologists have concurred, this attunement to the other's expressive body as addressable is manifest from early childhood onward (Merleau-Ponty, 1963; Reddy, 2008; Trevarthen, 1979; Tronick, 2007). Developmental psychologist Vasu Reddy draws attention to the experience of being the target of address:

> The breath-catchingness and warmth in receiving [a] smile are likely to be rather different from *observing* that smile directed at someone else. [...] Not only is the experience of the other person more immediate and more powerful in direct engagement, but it calls out from you a different way of being, an immediate responsiveness, a feeling in response, and an obligation to 'answer' the person's acts. (Reddy, 2008, p. 27)

Whatever else happens once we've answered the call of second-person address and we (attempt to) enter into a more sustained communicative process, the very moment of mutual embodied address is significant in its own right. Reddy links it to 'a different [responsive] way of being' and Husserl, at times, characterizes it as being *in contact*: 'in an act in which one I addresses the other [...] we understand each other and are spiritually together in mutual understanding, *in contact*' (Husserl, 1973b,

p. 211, our emphasis). Though touched on by Husserl, the phenomenon of *contact* has not received much phenomenological attention to the best of our knowledge.[6] Its fleeting and somewhat enigmatic nature makes it admittedly difficult to analyze in terms of structural experiential features. However, as we will now propose by looking at locked-in syndrome (LIS) as a limit case of embodied communication, the existential significance of contact—established in embodied mutual address—is hard to over-estimate.

2. The Breakdown of Embodied Mutual Address: The Case of Locked-In Syndrome

LIS is a rare medical condition most often caused by neurodegenerative diseases such as amyotrophic lateral sclerosis (ALS).[7] People with LIS have very limited muscle control and cannot move nor speak (anarthria). They do, however, have intact visual and auditory perception, consciousness, cognitive, and emotional abilities, and bodily sensations (American Congress of Rehabilitation Medicine, 1995).[8] In its most extreme form, i.e., when *complete*, LIS is characterized by a total loss of muscle-control, with even a person's eyes lacking the ability to blink.[9] In the future, people with complete LIS may be able to use a BCI to express some of their basic communication needs. BCIs are devices that can be controlled with brain activity in real time. It is, for instance, possible to control a computer with 'brain clicks' that are voluntarily generated by

---

6   Within the work of Husserl, the notion of 'contact' (or 'we-contact') doesn't appear as a recurring key technical term. In the *Oxford Handbook of Contemporary Phenomenology*, the notion of 'we-contact' is indexed only twice.

7   Numbers are estimated at 0.73 patients per 100.000 inhabitants in the Netherlands (Pels et al., 2017). ALS is a subtype of motor neuron disease (MND), which is sometimes also referred to as Lou Gehrig's disease.

8   We should note that it is not so straightforward to assess this 'inner intactness'. For instance, people who suffer from a stroke may transition from an unconscious coma towards a locked-in state (this was the case of Julia Tavalaro, discussed below). Moreover, in cases of ALS, there is a chance that patients develop comorbid neurological conditions such as dementia, which, when they become locked-in, is hard to assess.

9   There are three forms of LIS: classic, incomplete, and complete (Bauer, 1979). Physicist Stephen Hawking (1942–2018), who suffered from the neurodegenerative disease ALS, may be the most famous example of someone who was in *incomplete* LIS. He used AAC tech that he controlled with residual muscle control in his cheek.

the attempt to move a hand (Oxley et al., 2021; Vansteensel et al., 2016). Although this technology is still in its infancy, it is already allowing some research participants with LIS to produce speech-utterances without the usual requirement of moving their mouths, tongues, and breathing air through their vocal cords.[10]

If Merleau-Ponty is right about the body's constitutive role in our self and world relation, one would expect that being locked-in profoundly impacts upon a person's experiential life. Indeed, medical anthropologist Fernando Vidal, who works on the phenomenology of LIS, observes that 'for locked-in individuals, their medical condition represents a new manner of self-conscious existence and a novel experience of being in the world' (Vidal, 2020, p. 122). Devastatingly, one dimension of this new self and world experience recounted by many patients who recover from LIS is the experience of being treated as a mere physical object, not as an addressable subject (Nizzi, Blandin, & Demertzi, 2020).[11] The implications of finding oneself outside the space of contact, of *experiencing* one's own body as lived and addressable and yet *seen* by others as a mere Körper, is powerfully captured by Julia Tavalaro (1935–2003). Tavalaro became locked-in because of two strokes that paralyzed her from head to toe. For six excruciatingly long years, Tavalaro was misdiagnosed as being in a vegetative state (VS). VS and LIS are outwardly similar, in the sense that both conditions are characterized by the (near total) absence of motoric abilities and activity. However, whereas patients in VS have lost their conscious intentional directedness at the world as a space of meaning, a space where contact can be established, patients in LIS have not. For years, Tavalaro thus underwent the experience of being regarded as wholly un-addressable by her medical staff, hearing herself being referred to as 'the vegetable'. In her autobiography, which she was able to co-author using an AAC device called a 'switch-based scan', Tavalaro recounts the moment that one of her nurse practitioners finally recognized that she was in fact addressable:

---

10   For now, implantable speech-BCIs rely on large and heavy computers, which make them unfeasible for home-use.
11   This survey-study on the experience of personhood of people with LIS found that a large majority of the participants experience interactions that leave them feeling '"not respected as persons" but rather "treated as objects"' (Nizzi, Blandin, & Demertzi, 2020).

'Can you close your eyes, Mrs. Tavalaro?'

With these words, I am shocked back into reality. This is no dream. I'm actually *being spoken to*. I close my eyes. I open them and see Arlene's face.

'Can you blink twice?'

I do it. Silence fills the space between us. Her face shows shock and grief and happiness at once. In the previous six years, no one had thought to ask me these simple questions.

'Okay, Mrs. Tavalaro. I'd like you to respond with eye movements. Can you move your eyes up, like this?'

She rolls her eyes towards her forehead. I watch her do this. Then, with a quick movement of my eyes I feel my mind rise from the ocean depths of pain. For the first time in six years, *I feel whole*. (Tavalaro & Tayson, 1997, p. 121, our emphasis)

Here we witness a first-personal testimony of what it is like to go from being seen as un-addressable to establishing contact in mutual embodied address; to have one's blinks recognized as expressive and taken up by an other, whose face expresses in return 'with shock, grief, and happiness all at once'. As we saw earlier, Husserl proposes that the addresser and addressee unify when they are in contact. Tavalaro, who describes feeling 'whole' and attuned to reality again in the moment of contact establishing mutual embodied address, seems to suggest something more fundamental: not only do we unify with the other, but we also become unified within ourselves and with the world as a shared reality (recall Merleau-Ponty's claim that people are 'destined to the world' where it is 'in the world that [they] know [themselves]').[12] Talavaro's testimony urges us to take seriously that when a person finds herself outside the space of contact, when a person's bodily visibility as addressable is hidden from view, her grip on the experiential world and her grip on herself as a unified subject of experience are tenuous at best. By the same token, it urges us to recognize the deep meaning of what could easily be dismissed as a mere fleeting moment of embodied communication: in the blink of an eye, contact can be established through mutual embodied address. This contact has a profound existential significance, enabling not just an act of communicative exchange but unifying and reopening a locked-in person's compromised self and

---

12 This aligns with work from phenomenologists Richard Zaner (2003) and Lisa Guenther (2013).

world relation. Dramatically put, even though it only requires the smallest of gestures, what is at stake in the moment of embodied mutual address is, in a sense, *everything*.

3. 'I Wanna Be Able to Sound Sarcastic': How AAC Tech Constrains Embodied Enrichment

In the previous section we made a case for the transformative significance of contact, established through mutual embodied address. Being seen as a target of address and having one's response taken up by the communicative other seems capable of transforming one's experiential relationship to oneself and the world in profound ways. While address is, in that sense, *everything*, we must simultaneously acknowledge its limits. Mutual embodied address, established in a moment of contact, constitutes just the (enabling) beginning of embodied interpersonal communication. As Husserl proposes, 'every successful understanding of what occurs in others has the effect of opening up new associations and new possibilities of understanding; and conversely [...] every such understanding uncovers my own psychic life in its similarity and difference and, by bringing new features into prominence, makes it fruitful for new associations' (Husserl, 1960, §54). The enrichment of our understanding of the other, of our own psychic life and of 'new associations', described here by Husserl, is often unlocked through pre-reflective embodied processes of interpersonal responsiveness, with interlocutors perceiving and responding with near automaticity to the expressive embodied other. Unless our expressive resources are severely compromised, as for instance in the case of LIS, the lived expressive human body—unaided by additional expressive tools and technologies—shapes communicative processes in a vastly rich nuanced way, through:

- Movement, gesture, and positioning: e.g., pointing, waving, hugging, rocking, turning away, leaning in, etc.
- Posture: crouching, hunching, etc.
- Facial expressions: smiling, smirking, seducing, etc.
- Gaze (or the avoidance thereof)

- Sound: screaming, whispering, humming, laughing, crying, singing, etc.
- Tone: sounding funny, mad, engaged, etc.
- Rhythmic turn-taking (i.e., the temporal intervals with which we take up and respond the other's address), etc.

These expressions, movements, and rhythms are not mere 'bodily embellishments' of the content-transmissive speech acts that are typically highlighted when we think about communication and that figure prominently in AAC tech development (see Metzger et al., 2023). Perceived by the communicative other, they co-shape how communicative address is taken up and responded to in return. They inform the quality and direction of communicative interaction, as well as the ways in which we see the other, relate to ourselves, and attend to the world together. We introduce the notion of *embodied enrichment* to capture this embodied dimension of intercorporeality, where enrichment carries at least two meaningful aspects of communication: (1) embodied interaction *enriches* our individual experiential access to the world and the significances we perceive in it; (2) this experiential enrichment typically depends upon a mutual responsiveness to the mind-bogglingly *rich* array of expressive modalities that the human body is capable of.[13] Mentioning just a subset of the rich embodied expressions sketched above, Thomas Fuchs and Hanne de Jaegher, in their phenomenological analysis of intercorporeality, point out that:

> Grasping, pointing, handing over, moving towards, etc., are inherently meaningful and goal-directed actions [...] [that] invite a certain range of meaningful reactions (e.g., pointing to → gaze- following, handing over → accepting, moving forward → moving backward, etc.), *thus creating a common space of co-varying intentional movements*. (2009, pp. 470–472, our emphasis)

This common space of co-varying intentional movements, which presupposes the space of contact enabled by embodied mutual address,

---

13 In the field of 4E cognition, this is also referred to as *participatory sense-making* (De Jaegher & Di Paolo). We use the term embodied enrichment here for several reasons: (1) to emphasize that this concerns an embodied dimension of communication, (2) that what is at stake is enrichment, and (3) we also add two additional dimensions to the notion of enrichment in the next section that are not typically contained within the notion of participatory sense-making.

can depend enormously on the subtleties we can detect in one another's expressive bodies. It isn't just 'grasping, pointing, handing over, moving towards' that opens up a range of different communicative exchanges, it is grasping, pointing, and moving towards *in a particular way, with a particular rhythm and style*. There is, for instance, a perceivable qualitative difference (for those who possess the required visual machinery) between a grasping gesture performed with the intention to *compete* for an object versus the grasping gesture performed with the intention to *share* an object (Becchio et al., 2012). Such perceptually available subtle differences will have a decisive impact upon how we experience ourselves, others, and the interaction space in which we are embedded and to which we contribute as expressive interacting beings (Di Paolo & De Jaegher, 2007).

The frustration one can feel when losing access to one's rich range of expressive styles and habits, and the ability to fluidly respond to the bodily expressions of others, is captured powerfully by the late Colin Portnuff, a former software engineer and ALS patient who used his experience as an AAC tech user to educate AAC developers. Portnuff describes how many of the embodied dimensions of communication that typical communicators are able to take for granted are disrupted in AAC-mediated communication (e.g., eye-contact; the flow of rhythmic turn-taking; keeping up with the dynamics of group-communication). He also captures the embodied expressive limitations that he experiences as an AAC-user: 'I wanna be able to sound sensitive or arrogant, assertive or humble, angry or happy, sarcastic or sincere, matter of fact or suggestive and sexy' (Portnuff, 2006). Similar observations were made by two different AAC users interviewed by Caroline Bollen, one of the co-authors of this chapter:[14]

> sometimes people misinterpret what I think or how I feel when I'm using the [device]. I think it's because my body and my expressions don't always match what I'm saying. Sometimes people assume they know how I feel based on what my body is doing and they don't listen to what I'm telling them. One downside of the [device] is that it's hard to be expressive with it—for example to sound angry, sad, excited, etc. (Interviewee 1)
>
> What would make it so that I can identify with my device more would

---

14 The conduction of these interviews was approved by the Human Research Ethics Committee of TU Delft.

> be the possibility to change the intonation on the basis of the context. [...] Theoretically this is possible: there are three versions of [my device's] voice: a neutral one, a happy one, and a sad one. As far as I know there are no programs that make use of this, but I think it should be possible to indicate which emotion belongs to which part of the message. One could work with emoticons for extra accessibility.[15] (Interviewee 2)

While AAC tech has been invaluable in terms of supporting non-speaking people's communicative relations to the world, these testimonies underscore that this can nevertheless fall short of the embodied communicative enrichment many of us depend on for maintaining and deepening a successful communicative self and world relations. This will emphatically be the case if AAC design and research predominantly focuses on linguistic performance and propositional content-transmission, working with a limited conception of what it means to be a communicative self. We suggest that AAC tech, and communication technology more generally, should recognize (and be inspired by) the vast range of communicative resources that human bodies can be capable of and recognize the existential stakes of having access to these resources. This is not to say that this is altogether unacknowledged in the AAC space. In fact, there appears to be a growing interest in embodied enrichment, stemming in part from emerging technologies and developments in affective computing, which are opening up new affordances for communication (Feijt et al., 2023; Metzger, 2023). As we sketch in section 5, the analysis offered in this chapter can stand in the service of these emerging developments.

4. Embodied Communicative Diversity

It is imperative to be mindful of a danger when taking limit cases such as the ones described in the previous two sections as a methodological device for uncovering 'normal' experiential structures. The danger, perhaps lingering in our argument thus far, is that we end up underwriting the normativity of 'the normal'—that we see a limit case as merely a derivate form of 'full-fledged' communicative being-in-the-world. A phenomenological analysis of limit cases *can* but does not need to lead to such a reductive stance towards embodied communication—a

---

15 Translation from Flemish to English by Caroline Bollen.

stance that harbours problematic ableist biases.[16] One way to build upon phenomenological insights in order to circumvent such a narrow ableist stance on communication is by underscoring phenomenology's flexible expansive view of embodiment, according to which the embodied self's expressive resources are never fixed by what appears to be the 'natural' norm, but always capable of being extended and diversified through the habituated incorporation of tools external to the physical body. In the words of one of Bollen's interviewees, articulating the intimate connection forged between them and their AAC device, 'it's part of me. As time has gone by, I've seen it as my voice more and more' (interviewee 1).

We need not restrict ourselves to the modalities of (typically developed) unaided expression in order to identify and facilitate meaningful forms of communication and new ways of being as communicative selves. Recognizing this can help question normative biases that favour unaided expressivity, especially in their 'typical' form. If we don't attend to the diverse ways in which people can use their bodies to express themselves, we may be prone to thinking, for instance, that eye-contact or verbal expressions are necessary for communicative enrichment, or that rocking and flapping (examples of autistic embodied expressivity) are subpar or even pathological modes of expressivity. Such assumptions can, in turn, find their way into how AAC tech is designed (see Mankoff et al., 2010). Acknowledging and valuing the different ways in which people can be and thrive as expressive embodied beings is essential if AAC tech is to facilitate genuine communication, rather than enforce communicative norms that lead to 'neurotypical gatekeeping' (Bollen, 2023) or that are culturally hegemonic.[17]

In many ways, the field of AAC tech has already played an important role in accommodating and underscoring the validity of different communications styles and needs (Mirenda, 2009; Van Grunsven &

---

16 See Van Grunsven (2020) for a discussion of how different phenomenologically inspired approaches to autism can either harbour ableist tenets (as is the case in some of Shaun Gallagher's work) or embrace a neurodivergent perspective (exemplified in Hanne de Jaegher, 2013).

17 For an example of such a culturally hegemonic stance on what counts as meaningful language and expression, see Kim E. Nielsen's discussion of the significant role of sign-language in native American tribes and the Eurocentric dismissal and eventual eradication of this language (2012).

Roeser, 2022). In the context of non-speaking autism, for instance, it has signified a much more respectful alternative to the damaging practices of Applied Behavioral Therapy (ABA). ABA uses extensive 'positive reinforcement' strategies (sometimes subjecting young children to as much as forty hours of therapeutic intervention a week) in an effort to 'replace inappropriate behaviour', such as the rocking or flapping mentioned above, with 'socially accepted' forms of expression and communication.[18] In their blog post on the harm inflicted on autistic people through ABA therapy, Maxfield Sparrow writes:

> You want to always remember a few cardinal rules: behavior is communication [...] Communication is more important than speech. Human connection is more important than forced eye-contact. Trust is easy to shatter and painfully difficult to rebuild. It is more important for a child to be comfortable and functional than to 'look normal'.[19]

AAC tech, with its explicit emphasis on *alternative* communication strategies, has represented an important counter perspective on non-typical forms of communication that aligns with Sparrow's insistence on 'communication' as 'more important than speech'. That said, a significant amount of AAC interventions still prioritize speech acts. In a critical examination of this tendency, Donaldson, Corbin, and McCoy (2021) highlight the experiences of autistic adults who use AAC technology to complement speech in daily life. One of the trends they identify in their stories was an experienced pressure to use speech for communication rather than other modalities of communication, with one interviewee recounting:

> I learned to outwardly appear to speak well because there was a lot of social pressure to do so, but I was frequently being forced to speak when it was difficult. (Donaldson, Corbin, and McCoy, 2021)

Passages such as this one highlight that it is a common but mistaken view to assume that speech, when made available through technology,

---

18 The language of replacing inappropriate behaviour with socially accepted forms of communication is taken directly from the website of Autism Speaks, a deeply controversial and influential organization, largely responsible for the widespread availability, pursuit, and insurance coverage of ABA therapy in the US (See chapter 5 of Ashley Shew's *Technolableism*, 2023).
19 M. Sparrow (2016, October 20). ABA. *Unstrange Mind*.

is experienced as the preferred or even superior mode of communication for its users:[20]

> What makes communication successful for me is when I can use the method that works best for me in the moment, and when the other person just accepts that method. (Donaldson, Corbin, and McCoy, 2021)
>
> I love multimodal communication. My brain loves it. It is so much easier to communicate with multimodal communication. It is hard to try to force myself to one communication method when I can use multiple. Life is easier with multiple. Different methods have different advantage[s]. (Donaldson, Corbin, and McCoy, 2021)

Recognizing how wildly people's relationship to speech and their communicative styles and preferences can differ calls for a shift away from understanding AAC as an intervention aimed solely at restoring lacking abilities, towards an appreciation of AAC as a valuable extension of one's lived expressive body. Building upon that insight, the notion of *embodied enrichment*, as laid out in the previous section, should now itself be enriched, where we should refer to enrichment not in a twofold but in a fourfold sense:

1. Embodied interaction enriches our individual experiential take on the world.
2. This experiential enrichment typically depends upon a mutual responsiveness to the mind-bogglingly rich array of expressive modalities that the human body, unaided by technology, is capable of.
3. This rich array of unaided expressive modalities can take on many shapes, influenced by, among other things, factors of neurodiversity.
4. This expressive diversity should be acknowledged in technologies aimed at enriching people's expressive resources—technologies that the body, understood as lived, is able of to incorporate into its bodyschema, integrating it into a user's experiential self and world relation.

We propose that an appreciation of the diverse ways in which human

---

20   See Mel Baggs' video (Baggs, 2007), for their powerful message underscoring this point.

bodies can be expressive and communicative, paired with an appreciation of the (lived) body as a site of tool-incorporation, can highlight the powerful potential for AAC tech to introduce new creative modalities of communication without sustaining an ableist romanticized view of unaided, typically developed speech-oriented communication.

5. Some Practical Implications for AAC Tech

How can the AAC tech field (and its users) benefit from our theoretical-phenomenological account, which has highlighted three dimensions of embodied communication? We argue that the first dimension, the dimension of address, is crucial to highlight because it hammers home the profound existential significance of communication, which presupposes that one's body is seen by others as addressable. This dimension doesn't require much for its establishment. As we saw, a blink of an eye, when taken up by the other, can transform a locked-in person's experiential life, 'pulling them out' of a state of utter isolation and into a state in which they begin to feel like a 'whole person' again. This insight is not only phenomenologically illuminating, but it has consequences for how we engage with people who are compromised in their addressability and the importance we attribute to AAC-usage. Recognizing that the smallest of bodily exchanges, when constituting mutual embodied address, can have a profound bearing on a person's sense of self and openness to the world can affect the challenging process of deciding whether to pursue or forego a BCI intervention for a person with complete LIS, a decision that turns *in part* on the assessment of whether the form of communication that a BCI enables—which for now is still extremely cumbersome and minimal in terms of supporting embodied enrichment—is 'worth it'.[21] Beyond the case of LIS, AAC users with a variety of disabilities credit their AAC-usage with their becoming visible to others as addressable and within the space of contact. In the words of disability rights activist, AAC user, and AAC co-developer Michael B. Williams, his ability to use AAC to outwardly express his thoughts to others allowed him to 'demonstrate I am not the blob incarnate' (2012).

---

21 The existential significance of address could also help to explain the arguably surprising finding that people with LIS who are able to maintain minimal expressive resources still consider their quality of life to be fairly high (Lulé et al., 2009).

As we argued, while it is important to recognize the powerful existential meaning of establishing minimal communicative contact and being visible to others as an addressable embodied being, it is equally important to recognize how our communicative self and world relations depend upon embodied enrichment, facilitating reciprocal meaning-making. This has implications for the ways in which AAC tech is designed, including the kinds of expressive modalities that are prioritized. There continues to be a dominant emphasis on representational content-transmissive speech acts in the AAC tech space, where it is sometimes suggested that the availability of such speech acts suffices to fully 'restore' a person's lost access to communication (Van Balen et al., 2023). This is also reflected in how AAC tech is typically appraised. A recent meta-analysis showed that the way the 'success' of AAC technologies is measured predominantly focuses on the ability to make requests (Aydin & Diken, 2020). What is considered effectiveness in an 'intervention' is limited to this specific skill. This extremely narrow view of communication lacks much of what it means to be a communicative being. Relatedly, it threatens to dismiss potentially effective AAC technologies with significant communicative power if and when those technologies don't meet the requirement for the optimal making of requests. Crucially, the way the success of an AAC is measured and written about by researchers affects governmental and health insurance policy by informing technology assessment and appraisal, which, in turn, has been known to result in people being denied AAC devices (Romski & Sevcik, 2018). With its emphatic commitment to alternative communication, AAC technology should stand not stand in the way but should rather stand in the service of facilitating multimodal human communication in all of its rich facets. This can mean the difference between a person merely *surviving with* (*technology-mediated*) *speech* or a robustly *thriving with communication*.

The importance of pursuing multimodal forms of embodied communication is already acknowledged in some recent developments in alternative forms of technology-mediated communication, with, for instance, physiological biosignals such as heartbeat and respiration being used as sources of social information capable of opening new paths of interpersonal communication (Feijt et al., 2023). In a similar spirit, it is the expressed ambition of BCI-researchers Metzger et al. (2023) to build communication BCIs that acknowledge that 'speaking has rich prosody, expressiveness and identity that can enhance embodied communication beyond what can be conveyed in text alone' (p. 1037). With the notion of embodied diversity, we urge that efforts to enrich the design of AAC tech in multimodal ways means questioning ableist assumptions that can become operationalized in tech. This may require that technologists working in this space replace an emphasis on 'interventions', which often stem from an ableist mission of bringing disabled communicators into the space of 'the normal', towards an emphasis on what human-computer interaction researcher Rua Williams calls disability-led 'counterventions', which start emphatically from the lived experiences of disabled users rather than the normative assumptions from researchers (cf. Williams et al., 2023).

The phenomenologically inspired concepts introduced in this chapter can help to conceptualize such lived experiences and their implications for the design of AAC tech. In the course of everyday life, when things go as they should, mutual embodied address, embodied enrichment, and embodied diversity blend together in genuine communicative exchanges (see Fig. 10.1). But what the testimonials of different AAC tech users help to bring out is that these embodied dimensions of communication can come apart and fail to get off the ground in different ways. For instance, as we saw with Tavalaro, the experience of embodied mutual address can be established (and immensely important) without robust embodied enrichment being within reach. Likewise, a failure to recognize embodied diversity can set up asymmetrical communicative spaces in which some people are unable to express themselves in accordance with their expressive styles and needs, while this does not necessarily undermine embodied mutual address (that is, two interlocutors can continue to see each other as targets of mutual address while failing to find ways to engage in sustained embodied communication). At the same time, there are cases in which failures at the level of embodied diversity catalyze a full breakdown of embodied mutual address. This has occurred, for instance, in the context of autism. Autistic self-stimulatory behaviours such as rocking and humming (stimming) are now increasingly recognized as richly communicative (Kapp et al., 2019). Historically, though, it has been categorized as non-communicative and pathological, which, in turn, has contributed to the labelling of autistic people as non-communicative and non-addressable full stop (Van Grunsven, 2022). To the extent that AAC tech can embrace and mediate between divergent embodied communication styles, it thus has the potential to not only honour embodied diversity but also to help repair breakdowns in the very conditions necessary for someone to live a communicative life at all: embodied mutual address.

Consider, also, the way in which embodied enrichment and diversity, while ideally coinciding in real-life communication, can come apart. Embodied enrichment, phenomenologists have emphasized, often unfolds pre-reflectively, with communicative partners responding to each other's bodily cues and expressions with near automaticity and in a manner that contributes quietly to a shared mutually enacted relational domain. However, when two communicative partners exhibit communication styles, needs, habits, and preferences that are emphatically divergent from one another, one may feel oneself confronted with the challenge to resist habituated pre-reflective norms of embodied enrichment (e.g., expecting eye-contact, specific patterns of rhythmic turn-taking and distance-taking, certain intonation and cadence-styles to express emotion) in order to make room for embodied diversity. Recognizing this matters for the design of AAC tech. For instance, rapid advancements in machine learning seem to support functionalities that enable people with severe paralysis to use communication BCIs that augment expressed utterances with 'facial-avatar animation', enabling a person to express not merely that X but also their affective attitudes with respect to X (Metzger et al., 2023). Predictions made by a BCI about which affective states and expressive styles ought to accompany utterance X seem capable of contributing to BCI-mediated embodied enrichment. However, as BCI-made predictions about which affective states and styles ought to accompany a given speech act will, to an important degree, be built upon data sets that likely reflect neurotypical styles and preferences for affective expressivity, this creates a potential trade-off between the BCI facilitating experiences of embodied enrichment for some while also denying embodied diversity to others. Awareness of such trade-offs, which presupposes the conceptual distinction between embodied enrichment and embodied diversity, can open up choices at the levels of technological functionality and design that one otherwise might overlook.

In sum, insights pertaining to the failures and successes of embodied communication and the ways in which such failures and successes can come apart (or mutually reinforce one another) in the areas of embodied mutual address, embodied enrichment, and embodied diversity can fruitfully inform AAC tech design. In this chapter, we hope to have provided analytical tools that can stand in service of this work. At the same time, we call for further phenomenological research on the embodied dimensions of communication and the ways in which they are at play in the lives of AAC users. There are already many initiatives and methods aimed at better including AAC users in research and design processes as primary contributors (Beneteau, 2020). However, AAC tech users are still systematically excluded from research that is not directly related to AAC but that does inform how we theorize the nature and scope of human communication and our views about what it means to thrive as a communicator (Dee-Prince, 2021). We hope that the three dimensions of embodied communication that we have highlighted, and that we have arrived at in part through insights gleaned from the lived experiences of AAC users, can inform not only how AAC tech is designed and assessed, but also how we design and assess more mainstream communication technologies. Finally, we hope that the testimonials of AAC users, seen through the lens of phenomenological concepts and ideas, loops back into those concepts and ideas, thereby refining and diversifying our phenomenological understanding of the nature and meaning of human communication in all of its unaided and technology-aided complexities.

References

Aydin, O., & Diken, I. H. (2020). Studies comparing Augmentative and Alternative Communication systems (AAC) applications for individuals with autism spectrum disorder: A systematic review and meta-analysis. *Education and Training in Autism and Developmental Disabilities, 55*(2), 119–141.

Baggs, A. M. (2007). *In my language* [Video], https://www.youtube.com/watch?v=JnylM1hI2jc

Bauer, G., Gerstenbrand, F., & Rumpl, E. (1979). Varieties of the locked-in syndrome. *Journal of Neurology, 221*(2), 77–91, https://doi.org/10.1007/BF00313105

Becchio, C., Manera, V., Sartori, L., Cavallo, A., & Castiello, U. (2012). Grasping intentions: From thought experiments to empirical evidence. *Frontiers in Neuroscience, 6*(117), https://doi.org/10.3389/fnhum.2012.00117

Blackstone, S. W., Williams, M. B., & Wilkins, D. P. (2007). Key principles underlying research and practice in AAC. *Augmentative and alternative communication, 23*(3), 191–203.

Beukelman, D., & Mirenda, P. (2013). *Augmentative and alternative communication: Supporting children and adults with complex communication needs*. Paul H Brooks.

Bollen, C. (2023). Towards a clear and fair conceptualization of empathy. *Social Epistemology, 37*(5), 637–655, https://doi.org/10.1080/02691728.2023.2227963

Burwell, S., Sample, M., & Racine, E. (2017). Ethical aspects of brain computer interfaces: a scoping review. *BMC Medical Ethics, 18*(1), 1–11, https://doi.org/10.1186.s12910-017-0220-y

Cabrera, L. Y., & Weber, D. J. (2023). Rethinking the ethical priorities for brain–computer interfaces. *Nature Electronics, 6*, 99–101, https://doi.org/10.1038/s41928-023-00928-w

Carel, H. (2016). *Phenomenology of illness*. Oxford University Press.

Donaldson, A. L., corbin, e*, & McCoy, J. (2021). 'Everyone deserves AAC': Preliminary study of the experiences of speaking autistic adults who use augmentative and alternative communication. *Perspectives of the ASHA Special Interest Groups, 6* (2), 315–326, https://doi.org/10.1044/2021_PERSP-20-00220

Eilan, N. (2020). Other I's, communication, and the second person. *Inquiry*, https://doi.org/10.1080/0020174X.2020.1788987

Feijt, M. A., Westerink, J. H., De Kort, Y. A., & IJsselsteijn, W. A. (2023). Sharing biosignals: An analysis of the experiential and communication properties of interpersonal psychophysiology. *Human–Computer Interaction, 38*(1), 49–78.

Fuchs, T. (2017). Intercorporeality and interaffectivity, In C. Meyers, J. Streeck, & J. Scott Joradan (Eds), *Intercorporeality: Emerging socialities in interaction* (pp. 3–24). Oxford University Press.

Fuchs, T., & Jaegher, H. D. (2009). Enactive intersubjectivity: Participatory sense-making and mutual incorporation. *Phenomenology and the Cognitive Sciences, 8*(4), 465–486, https://doi.org/10.1007/s11097-009-9136-4

Gilbert, F., Ienca, M., & Cook, M. (2023). How I became myself after merging with a computer: Does human-machine symbiosis raise human rights issues? *Brain Stimulation, 16*(3), 783–789, https://doi.org/10.1016/j.brs.2023.04.016

Guenther, L. (2013). *Solitary confinement: Social death and its afterlives*. University of Minnesota Press.

Guenther, L. (2021). Six senses of critique for critical phenomenology. *Puncta: Journal of Critical Phenomenology*, 4(2), 5–23, https://doi.org/10.5399/PJCP.v4i2.2

Haselager, P., Vlek, R., Hill, J., & Nijboer, F. (2009). A note on the ethical aspects of BCI. *Neural Networks*, 22(9), 1352–1357, https://doi.org/10.1016/j.neunet.2009.06.046

Husserl, E. (1960). *Cartesian meditations*. Martinus Nijhoff.

Husserl, E. (1973). *Zur Phänomenologie der Intersubjektivität: Texte aus dem Nachlass, vol. ii, 1921–1928*. Springer.

Jaegher, H. D., & Paolo, E. D. (2007). Participatory sense-making: An enactive approach to social cognition. *Phenomenology and the Cognitive Sciences*, 6(4), 485–507, https://doi.org/10.1007/s11097-007-9076-9

Johar, S. (2016). *Emotion, affect and personality in speech*. Springer.

Kapp, K. S., Steward, R., & Crane, L. (2019). 'People should be allowed to do what they like': Autistic adults' views and experiences of stimming. *Autism*, 23(7), 1782–1792. https://doi.org/10.1177/13623613

Lulé, D., Zickler, C., Hä Cker, S., Bruno, M. A., Demertzi, A., Pellas, F., Laureys, S., & Kü Bler, A. (2009). Life can be worth living in locked-in syndrome. *Progress in Brain Research*, 177, https://doi.org/10.1016/S0079-6123(09)17723-3

Mankoff, J., Hayes, G., & Kasnitz, D. (2010, October 25–27). Disability studies as a source of critical inquiry for the field of assistive technology. Proceedings of the 12th International ACM SIGACCESS Conference on Computers and Accessibility, ASSETS 2010, Orlando, Florida, USA.

Maslen, H., & Rainey, S. (2021). Control and ownership of neuroprosthetic speech. *Philosophy and Technology*, 34(3), 425–445, https://doi.org/10.1007/s13347-019-00389-0

Meindl, P., & Zahavi, D. (2023). From communication to communalization: a Husserlian account. *Continental Philosophy Review*, https://doi.org/10.1007/s11007-023-09601-7

Merleau-Ponty, M. (1963). *The Structure of Behaviour*. Beacon Press.

Merleau-Ponty, M. (2012). *Phenomenology of perception*. Routledge.

Metzger, S. L., Littlejohn, K. T., Silva, A. B., Moses, et al. (2023). A high-performance neuroprosthesis for speech decoding and avatar control. *Nature*, 620(7976), 1037–1046.

Mirenda, P. (2009). Introduction to AAC for individuals with autism spectrum disorders. In P. Mirenda & T. Iacono (Eds), *Autism spectrum disorders and AAC* (pp. 3–22). Paul H Brooks.

Nielsen, K. E. (2012). *A disability history of the United States* (Vol. II). Beacon Press.

Nizzi, M. C., Blandin, V., & Demertzi, A. (2020). Attitudes towards personhood in the Locked-in Syndrome: from third-to first-person perspective and to interpersonal significance. *Neuroethics, 13*(2), 193–201.

Osler, L. (2021). Taking empathy online. *Inquiry*, 1–28.

Oxley, T. J., Yoo, P. E., Rind, G. S., Ronayne, S. M., et al. (2021). Motor neuroprosthesis implanted with neurointerventional surgery improves capacity for activities of daily living tasks in severe paralysis: first in-human experience. *Journal of Neurointerventional Surgery, 13*(2), 102–108, https://doi.org/10.1136/NEURINTSURG-2020-016862

Portnuff, C. (2006). AAC: A user's perspective [Video]. *AAC-RERC* Webcast series. Oregon Health and Science University, https://www.youtube.com/watch?v=ldXC3FbShn0

Ratcliffe, M. (2014). *Experiences of depression: A study in phenomenology*. Oxford University Press.

Reddy, D. V. (2008). *How infants know minds* (1st edition). Harvard University Press.

Romski, M. A., & Sevcik, R. A. (2018). The complexities of AAC intervention research: emerging trends to consider. *Augmentative and Alternative Communication, 34*(4), 258–264.

Shew, A. (2023). *Technoableism*. Norton Shorts Series.

Tavalaro, J., & Taylon, R. (1997). *Look up for yes*. Kodansha America Inc.

Trevarthen, C. (1979). Communication and cooperation in early infancy. A description of primary intersubjectivity. In M. Bullowa (Ed.), *Before speech: The beginning of human communication* (pp. 321–347). Cambridge University Press.

Tronick, E. (2007). *The neurobehavioral and social-emotional development of infants and children*. W. W. Norton & Company.

Vidal, F. (2020). Phenomenology of the locked-in syndrome: An overview and some suggestions. *Neuroethics, 13*, 119–143, https://doi.org/10.1007/s12152-018-9388-1

Van Balen, B., van Grunsven, J., Vansteensel, M., & IJsselsteijn, W. (2023). Brain Computer Interfaces: Kunnen breincomputers een stem geven aan niet-sprekenden? *Wijsgerig Perspectief, 63*(1), 16–23.

Van Grunsven, J. (2020). Perceiving 'other' minds: Autism, 4E Cognition, and the idea of neurodiversity. *Journal of Consciousness Studies, 27*(7–8), 115–143.

Van Grunsven, J. (2021). Perceptual breakdown during a global pandemic: Introducing phenomenological insights for digital mental health purposes. *Ethics and Information Technology, 23*, 91–98.

Van Grunsven, J. & Roeser, S. (2022). AAC technology, autism, and the empathic turn. *Social Epistemology, 36*(1), 95–110.

Van Grunsven, J. (2022). Enactivism and the paradox of moral perception. *Topoi, 41,* 287–298, https://doi.org/10.1007/s11245-021-09767-w

Vansteensel, M. J., Pels, E. G. M., Bleichner, M. G., Branco, M. P., et al. (2016). Fully implanted brain–computer interface in a locked-in patient with ALS. *New England Journal of Medicine, 375*(21), 2060–2066.

Wickenden, M. (2011). Whose voice is that?: Issues of identity, voice and representation arising in an ethnographic study of the lives of disabled teenagers who use Augmentative and Alternative Communication (AAC). *Disability Studies Quarterly, 31*(4).

Williams, M. B. (2012). How far we've come, how far we've got to go: Tales from the trenches [Video]. https://www.youtube.com/watch?v=f14uio_2tNk0

Williams, R. M., Boyd, L., & Gilbert, J. E. (2023, April). Counterventions: A reparative reflection on interventionist HCI. In *Proceedings of the 2023 CHI Conference on Human Factors in Computing Systems* (pp. 1–11). ACM.

Young, I. M. (1980). Throwing like a girl: A phenomenology of feminine body comportment motility and spatiality. *Human Studies,* 137–156.

Zaner, R. M. (2003). Sisyphus without knees: Exploring self-other relationships through illness and disability. *Literature and Medicine, 22*(2), 188–207.

Epilogue

Jochem Zwier and Bas de Boer

In circling back to where we started, this volume took Martin Heidegger's and Maurice Merleau-Ponty's phenomenological responses to Edmund Husserl as a point of departure. We deemed it relevant to begin there, since Heidegger's prioritization of practical involvement in being-in-the-world, Merleau-Ponty's emphasis on bodily involvement, as well as the way these authors address these issues as pertaining to how the world appears, decidedly bring phenomenological inquiry to bear on technology. It is accordingly no surprise that the question concerning technology becomes a central concern for Heidegger, and that the relation between the being of the body and the being of the world occupies Merleau-Ponty at considerable length. Neither is it a surprise that the philosophy of technology has taken many cues from the works of these authors, as evidenced by the frequent occurrence of references in postphenomenology's followers and detractors.

This of course tells a rather orthodox or traditional story of the way philosophy of technology and phenomenology came to meet, with the protagonists being the usual suspects (Husserl, Heidegger, Merleau-Ponty). Although not particularly original in this sense, our approach has the advantage of offering an introduction to readers that are less familiar with the affair of phenomenology and the philosophy of technology, while simultaneously asking how the work of contemporary phenomenologists of technology relates and responds to these traditional figures. As mentioned in the introduction, we considered it sensible to categorize these responses along the lines of method (how does phenomenology access or approach technology?); technology as phenomenon (what does it mean to take technology as phenomenon, rather than as something else?

How does it appear as object?); and praxis (what do phenomenological inquiries bring to bear on technological practice or practices?).

Given this approach and way of structuring, the present moment calls for posing the evaluative question as to whether our approach was fruitful. What do we learn when surveying the contributions that make up the present volume?

A first lesson consists in the observation that, similar to what Friedrich Nietzsche once remarked about the will: phenomenology only appears singular as a term. This is to say that when reading through this book, one encounters many perspectives that all make reference to phenomenology in highly divergent ways. While some authors take phenomenology to mainly refer to the careful examination of lived experience, others read it through a more hermeneutic and even socio-historical lens, while still others seek to infuse phenomenology with other empirical methods from science and technology studies (STS), media studies, and sociology. If the present volume adequately captures the lay of the land, we learn that a central, overarching perspective on 'the' phenomenological method or 'the' way of inquiry is no longer sought after. Rather than extensive discussions on the ultimate ambitions of phenomenology as a way of philosophical inquiry, we encounter a variety of approaches that draw on and borrow from phenomenological insights. It thus appears that we have considerably strayed from Husserl's endeavour to develop phenomenology as a 'rigorous science' (Husserl, 2002) that would offer a transcendental foundation for all the other sciences.

Perhaps we must no longer speak of phenomenology of technology, but of phenomenologies of technologies. While a proper evaluation of this development lies beyond the scope of the present volume, we can draw attention to two noteworthy aspects. On the one hand, it could be argued that the current, somewhat loose and pluralized way of practicing phenomenology carries the merit of opening novel avenues for questioning technology, and of extending inquiries into different technological domains including medical contexts and the uses and abuses of social media. It could be argued (as has repeatedly been done) that such extensions of phenomenology have the merit of carrying phenomenology away from the abstractions often preferred by academic discourses to domains where technological phenomena are routinely encountered in practice.

On the other hand, and this brings us to a second lesson, we can also observe an increasingly distinct reaction to the aforementioned pluralization of phenomenology. As noted in the introduction, this reaction is anticipated by the critique of postphenomenology's empiricism, as found in attempts to rehabilitate technology as an ontological, specifically Earthly or planetary, theme. The methodical chapters of the present volume further demonstrate this reaction, as it is becoming increasingly clear that next to ongoing pluralizing and interdisciplinary approaches, the 'classical' phenomenological question concerning the whole of being is resurfacing. We are thereby reminded of Heidegger's statement that 'metaphysical inquiry must be posed as a whole and from the essential position of the existence (*Dasein*) that questions' (1998, p. 82), of Merleau-Ponty's project where 'the essential is to know precisely what the being of the world means' (1968, p. 6) and, with respect to technology specifically, of the notion of standing reserve, which for Heidegger 'designates nothing less than the way in which everything presences (*anwest*)' (Heidegger, 1977, p. 17). We here find 'whole' and not 'wholes', we read 'the being of the world' and not 'beings of the worlds', we read about '*the* way' (*die* Weise) and not ways.

Does this then imply the return to Heidegger's characterization of the technological whole understood as standing reserve, as expressed in the example of the airliner that is 'ordered to ensure the possibility of transportation. For this it must be in its whole structure and in everyone of its constituents parts, on call for duty, i.e. ready for takeoff' (Heidegger, 1977, p. 17)? As the chapters from the section on method demonstrate, this revisiting of this traditional phenomenological theme does not simply imply the restoration of what Heidegger and Merleau-Ponty said. Rather, what appears to be resurfacing is a renewed questioning of how this whole and its relation to technology must be thought. For one, it remains questionable whether one can speak of living in *a singular* whole or whether pluralism fractures this. Further, the question becomes how the whole must be characterized: must it be addressed as world? As Earth? As Epoch? As historical-hermeneutic coherence? Must technology be pluralized as many technological things themselves? Or does technology found a whole in the sense of a planetary, now increasingly necessary geo-engineered whole? Whatever the answers, it can at least be surmised that the present volume documents both the ongoing pluralization of phenomenological approaches to technologies as well as attempts to address technology as a whole.

A third lesson concerns the political. In the philosophy of technology, it has by now become a common trope to refute ideas about technologies being politically neutral instruments wielded by subjects who would bear exclusive political agency. From Langdon Winner's identified racist bridges to algorithms of oppression, from planned obsolescence to hostile design, the statement that technologies 'have politics' or at least carry political relevance has more or less become a truism. Various chapters collected here similarly make the passage to the political, whether in terms of material hermeneutics, the de-politization and re-politization of social media, the way phenomenology can be combined with activism, or the outsourcing and therefore becoming political of reproduction. It may thus be clear that the phenomenological perspectives presented in these pages are not isolated to theoretical labour but also engage political practice. That said, a couple of observations must be made on this point.

Although we find numerous analyses of how phenomenological analysis of technology lays bare a political dimension belonging to technology, we do not find a sustained and systematic treatment of said dimension. It is one thing to argue that technologies mediate how political issues arise (just think of self-driving cars and accountability, just think of vaccination and mandates, etc.), it is quite another to ask what a 'political issue' means from a phenomenological perspective, what exactly is experienced when something is regarded or phenomenologically 'intended' as being 'political', or how being-in-the-world relates to being-in-the-polis. While such questions are of course beyond the purview of this book, it does indicate a point of contention that may be worth exploring further. It is perhaps remarkable that, in discussing political aspects, all the authors of the present volume argue that phenomenology is too limited and lacks the wherewithal to address political issues. One calls for a more socio-culturally sensitive material hermeneutic, another for a combination of phenomenology and critical theory, yet another seeks to infuse phenomenological analysis with explicitly ethical concepts of dignity and flourishing. It appears that phenomenology's *analytically descriptive* forte limits its *politically prescriptive* relevance.

This situation is not new. Phenomenology has often been accused of lacking political and ethical thrust. Authors like György Lukács and Theodor W. Adorno have long since criticized the phenomenological method for precisely bracketing everything political. From a materialist-dialectical perspective, phenomenology may ask *how* something appears, but tends to overlook the fact that this 'how' is thoroughly embedded in relations of production. Yes, a phenomenologist can elucidate the fore-understanding at play upon entering a classroom by explicating how, before any explicit or formal cognitions, we have always-already understood where students are to sit and the lecturer to stand. Yes, a phenomenologist can characterize how all these items in the classroom (lectern, chairs, tables) are primarily practically grasped as for-something and thus exist in an equipmental totality that is encountered before said items appear as distinct objects for a theoretical gaze. Yet this says nothing of the exploitative labour that makes the lecterns, chairs, tables, etc. possible. It says nothing about where the wood for the tables is sourced from. It says nothing about the pollution resulting from the production process.

Furthermore, phenomenology has often been criticized for its focus on experience as individual experience. Husserl famously grappled with the relation between his notion of the *ego* and the question of intersubjectivity. Heidegger indeed speaks of being-with and being-alongside others in his descriptions of how *Dasein* navigates the world, but mostly emphasizes individual existence, for instance in how mortal *Dasein* must face its potential death on its own, a 'mineness' that first individuates *Dasein* as a singular, authentic entity. Merleau-Ponty's focus on the body and concomitant distinction between the lived body (*Leib*) and body-as-object (*Körper*) similarly seems to prioritize individual experience. For all its merits, it is not difficult to see how this individualistic focus can serve as an obstacle to traversing to political questions that are necessarily intra-individual, or even how phenomenology could be criticized as ideological in the sense that in merely looking at individual experience, it quietly accepts the place of this individual in society.

These admittedly reductive portrayals of phenomenology and its political critiques reflect a tension at the heart of phenomenological analysis and political praxis. The chapters that touch on the political in this book appear to grapple with the same tension. It would of course be folly to attempt to solve or dissolve this tension here. The lesson rather seems that this tension continues unabatedly in contemporary phenomenology of technology, leading to the question of how it can be rendered fruitful.

Given this tension, it is all the more striking that the name of Bernard Stiegler remains largely absent in these pages. Striking, because Stiegler's oeuvre is on the one hand clearly rooted in the phenomenological tradition, whilst on the other hand informed by more (post)structuralist, anthropological, and ultimately psycho-analytical approaches. Through the fusing of these traditions, Stiegler seems to offer a systematic framework for integrating phenomenological analysis of technology with renewed political praxis, notably a praxis of care. In closing, it is worth exploring this somewhat further as it offers a potential marriage between phenomenology and having an explicit eye for sociopolitical concerns.

Stiegler ends the introduction to his first book *Technics and Time I* by stating that his work 'call[s] in question Heidegger's claim that "the essence of technics is nothing technical (1977, 35)"' (1998, p. 18).[1] He makes this claim, however, on the basis of a dialogue with phenomenology. One of the key entry-points to his analyses of technics is Husserl's *Crisis of the European Sciences* from which Stiegler derives that 'the technicization of science constitutes its eidetic *blinding*' (Stiegler, 1998, p. 3). As mentioned in the introduction, according to Husserl, the work of Galileo marked a break with the lifeworld— it turns a blind eye to the lifeworld by creating a world exclusively understood in mechanistic and scientific terms. As Husserl describes, whereas initially it was clear that Galileo's arithmetic descriptions of the world were to be understood as idealizations quite different from the world in which they originate, modern philosophy endowed these idealizations with metaphysical primacy, such that their connection with the lifeworld was lost (Husserl, 1970, p. 90, p. 221). The forgetting of this initial connection is the ground of Husserl's diagnosis that the European sciences are in crisis.

---

1   We limit ourselves here to how Stiegler takes inspiration from phenomenology in the *Technics and Time* series, which arguably lays the foundation for his philosophy.

Stiegler builds on Husserl's diagnosis and connects it to Heidegger's characterization of modern technology as enframing. On the one hand, Stiegler maintains that Husserl's diagnosis according to which modern science forgets its connection with the lifeworld is intensified in Heidegger's assessment of modern technology as enframing, where the forgetfulness of being characteristic of Western metaphysics finds its culmination and is therefore 'the extreme danger' (Heidegger, 1977, p. 28). On the other hand—and this is why this forgetfulness manifests experientially—the existential constitution of *Dasein* takes place through its interaction with equipment, such that its relation with the world is always shaped through technicity (Stiegler, 1998, pp. 4–5). Here Stiegler is also inspired by phenomenology. Just as Heidegger, he understands humans as *Dasein* that is fundamentally temporal: 'it has a past on the basis of which it can anticipate and thereby be' (Stiegler, 1998, p. 5). Hence, existence is anticipatory existence, and how anticipation takes place is crucially structured by *Dasein's* interactions with technologies. Stiegler therefore speaks of 'technics and time'.

To further clarify this, Stiegler turns to Husserl's *On the Phenomenology of Internal Time Consciousness*. Through a critical reinterpretation of Husserl's notions of retention and protention, Stiegler attempts to characterize how technics structures anticipation, which eventually leads to the development of the notion of *tertiary memory*. According to Husserl, our perception of temporal phenomena must be understood as a process of modification, such that retentions and protentions are constitutive of present perception (Stiegler, 1998, p. 246). Husserl gives the example of hearing a melody: 'at any particular time there is always a tone (or tone-phase) in the now-point. The preceding tones, however, are not erased from consciousness. Primary memory of the tones that, as it were, I have just heard and expectation (protention) of the tones that are yet to come fuse with the apprehension of the tone that is now appearing and that, as it were, I am now hearing' (Husserl, 1991, p. 37, cited in Stiegler, 1998, p. 247). Stiegler generalizes this structure of retention-protention to the perception of any object—after all, to exist is to exist temporally, such that any perception is conditioned by the past as well as oriented towards the future.

Husserl makes a distinction between *primary* retention and *secondary* retention: the former refers to the lived experience of temporal extension by means of retentions in the here-and-now—like in the above example of hearing a melody *as* melody—whereas the latter is understood as a representation of an earlier perception and hence derivative (like in recognizing a melody as a theme from Beethoven, e.g., Stiegler, 2008, p. 6). According to Stiegler, however, temporality is to be understood fundamentally historically, which demands 'that the already-there is not lived but inherited, constituted outside any perceptions, [yet] nevertheless constitutive of presence as such—and this is why temporality cannot be conceived in terms of the "now"' (Stiegler, 1998, p. 248). In Stiegler's view, then, temporality is constituted through technics—through originary prostheticity. Technical objects are 'before anything else, memory' (Stiegler, 1998, p. 254): even basic flint tools already carry an exteriorized experience such as 'hammering', where this exterior memory trace can be passed on to be interiorized or re-membered by subsequent generations. Writing—that is to say, *memoirs*—can accordingly be seen as an explicit and obvious iteration of this exteriorization-interiorization dynamic that for Stiegler belongs to technics as such. This makes it so that our perceptions are grounded in retentions that we have technically inherited, which also constitute protentions and hence anticipation.

Stiegler's central term *tertiary memory* or *tertiary retention* denotes that the technical constitution of perception is thus clearly inspired by Husserl's phenomenology of temporal perception. At the same time, since this phenomenological constitution is carried by the memory-trace of technics, Stiegler can go on to fuse the phenomenological insight regarding temporality with political questions, which then circle around *caring* for the trace. If anticipation, retention, and protention are central to the existence of *Dasein*, and if these are not simply a-priori given but result from the re-memberance of technical memory traces, than both the care for these traces and the techniques of re-memberance become politico-ethical questions. We are of course reminded (no pun intended) of Plato's *Meno*, where knowledge is a distinct question of remembering and where upbringing or *paideia* can be understood as the art or technique of remembering well (e.g., Socrates helping the boy remember, midwifing the memory as it were). We are further reminded of the Stoa, where a right upbringing was considered in terms of remembering the *loci classici* (of, above all, Homer). All of these are instances of careful and attentive re-membering, and it is by means of these that we become individuated as well-formed individuals.

For Stiegler, such care and attention now become urgent questions in our time where, to put it bluntly, hyperindustrial technologies tend to capture care and attention, engendering not the individuation of well-formed individuals, but leading to disindividuation and therefore dehumanization. We may think of social media platforms that tends towards offering instant gratification, of repetitive video games that capture 'dopamine rush' attention while hardly inviting or even blocking the learning, careful re-membrance and therefore individuation to be gained from re-membering the lessons of Homer and Socrates. Here, Stiegler warns of the enormous danger of the disindividuated and therefore inhuman, and attempts to develop a countervailing politics of attention.

The intricacies of how toxic forms of attending to the technical memory-trace can be distinguished from curative ones cannot be covered here, but it may be clear that Stiegler's reading of phenomenology and its technical-memorial underpinning may open a way to more systematically address the aforementioned tension between phenomenology and the politico-ethical. We previously remarked that at least in the contributions collected here, a sustained examination of what 'the political' might mean from a phenomenological perspective on technology remains absent. For Stiegler, the phenomenon of the political or rather politico-ethical precisely becomes a technical phenomenon, both in the sense that the memory trace to be cultivated *is* technics (as tools, as buildings, as books, i.e., as recordings of culture so to speak) as well as the sense of developing techniques *against* the capture and short-circuiting of care and *paideia* by hyperindustry and contemporary media technologies, and *for* their cultivation.

In sum then, besides offering a documentation of present-day work in phenomenology and technology, the present volume demonstrates an ongoing discussion between the pluralization of phenomenologies of technology on the one hand and a singularization of *the* phenomenon of (planetary) technology on the other. It further demonstrates that wherever one lands with respect to this discussion, the passage to the political remains fraught with difficulty, which may explain why it is hardly undertaken in a systematic way, at least on the pages making up the present volume.

Were one to give this a positive spin, one could argue that being exhaustive was never on the list of ambitions for this book. This is to say that gathering together the present chapters' authors not only shows what is *actually* being worked on today, but also highlights a *potential* for further developments in the (political) phenomenology of technology. As suggested, the work of Stiegler may well open avenues for following up on this potential, avenues that will likely traverse the lands of critical theory as well, since the question of attention is also that of capitalism (e.g., hyperindustry) and of desire (e.g., culture-industry), two themes often addressed in Critical Theory. The fact that neither the latter nor Stiegler is frequently mentioned in these pages is perhaps best read as an invitation.

Phenomenology concerns the 'how' of how things appear. It may have become clear that this 'how' cannot be considered in isolation from technology. Yet it may also have become clear that this says very little indeed. If unhindered by stylistic concerns, one could say that the question remains how the 'how' of the technological phenomenon is to be addressed. Perhaps the 'how' primarily refers to a plurality of artificial things mediating how other things appear. Perhaps the world on a geo-engineered Earth attests to a singular mode of appearance. Perhaps how things appear depends on how one attends, cares, and re-members the memory trace by which appearance becomes possible. As the 'how' of the 'how' continuously changes in light of technological developments, phenomenology is perhaps never exhausted as Husserl had feared towards the end of his life, but instead is compelled to (re)invent itself ever anew.

References

Heidegger, M. (1977). *The question concerning technology and other essays* (W. Lovitt, Trans.). Harper.

Heidegger, M. (1998). What is metaphysics? (D.F. Krell, Trans.). In W. McNeill (Ed.) *Pathmarks* (pp. 82–96). Cambridge University Press.

Husserl, E. (1965). Philosophy as Rigorous Science. In Q. Lauer (Ed.), *Phenomenology and the crisis of philosophy*. Harper.

Husserl, E. (1970). *The crisis of the European sciences and transcendental phenomenology* (D. Carr, Trans.). Northwestern University Press.

Merleau-Ponty, M. (1968). *The visible and the invisible*. Northwestern University Press.

Stiegler, B. (1998). *Technics and time, 1: The fault of Epimetheus* (R. Beardsworth & G. Collins, Trans.). Stanford University Press.

List of Figures

Fig. 8.1	Instagram post by Cindy Sherman. Photo by Cindy Sherman (2020), public Instagram account, https://www.instagram.com/cindysherman/	p. 206
Fig. 10.1	Diagram illustrating the three interrelated dimensions of embodied communication. Figure created by authors (2024).	p. 244

Index

ableist bias 255, 258, 260
absence 21, 57, 113, 175, 190–192, 195, 201–205, 208–211, 238, 249, 272, 275
abstraction 3, 38–40, 44, 78, 86, 111, 122, 134, 146, 148–149, 268
acceptio 16–17, 35–45
access 19, 30, 33, 36–40, 45–46, 63, 75, 109, 137, 168, 243, 252–254, 259, 267
Achterhuis, Hans 134
action 8, 16, 19, 75–76, 85, 91, 102, 106, 108, 144, 149–150, 179, 196, 200, 202, 224, 235
activism 18, 97–99, 102–103, 106, 114–115, 258, 270
actor-network theory 15, 101, 104, 128
actuality-potentiality 81, 83, 90, 92, 146, 161, 191, 195, 200–201, 205–206, 210
Adorno, Theodor W. 138, 271
affect 41–42, 130, 150, 172, 216–217, 258
affective gaze 223
affective states 261
affordance 61, 108, 150, 229, 234, 241, 254
Agamben, Giorgio 46
agency 123, 128–129, 139, 216–217, 219–222, 226–229, 236–238, 242, 270
  agents 76, 128, 202, 216–217, 219–222, 224–229, 232, 236, 242–243
Ahmed, Sara 113
Akrich, Madeleine 109
Alfano, Mark 220–221
algorithm 2, 104–105, 108, 182, 233, 235, 270
alterity relations 167–168, 203
alternative communication strategies 256
alternative communication technology 21, 242
amyotropic lateral sclerosis (ALS) 248, 253
Anders, Gunther 156
animal nature 226
Anthropocene 12–14
anti-essentialism 98, 100–101
anti-foundationalism 98
appearance 5, 10, 13, 17, 43, 59–61, 78, 85–86, 90, 121, 204, 276
Arendt, Hannah 101
Aristotle 9
art 55, 68, 89, 92, 197, 205, 274
artefacts 10, 12, 15, 18–19, 27–30, 35, 42, 46, 54, 59, 68, 80, 108, 124–127, 131, 135, 139, 167, 179, 216, 221, 226
Artificial Intelligence (AI) 18, 20, 27–29, 34, 46, 49, 59, 68, 70–71, 165–166, 168, 171–173, 178–182
artificial wombs 143
artists 88, 189–195, 197–201, 203–204, 206, 208, 210–211
assisted reproductive technology (ART) 19, 143–145, 148, 154–155, 159–160, 162
attention 11, 20–21, 59, 92, 123, 125, 129, 134–135, 152, 158, 165–166, 174–182, 203, 209, 215–238, 247–248, 268, 275–276
augmented and alternative communication (AAC) 21, 242–245, 249, 251–262
augmented reality (AR) 168, 171
authenticity 196–197, 199, 211
automatic actions 228
automaticity 251, 261
autonomization 149–152
autonomy 58–59, 104, 124, 128, 152, 217, 219–221, 226

autonomy of technology 59, 128
awareness 113–114, 123, 176–177, 195–196, 217, 219, 227, 229

background relations 168, 192, 203–204, 210
Barad, Karen 102
being 2–16, 21, 28, 30–41, 43, 46, 48, 55, 57–61, 68, 70, 73, 75–79, 81, 85–88, 90, 97, 104, 107, 114, 125, 128, 131, 136–137, 140, 150, 152, 156, 174, 177, 179, 191–192, 195–199, 206–209, 211, 215, 219–220, 222–223, 225–229, 231, 234, 236–237, 243, 247, 249–250, 254–256, 259–260, 267, 269–271, 273, 275–276
being-in-the-world 4–7, 9–13, 31–33, 37, 137, 219, 225–227, 254, 267, 270
beings 6–7, 11–14, 21, 32–37, 39–41, 54–56, 58–60, 62, 104, 111, 131, 225, 227, 241, 253, 255, 269
bias 2, 29, 44, 48, 58, 66, 105, 111, 130, 132
biosignals 259
biosphere 46–47
bodily comportment 108, 246
body 7–9, 11, 19, 65–66, 84, 106, 143–144, 147, 157, 159, 161, 165, 167–172, 174–176, 180–183, 196, 208, 222, 225, 227, 242–243, 245–247, 249, 251–253, 255, 257–258, 267, 271
body schema 8, 11, 165, 167, 243
Borgmann, Albert 100
Bourdieu, Pierre 58, 101, 109
Braidotti, Rosi 182
Brain-Computer Interface (BCI) 243, 248, 258–261
Brentano, Franz 2
Burnham, Bo 190, 208–210

capacities 20, 85, 89, 165
capitalism 76–77, 101, 175, 276
care 21, 28, 151–152, 200, 208–209, 226, 272, 274–275

Cartesian worldview 7, 61, 83, 135
case studies 19, 122, 131–132, 166, 200
Cassirer, Ernst 63, 68
Castoriadis, Cornelius 74
causality 88
cell phones 172, 176–179, 182
challenging-forth 13, 145–146
Cheong, Marc 196
classical phenomenology 165–166, 168, 175–176, 181–182
climate change 48, 101
co-constitution 48, 78, 98–99, 104–106, 115, 191, 204
Coeckelbergh, Mark 109, 124
cognitivism 21
communication 21–22, 55, 62, 70, 84, 86, 242–248, 250–262
computer simulation 106
concretization 87–88, 90–91, 146–147, 161
conditioning 16, 83, 85–86, 129–130, 133, 137–138, 140, 273
conditions of possibility 30, 54, 66, 68, 71, 134
consciousness 4, 7, 22, 30–31, 45, 62, 79–85, 122, 128, 191, 194–196, 202, 218, 248, 273
consent 159, 217, 221
constitution 1, 3–4, 6–11, 19, 27, 29, 31–32, 44, 46–49, 58, 61, 78–81, 83, 86–87, 90, 98–99, 101–102, 104–106, 109, 115, 122, 124, 127, 135–136, 148, 154, 191, 204, 241, 251, 258, 272–274
constructivism 19, 111, 144–145, 147–148, 154, 156
content 17, 29, 31–32, 34, 39–49, 76–77, 83, 159, 172, 179, 189–190, 197, 199–200, 208–211, 220, 231–232, 234–235, 238, 243–244, 252, 254, 259
counterventions 260
crisis of the European sciences 272
critical phenomenology 97
critical theory 125, 270, 276

critique 3, 9, 18–20, 55, 58, 68, 70, 73, 78–80, 82–83, 98–102, 105, 114–115, 200, 269, 271
cryopreservation 149
cryptocurrency 20, 172–173, 181
  digital coins 172
cultural hegemony 255
culture industry 276
cyborg relations 64–65

DALL-E 172, 181
Dasein 5, 7, 54–55, 58–59, 269, 271, 273–274
data 3, 28, 49, 61, 105, 172, 261
decision-making 104–105, 221, 244
Deep Dream Generator 172, 181
deficiency 156, 245
dehumanizing gaze 223
de Jaegher, Hanne 252
delegation 173, 179
Deleuze, Gilles 173
democracy 16, 101
Derrida, Jacques 74, 84
design 16, 20, 79, 98, 104, 106, 108, 110, 114, 123, 172, 217, 243–245, 254, 260–262, 270
  design ethics 123
designers 16, 27, 59, 123, 171, 189–190, 192, 194, 197, 210–211
desire 155–156, 246, 276
determined negations 192, 202, 204, 210
developmental psychology 247
devices 46, 98, 105, 107–110, 114, 148, 151, 171, 175, 248–249, 253–255, 259
Dewey, John 105, 122
dialectics 19, 77–79, 144, 154–155, 191–192, 196, 200, 204, 207, 210, 271
digitality 135
digital power relations 191
digital technologies 27–28, 49, 108, 135, 165, 176, 181–183, 209
digital twins 28, 49

Dilthey, Wilhelm 63
disability 21, 109, 242, 258, 260
disabled embodied communication 245
disembodiment 153, 160, 170
disindividuation 275
disruptive technologies 27, 29, 32, 34–35, 216
dominant stabilities 19, 109–110
Dostoevsky, Fyodor 224
dystopian one-dimensionality 190

Earth 9, 14, 17, 35, 46–48, 170, 269, 276
ecology 17, 30, 34–35, 40, 42, 44, 46–49, 88–89, 101, 105–106
economy 2, 9, 21, 27, 54, 68, 158, 175, 198, 227
ecosystem 28, 46
Eco, Umberto 56, 62–63
education 104–106, 147
Ellul, Jacques 66
embodied diversity 21, 243, 245, 247, 260–262
embodied enrichment 21, 243, 245, 252, 254, 257–262
embodied ground for attending to others 226
embodied minds 225
embodied mutual address 243, 245, 248, 251–252, 260–262
embodied perception 20, 172
embodiment 7, 9, 11–12, 20–21, 67, 69, 74, 122, 165–168, 170, 172–174, 181–183, 203, 225, 241–242, 245–246, 255
embodiment relations 20, 166–167, 170
embrainment 20, 182–183
emerging technologies 30, 34, 48, 254
empathy 222, 224–225, 227, 233, 238
empirical philosophy 131
empirical turn 19, 42, 66, 122, 124, 131, 134, 139
empiricism 3, 15, 17, 19, 29, 42, 54, 66, 69–70, 79, 88, 91, 122, 124,

131–134, 136–140, 144, 146, 193, 200, 268–269
enactment 17, 31–33, 35, 41–44, 46–49
enframing 6, 11, 13, 144, 146–148, 150, 160–161, 273
engineering 37, 66, 144, 269, 276
entanglement 191–192, 194–195, 202, 204, 209–210
Entbergen (mode of revealing) 145
epistemic injustice 111
epistemology 111, 113–114, 122
epoché 30, 45–46, 48, 60, 65
equipmental totality 271
Esposito, Roberto 74
essence 10, 13, 22, 41, 55, 58–59, 67, 97, 154, 194, 196, 198, 207, 272
essentialism 1, 15–16, 29, 35, 41–42, 44, 48, 98–101, 124
establishment 73, 108, 258
ethics 2, 70–71, 102, 104–106, 114, 123, 215–217, 219–220, 231
 ethics of design. *See* design: design ethics
European Commission 28
existentialism 4, 63, 196, 200
existential phenomenology 191–192, 195
experience 1, 3–5, 7–11, 14–16, 20–21, 27–28, 30–32, 34–36, 38, 43, 45–46, 48, 56, 60–61, 75, 78–80, 82–85, 87–90, 97, 104, 106–108, 111, 113–115, 121–132, 134–135, 137–140, 147, 151, 156–157, 161, 165–168, 170–173, 175–179, 181–182, 190–192, 194–196, 200–202, 204–206, 208–210, 217–219, 222–227, 229–231, 236, 241–245, 247, 249–250, 253, 256–257, 260–262, 268, 270–271, 273–274
expression 32, 70, 74, 77, 84–86, 88, 91, 189, 191, 255–256
expressive human body 251
expressive modalities 252, 257, 259
extreme danger 273

Facebook 203, 234

facial recognition 114
factuality 30, 45
familiarity 7–9
Feenberg, Andrew 16, 19, 101, 143, 145–157, 161
feminism 102, 104, 111, 113–114, 144, 148, 158–159
feminist phenomenology 111, 113, 144, 159
field of awareness 113, 176
first-person perspective 20, 128–129
flow 85, 90, 113, 162, 242, 246, 253
foetuses 158
Food and Drug Administration (FDA) 144–145
foreground 177
for-itself 196, 200, 207
formalization 38–41, 131
Franklin, Sarah 76, 154–157, 162
friendship 1, 54, 155
Fuchs, Thomas 243, 247, 252
Fukuyama, Francis 198
fungibility 145–146, 148, 157–161

Gadamer, Hans-Georg 17, 53, 55, 60, 63, 71
Galilei, Galileo 272
Gallagher, Shaun 8, 222–223, 226
gaze 3, 91, 149, 175, 181, 217, 222–223, 225, 227–229, 233–235, 237–238, 247, 252, 271
Gegenstand 146
Gehlen, Arnold 9
gender 154–155, 158, 204, 231–232
general attentiveness 218
generalization 38–41, 122, 227
gesture 219–220, 235, 251, 253
Guattari, Félix 173
Gyngell, Christopher 144, 154

habit 7–8, 12, 57, 110, 115, 193, 201, 219, 253, 261
habitat 150
habituation 98, 108, 114, 242, 255, 261
Han, Byung Chul 231
Haraway, Donna 102, 111, 176

Harding, Sandra 111–112
Harman, Graham 126
Heidegger, Martin 2, 4–7, 9–11, 13–14, 16–17, 19, 28–38, 40–42, 44, 48, 53–55, 58–61, 63, 66, 71, 122, 135, 137–138, 144–148, 154, 157–162, 267, 269, 271–273
hermeneutic circle 33, 67
hermeneutic phenomenology 17, 29–30, 32–35, 40, 42, 44, 46–49, 54, 68–69, 169
hermeneutic relations 69, 167, 172–174, 183
hermeneutics 15, 17, 31, 34, 53–60, 62–63, 66, 68–71, 131, 202, 270
history 75–77, 80–83, 86, 88–89, 92, 108, 115, 137, 150, 160, 219, 229
homelessness 110, 114, 229
hostile design 110, 270
human condition 1, 156, 195–196
human-technology relations 10–12, 19, 21, 27, 29–30, 45, 98–99, 101, 107–109, 114, 122, 127, 129–133, 139, 193, 196, 203, 210
Husserl, Edmund 2–3, 7, 10, 14, 16, 20, 22, 30–32, 38–39, 41, 45–46, 54, 57, 64, 74–75, 77, 80–84, 90, 122, 127, 137, 166, 174, 202, 244, 246–248, 250–251, 267–268, 271–274, 276
hyperindustrial technologies 275

idealism 5, 17, 53, 57–60, 64–65
identity 1–2, 82, 153–157, 162, 191–192, 194–201, 205–206, 208, 210, 230–231, 236–238, 260
Ihde, Don 10–11, 20, 27, 29, 34, 53, 63–64, 66–67, 69, 98–100, 106–107, 115, 121–122, 125–126, 129, 131, 136, 165–170, 172, 191–195, 200–206, 210
imagination 20, 77, 79, 82, 91, 165–166, 168–174, 181–182
incorporation 8, 101, 242, 255, 258
individuality 228, 232
individuation 86, 90–91, 271, 274–275

industrialization 28, 148
influencers 233, 235–237
inforgs 233
information 1, 147, 179–180, 199, 223, 232–233, 237, 243, 259
Ingarden, Roman 54
in-itself 195, 207, 222
Instagram 189–190, 197, 201, 203, 206–207, 210
institution 17–18, 73–75, 77–92, 159, 178
instrumental explanation of technology 146
instrumentalization 6, 28, 147–149, 151–152, 156
   primary and secondary instrumentalization 148–149, 151–152
intention 58–59, 61, 67, 70, 76–77, 127, 131, 218, 238, 247, 253
intentionality 3, 7–10, 12, 30, 78, 128–130, 136–137, 166, 173–174, 202, 242, 249, 252
interconnectedness 28, 69, 225, 241
intercorporeality 243–244, 252
interdisciplinary approaches 98–99, 269
interpersonal communication 243–244, 251, 259
interpretation 20, 32–34, 53, 56–58, 61–63, 69, 87, 105, 149, 167, 169, 193, 198, 204
interpretivism 62
inter-relationality 128–129, 136
intersubjectivity 18, 83–84, 86, 90, 137, 198, 271
intuition 58, 84, 204
invention 41–44, 47–48, 83, 159, 179
invisibility 144, 161, 225–226, 229, 233, 237
in vitro fertilization (IVF) 143–146, 148–162
in vitro gametogenesis (IVG) 19, 143–146, 148, 150, 159–162
involuntary attention 219

Janus-faced technology 189
Jaspers, Karl 54

Kant, Immanuel 35–36, 171, 221
Kapp, Ernst 9, 260
Kehre 55
kinship 154–155, 162
Körper 84, 246, 249, 271
Körper-Leib distinction 271

language 19, 34, 60, 81, 84–85, 92, 169, 180, 193, 208
Latour, Bruno 128, 173, 179
layers-plateaus 174
Lefort, Claude 74, 82, 84
Leib 246, 271
Lemmens, Pieter 12–13, 48, 100, 125, 133–134, 199
Levinas, Emmanuel 222, 224
lifeworld 20, 67, 122, 124, 127, 131, 133, 137, 140, 148–149, 151, 169, 191, 195, 205, 272–273
limit cases 22, 242, 245–246, 248, 254
linguistics 29, 33–34, 53–54, 60, 63, 68, 254
lived experience 4, 9–10, 16, 21, 60, 165, 242–243, 245, 260, 262, 268, 273
locked-in syndrome (LIS) 248–249, 251, 258
Lukács, György 18, 74–75, 77–83, 86–87, 90, 271

machine learning 104–105, 261
macro-perspective 29
Marxism 78
Marx, Karl 9, 68
material 13, 17, 34–35, 39–40, 46–47, 53, 56, 63–68, 70, 76, 82–83, 85–87, 89, 91–92, 111, 122, 124, 146, 157–158, 160, 200, 202, 270
material hermeneutics 17, 34, 63, 202, 270
materiality 35, 40, 46–48, 54, 63, 70, 135
matrix 77, 79, 82, 85–86, 89–90, 181

McLuhan, Marshall 135, 198
meaning 1, 3, 5, 27–28, 31–35, 43, 53, 55–56, 59–61, 76–77, 79–82, 84–85, 89–90, 135, 159, 167, 169, 172–173, 180, 194–196, 198, 205, 221, 233, 247, 249–250, 259, 262
meaningful world 30, 34, 241
mediation 10, 17–19, 57, 69, 99, 103–106, 115, 121, 123, 125–131, 133, 136–137, 139, 151–152, 167, 170–171, 190, 192, 194, 204, 209–210, 236
mediation theory 99, 104–105, 190, 192, 210
medical anthropology 249
memory 157, 179, 273–276
mental health 193
Merleau-Ponty, Maurice 4, 6–9, 11, 14, 18, 20, 64, 74–85, 87–92, 122, 137, 166–167, 169, 174–175, 178, 181, 225, 241–244, 246–247, 249–250, 267, 269, 271
metaphysics 5, 28, 32, 41, 100, 123, 133, 138, 200, 269, 272–273
meta-stability 82
methodology 3, 14–18, 32–35, 37–39, 41, 44, 46, 48–49, 61, 63, 69, 71, 73–74, 76, 79, 82–83, 86, 121, 131–132, 135, 137–139, 144, 165, 192, 195, 199–200, 210, 257, 262, 267–269, 271
micro-perspective 29
milieu 7
mineness 271
moods 14
moral agency 216–217, 220–222, 224–229, 232, 236–238
morality 133
moral patiency 220, 226
moral relations 21
motherhood 147, 149, 151, 153, 158–160, 227–228, 232, 237
mother nature 153
movement 12, 14, 80, 146, 170–171, 175, 200, 250
multi-attentions 168, 176–178,

181–182
multimodal communication 257, 259–260
multistability 18, 98–100, 106–107, 109–110, 115, 132, 169, 190, 201
multi-tasking 20, 175–176, 179, 181, 215
Murdoch, Iris 227, 232, 237
Musk, Elon 233, 236

National Socialism 54
nature 19, 31, 38, 57, 60–62, 65, 69–70, 77, 84, 104, 125, 144–146, 149, 153, 156, 158, 161–162, 198, 226–228, 248, 262
Necker Cube 169–170
negation 192, 195, 200, 202, 204–205, 210
neural network 180
neuroscience 180
neurotypical gatekeeping 255
neutral tools 154, 199
new materialism 102, 104
Nietzsche, Friedrich 268
nihilation 195, 204, 208
noema 30, 45
noesis 30, 45
non-human entities 28, 36, 236
non-use 191, 201, 204, 210
normality 245, 254, 256, 260
normativity 70, 108, 246, 254–255, 260
nothingness (le néant) 20, 190–192, 194–197, 200–211
Notini, Lauren 144, 154, 160

objectification 19, 79, 90, 146, 152, 157, 161, 222
objectivity 2, 4, 8, 36–37, 58, 64, 69, 76–77, 82, 85–87, 89–91, 104, 112, 136, 140, 149, 174
object-oriented ontology 135
objects 3–5, 7–10, 13, 15, 18–19, 31–33, 39, 60–64, 68–69, 74, 78–80, 82–86, 89–91, 102–103, 107, 109–110, 113, 122, 126, 128–129, 132, 135–136, 139, 144, 146, 148–151, 153, 157–

161, 166, 171, 174–181, 195, 207, 216, 218, 221–224, 242, 246–247, 249, 253, 268, 271, 273–274
Obsolescence of Man, The 156
offline 209, 229, 234–235, 237
online others 237
ontic level 12–14, 16–17, 29, 32, 34–38, 40–42, 44–48, 53, 55, 58, 61–62
ontology 6, 12–14, 16–17, 28–30, 32, 34–37, 39, 41–45, 47–48, 53–55, 57–58, 61, 63, 66, 90, 92, 102–103, 122, 126, 128, 135, 137, 145, 154, 192, 202, 210, 269
openness 35, 61, 258
originary prostheticity 274
otherness 58, 61–62, 71, 170
other-oriented attention 21, 216, 222, 224, 227–229, 236
oversharing 209

painting 83, 87–88, 90–91
Panofsky, Erwin 63
passive synthesis 77, 81, 128
pathology 255, 260
Peirce, Charles Sanders 56, 61
perception 7–8, 19–20, 30, 36–38, 40–41, 44, 67, 69, 74, 88, 99, 106, 110, 113, 115, 149, 153, 169–174, 176, 181–182, 191, 193, 195–196, 216, 218–219, 225, 227, 237, 248, 273–274
peripheral vision 176
phenomenology of attention 21, 175, 217, 221–222
phenomenology of technology 15, 17, 28–29, 48, 54, 64, 68–69, 97, 144–145, 147, 159, 268, 272, 276
philosophy of technology 1–2, 6, 8–9, 12–19, 22, 48, 53, 58–59, 63, 66–67, 73–74, 78, 92, 103, 113, 122, 126, 131, 133, 137, 192, 267, 270
plandids 189, 206
plasticity 82
plateaus 20, 171, 173–174
Plato 274

plundering 159
point of view (POV) 58, 136, 149, 153, 169–171, 173–174
politics 2, 9, 17–19, 27, 70–71, 73–77, 79, 81–82, 85, 88, 91–92, 98–99, 101–103, 105–106, 109–111, 113–115, 123, 177, 198, 231–232, 270–272, 274–276
Portnuff, Colin 253
positive science 2–3, 15, 22, 30
posthumanism 66, 102
postmodernism 98, 171
postphenomenology 9–12, 16–20, 27, 29, 35, 48, 53, 63–69, 73, 97–115, 121–140, 165–166, 168, 170, 181, 183, 190–194, 199–203, 207, 210–211, 267, 269
potentiality 81, 83, 90, 92, 146, 161, 191, 195, 200–201, 205–206, 210
power 4, 68, 78, 85–86, 88–89, 99, 109, 111–112, 114, 127, 146, 151, 153, 161, 191, 259
practical involvement 267
pragmatism 10, 15, 17, 53, 55–56, 62, 66, 98, 100, 102, 122, 126–127, 130, 137, 177, 205, 210
pregnancy 143, 151–153, 156–158
prejudice 57–58, 99, 151, 227, 232
present-at-hand 5, 10, 36, 60
press, the 291
presupposition 2, 7–8, 14, 21, 30, 38, 41, 44, 59, 61, 78, 82, 122, 159, 174, 177, 218, 220, 252, 258, 261
primacy of perception 170–171, 182
production 19, 28, 90, 144, 150–151, 155, 158–159, 169, 271
propositional content 243–244, 254
prosthesis 65–66
protention 273–274
psychic life 251
psycho-analysis 272
psychological meaning 247
psychology 2, 15, 140, 193, 220, 247

quasi-disembodied perspective 170

racism 59, 99, 270
rationalization 29
ready-to-hand 5, 10, 60
reality 3, 6, 10–11, 13–14, 27, 30, 60, 65, 68–69, 71, 104, 138, 155, 168, 170–172, 181, 191, 199, 250
recognition 21, 114, 153, 179, 198, 225–229, 236, 238
Reddy, Vasu 247
relation 4, 10, 13–14, 17, 21, 27, 29–33, 36–37, 43–45, 57–58, 82, 84, 86, 89–90, 99, 108, 126–129, 132, 137, 175, 190, 196, 199, 201–205, 209–211, 223, 243, 249, 251, 257, 267, 269, 271, 273
relational approaches 136
relational ontology 103, 128, 192, 202, 210
relational strategies 108
representation 3, 8, 70, 105, 172, 274
reproductive body 19, 143–144, 146–148, 157, 160
reproductive enframing 147–148, 150, 160
responsibility 105, 123, 196, 205, 219–222, 228
retention 273–274
rhythms 252–253
Ricœur, Paul 53, 57–61, 68, 71, 198
rigid salience hierarchies 232
rigorous science 268
Rorty, Richard 62

salience 180, 218–219, 224, 228–229, 231–232, 237
sardine cans 66
Sartre, Jean-Paul 4, 20, 74–75, 189–205, 207–211, 222
Savulescu, Julian 144, 154, 160
scanning 175, 179
Scharff, Robert 29, 100, 138
Scheler, Max 54, 78
schematization 172
Schutz, Alfred 27
science 2, 9, 37, 70, 91–92, 97, 101,

111–112, 133, 140, 161, 268, 272–273
science and technology studies 101, 268
science studies 2
scientific gaze 3, 223
sedimentation 8, 84–85, 115
self 3, 13, 17, 19–22, 31, 33, 45, 56–59, 61, 64, 78, 123, 131, 146, 150, 152, 154–157, 161, 189, 191–192, 194–199, 205–206, 209, 211, 217, 225, 242–243, 249–250, 254–255, 257–260, 270
self-expression 189, 191
selfies 190, 206, 210
self-portraits 206
semiosis 56, 61
Sen, Amartya 198–199, 205
Sense and Significance 168, 202
sense-making 89, 192, 194, 196–197, 201
sensorimotor body-schema 243
shame 156–157
Sherman, Cindy 190, 206–207, 210
signifiers 56, 70
signs 56, 61, 89, 222, 227
Simondon, Gilbert 59
situatedness 36, 99, 111, 113, 201
skimming 175
social bubbles 221–222
social constructivism 19, 144–145, 147–148, 154, 156
socially disruptive technology 216
social media 1–2, 20–21, 189–201, 203–211, 215–216, 219, 221, 227, 230, 232, 268, 270, 275
  ethics 215–216
social media platforms (SMPs) 215–216, 220, 231–233, 235
social objects 74, 85–86, 89–90
society 27, 63, 66, 70, 79–80, 86, 112, 125, 143, 149, 193, 206, 271
socio-ethical decision making 104, 244
solipsism 58, 61–62, 83–84

Sorensen, Roy 202, 204
space 38–41, 69, 78, 84, 109, 113–114, 125, 161, 171, 210, 233, 237, 249–250, 252–254, 258–260
speech 33, 77, 84, 219, 243–244, 249, 252, 256–259, 261
spontaneous rearrangement 218
standardization 21, 147, 156
standing reserve 146–147, 159, 162, 269
standpoint theory 111
Stiegler, Bernard 272–276
stimming 260, 264
style 37, 76–77, 79, 83, 91, 98, 102, 253
subjectification 153, 156
subjectivity 4, 20, 31, 36, 45, 55, 58, 69, 76, 79–82, 84, 86–87, 90–91, 122, 128, 132, 136, 140, 152, 156–157, 171, 218, 222, 225
subject-object dichotomy 128
subjects 19, 55, 58, 64, 83, 102–103, 112, 128, 136–137, 144, 148, 221–224, 270
suppositio 35, 37–38
surveillance 28, 110, 113–114
symbols 17, 53–54, 56, 65–68, 76–77, 82, 85–86
Szilasi, Wilhelm 78–79

Tavalaro, Julia 249–250, 260
Techné 177
technical objects 18, 91, 148–149, 151
technicization 272
technics 16, 91–92, 131, 180, 272–275
technological artefacts 1, 10, 15, 18, 46, 54, 68, 124, 126–127, 139, 179, 216, 221
technological mediation 10, 17–19, 99, 103–106, 121, 125–127, 129–131, 133, 136–137, 139, 170
technological mediation theory 99, 105
techno-optimism 123
techno-solutionism 70
technosystem 143

temporality 76, 82, 85, 90–92, 252, 273–274
terrestrials 9, 12–13, 48
tertiary retention 274
text 34, 58, 62–63, 74–75, 171–172, 179, 182, 196–197, 199, 260
The Idiot 224
  Myshkin 224
thematic perception 17, 30, 38, 40–41, 44–45, 242
theoretical attitude 41
thought 3–4, 7, 9, 17, 33, 55, 74, 76, 80, 88, 98, 138, 144, 157, 174–175, 190, 210, 250, 269
time consciousness 273
tools 5, 8, 10–12, 28, 34, 148, 153–154, 192, 203, 241–242, 251, 255, 262, 274–275
totality 5, 18, 31, 77, 79–80, 82–85, 87, 89–91, 271
toxic impacts of technology 193
trajectory 22, 76–77, 82–83, 86, 91, 108
transcendentalism 22, 31–32, 36–37, 45–46, 54–55, 59, 64, 71, 74, 79–80, 133–134, 200, 268, 276
transcendental reduction 45–46
transduction 17, 30, 45–46, 48
transhumanism 66
transparency 11–12, 65, 67, 114, 172
Trump, Donald 220, 233, 236
Twitter 230, 232, 236–237

umwelt 150
unthought 80, 87
usage 65, 70, 109–110, 170, 176, 215, 243, 258
user manipulation 217

users 2, 9, 15–16, 20–21, 103–104, 107–110, 113, 131, 139, 150, 153, 156–157, 161, 171, 175, 197, 215–217, 219–220, 232–235, 237, 243, 245, 253, 257–258, 260, 262

Van Den Eede, Yoni 98, 126, 133, 135
variational theory 122, 169
Verbeek, Peter-Paul 11, 15–16, 63, 69, 98–99, 101, 103–105, 109, 122–123, 126–129, 131–134, 136, 168, 191–192
Vidal, Fernando 249
virtuality 8, 20, 87, 89, 171, 181–182, 197, 206
vocation 19, 151–154, 156–157
vulnerability 21, 194–195, 205

Watzl, Sebastian 178, 217–218, 228
Web 2.0 189, 197
Weber, Max 74–80, 85, 90
web of relations 90
well-being 152, 196, 198, 211, 215, 220
Whiteley, Ella 231
whole 4, 12–15, 28, 32, 76–77, 82, 91, 147, 149, 152, 178, 209, 236, 250, 258, 269–270
wicked problem 198–199, 210
wilful non-perception 225
Williams, Rua 260
Winner, Langdon 59, 270
writing 4, 32, 74, 77, 83–84, 86, 90, 92, 107–108, 144

Zahavi, Dan 225, 246

About the Team

Alessandra Tosi was the managing editor for this book.

Annie Hine and Adèle Kreager proof-read this manuscript. Annie compiled the index. The authors created the Alt-text.

Jeevanjot Kaur Nagpal designed the cover. The cover was produced in InDesign using the Fontin font.

Cameron Craig typeset the book in InDesign and produced the paperback and hardback editions. The main text font is Tex Gyre Pagella and the heading font is Californian FB.

Cameron also produced the PDF and HTML editions. The conversion was performed with open-source software and other tools freely available on our GitHub page at https://github.com/OpenBookPublishers.

Jeremy Bowman created the EPUB.

Raegan Allen was in charge of marketing.

This book was peer-reviewed by Prof Jan Kyrre Friis, University of Copenhagen, and Prof J. du Toit, School of Philosophy, North-West University, South Africa. Experts in their field, these readers gave their time freely to help ensure the academic rigour of our books. We are grateful for their generous and invaluable contributions.

This book need not end here...

Share

All our books — including the one you have just read — are free to access online so that students, researchers and members of the public who can't afford a printed edition will have access to the same ideas. This title will be accessed online by hundreds of readers each month across the globe: why not share the link so that someone you know is one of them?

This book and additional content is available at:
https://doi.org/10.11647/OBP.0421

Donate

Open Book Publishers is an award-winning, scholar-led, not-for-profit press making knowledge freely available one book at a time. We don't charge authors to publish with us: instead, our work is supported by our library members and by donations from people who believe that research shouldn't be locked behind paywalls.

Why not join them in freeing knowledge by supporting us:
https://www.openbookpublishers.com/support-us

Follow @OpenBookPublish

Read more at the Open Book Publishers BLOG

You may also be interested in:

Science as Social Existence

Heidegger and the Sociology of Scientific Knowledge

Jeff Kochan

https://doi.org/10.11647/obp.0129

Forms of Life and Subjectivity

Rethinking Sartre's Philosophy

Daniel Rueda Garrido

https://doi.org/10.11647/obp.0259

Ethics of Socially Disruptive Technologies

An Introduction

Ibo van de Poel, Lily Eva Frank, Julia Hermann, et al. (Eds)

https://doi.org/10.11647/obp.0366

www.ingramcontent.com/pod-product-compliance
Lightning Source LLC
Chambersburg PA
CBHW050208240426
43671CB00013B/2255